Glossator: Practice and Theory of the Commentary

Volume 7

GLOSSATOR

VOLUME 7

THE MYSTICAL TEXT (BLACK CLOUDS COURSE THROUGH ME UNENDING . . .)

Edited by
Nicola Masciandaro & Eugene Thacker

http://glossator.org

ISSN 1942-3381 (online)
ISSN 2152-1506 (print)
ISBN-13: 978-1482689181
ISBN-10: 1482689189

Nicola Masciandaro, Editor
Glossator: Practice and Theory of the Commentary
Department of English
Brooklyn College, The City University of New York
2900 Bedford Ave.
Brooklyn, NY 11210
glossatori@gmail.com

Cover image: St. Paul, by Nicholas Tournier (1625). Public domain.
Source: http://commons.wikimedia.org/wiki/Category:Nicolas_Tournier

Glossator 7: The Mystical Text (2013)

CONTENTS

Karmen MacKendrick   209
THE VOICE OF THE MIRROR: STRANGE ADDRESS IN
HILDEGARD OF BINGEN

It is always surprising to discover that the great mystics produced so much, that they left so many treatises. Undoubtedly their intention was to celebrate God and nothing else. This is true in part, but only in part. We do not create a body of work without attaching ourselves to it, without subjugating ourselves to it. Writing is the least ascetic of all actions . . . The mystics and their "collected works." When one addresses oneself to God, and to God alone, as they claim to do, one should be careful not to write. God doesn't *read* . . .

– E. M. Cioran, The Trouble with Being Born

IN PRIORA EXTENDENS ME: CONFESSIONES, IX.x.23-25

Kevin Hart

"Augustine is for me the Prince of Mystics, uniting in himself, in a manner I do not find in any other, the two elements of mystical experience, viz. the most penetrating intellectual vision into things divine, and a love of God that was a consuming passion."[1] Thus Dom Cuthbert Butler in a commanding book of 1922. Not everyone would agree with him, and some readers of Christian mystical literature would give the palm to John of the Cross, Theresa of Ávila, or one of several others, Thomas Aquinas not being an outrider.[2] Dom Cuthbert's book is entitled *Western Mysticism*, though we are not to suppose a contrast with the mysticisms of Buddhism and other Eastern religions. He is concerned entirely with the Latin West, and the adjective in his title serves to exclude Orthodoxy.[3] Not that he proposes a

---

I would like to thank John F. Miller and Tony Kelly for their comments on an earlier version of this essay. Also I should like to thank the members of the Philosophy Colloquium at the Australian Catholic University for inviting me to present this paper in an earlier form, and the Cistercian Fathers of the Abbey of Notre Dame, Tarrawarra, who heard a shorter version of the whole and engaged me in a memorable conversation about Augustine.

[1] Dom Cuthbert Butler, *Western Mysticism: The Teaching of Augustine, Gregory and Bernard on Contemplation and the Contemplative Life,* 2nd ed. (1926; New York: Harper and Row, 1966), 20. The book was originally published in 1922 and then a section entitled "Afterthoughts" was added for the 1926 edition. It is worth noting that at first Dom Cuthbert did not think of including Augustine in the book: "It was an afterthought to include St Augustine," he writes in the Preface (xi).

[2] See Denys Turner, *Faith, Reason and the Existence of God* (Cambridge: Cambridge University Press, 2004).

[3] See Butler, *Western Mysticism*, 88. I presume that Dom Cuthert also wishes to exclude Eastern Catholicism from consideration.

1

comprehensive survey of the mysticism of all Latin Christianity, for
by "western mysticism" he means that of "Cassian, Gregory, and
Bernard," finding that "St Augustine's mysticism stands somewhat
apart" from theirs.[4] The Prince stands to the side of his people. Of
course, Cassian's teaching draws deeply from Eastern Christianity,
and one might point out that the Eastern Church veers away from
lauding individuals and their experiences.[5] The Orthodox would
be unlikely to use an expression such as "Prince of Mystics," and
might also question the completeness of the "two elements." But let
the claim stand, let the criteria not distract us, and let us focus
sharply on Augustine.

Dom Cuthbert is thinking of passages in eight texts: *De animæ
quantitate* (387-88), 74-75; *Enarrationes in Psalmos* (392-422), xli;
Confessiones (397-401), VII. xvi. 22, IX.x.23-25; *De Genesi ad litteram*
(401-15), xii; *Contra Faustum Manicheum* (404) xxii. 52-58; *De
videndo Deo (Ep.* 147) (413-14); *De civitate Dei* (413-27), xix.1, 2, 19
(413-27); and *Sermones,* ciii, civ (dates uncertain). Other texts could
be cited, especially with respect to one or another aspect of
contemplatio: *De Ordine* (386-87), II. ii. 51, *De musica* (387-91), VI.
xii. 36-37, *De Genesi adversus Manicheos* (387), I.xxv.43, and *De
trinitate* (399-422/26), i.17-18, 31 all come to mind. Taken together,
these texts span Augustine's mature life as a Christian and establish
a wider range than Dom Cuthbert's "two elements" suggests. They
pass from a delineation of the seven levels of the soul and further
gradations of rapture and vision, to testimony of direct experience
of God, to a meditation on the passage from the visible to the
invisible, to pondering the various merits of the *vita activa* and the
vita contemplativa, to making a case for the leisure to engage in
contemplation, to reflection on whether we shall see God with the
eyes of the flesh, and to the statement that the sole reason for
philosophizing is devoting oneself to the ultimate good.[6] Yet Dom

---

[4] See Butler, *Western Mysticism,* 130.
[5] See Vladimir Lossky, "Theology and Mysticism in the Tradition of the
Eastern Church," *The Mystical Theology of the Eastern Church,* trans.
Members of the Fellowship of St Alban and St Sergius (London: J. Clarke,
1957), 20-21.
[6] See, in order, Augustine, *The Greatness of the Soul,* in *The Greatness of the
Soul, the Teacher,* trans. Joseph M. Colleran, Ancient Christian Writers
(New York: The Newman Press, 1950), 104-6, 109, along with *The Literal
Meaning of Genesis* in *On Genesis,* ed. John E. Rotelle, intro., trans. and notes
Edmund Hill, The Works of Saint Augustine I/13 (Hyde Park, NY: New

Cuthbert devotes sustained attention to only two passages: *Enarrationes in Psalmos*, xli and *Confessiones*, IX.x.23-25. The former includes a fundamental piece in the history of *contemplatio*, and the latter has become a major text in the history of what we moderns call "mysticism."

I wish to offer a commentary on the latter text, knowing all too well that I am far from being the first to do so: It is one of the most celebrated yet most intensely debated short documents in the history of Christianity.[7] I begin by drawing attention to a distinction entertained by Dom Cuthbert in his choice of texts and his discussion of those he selects, namely that between "mystical experience" and "contemplation." It will send me back to some of the other passages that he lists. Are "mystical experience" and "contemplation" different ways of saying the same thing? Or are

---

City Press, 2002), 465, 470, 494, 499; *Expositions of the Psalms 33-50*, ed. John E. Rotelle, trans. and notes Maria Boulding, The Works of Saint Augustine III/16 (Hyde Park, NY: New City Press, 2000), 240, 244; *Confessions*, trans. and intro. Henry Chadwick (Oxford: Oxford University Press, 1991), 170-72; *Answer to Faustus a Manichean*, ed. Boniface Ramsey, intro., trans. and notes Roland Teske, The Works of Saint Augustine I/20 (Hyde Park, NY: New City Press, 2007), 333-39 and *Sermons*, ed. John E. Rotelle, trans. and notes Edmund Hill, The Works of Saint Augustine III/4 (Brooklyn, NY: New City Press, 1992), 76-87; "A Book on Seeing God," *Letters 100-155*, ed. Boniface Ramsey, trans. and notes Roland Teske, The Works of Saint Augustine II/2 (Hyde Park, NY: New City Press, 2003), 319-49; *City of God*, 7 vols. (Cambridge, MA: Harvard University Press, 1960-72), VI, trans. William Chase Greene, 107.

[7] See, in particular, A. Mandouze, "'L'extase d'Ostie', possibilités et limites de la méthode des parallèles textuels," *Augustinus Magister: Congrès International Augustinien, Paris, 21-24 Septembre 1954* (Paris: Études Augustinniennes, 1954), 67-84, and *Saint Augustin: L'aventure de la raison et de la grâce* (Paris: Études Augustiniennes, 1968), Paul Henry, *The Path to Transcendence: From Philosophy to Mysticism in Saint Augustine,* trans. and intro. Francis F. Burch (1938; Pittsburgh: Pickwick Press, 1981), Suzanne Poque, "L'Expression de l'anabase plotinienne dans la prédication de saint Augustin et ses sources," *Recherches augustiniennes*, 10 (1976), 186-215, Andrew Louth, *The Origins of the Christian Mystical Tradition: From Plato to Denys* (Oxford: Clarendon Press, 1981), ch. 7, J. J. O'Donnell, ed., Augustine, *Confessions*, 3 vols. (Oxford: Oxford University Press, 1992), III, 122-37, and Jean-Luc Marion, *In the Self's Place: The Approach of Saint Augustine*, trans. Jeffrey L. Kosky (Stanford: Stanford University Press, 2012), ch. 7.

they quite different things? Or is it that "mystical experience" is the end point, for some, of "contemplation"? I leave these questions to resonate for a while, as I do the question at the heart of the commentaries I have mentioned: The character of the experience, if it is one, that Augustine and his mother appear to have had. Is it Christian, Neo-Platonic, or somehow both at once? Yet rather than be guided by questions that come from reflections by other readers of the text, I shall take my cues from the text itself, and seek to re-phrase, if need be, and answer the questions in the light of what it reveals of itself.

The piece begins, as is well known, with a reference to Monica, Augustine's mother. The preceding pages have recalled her childhood, her weakness for wine, her marriage, and her widowhood; and this evocation of her entire life is introduced by her death ("my mother died" [IX. viii. 17]) and, within only a few words, by an allusion to Augustine's birth or, better, double birth ("into the light of time. . . into the light of eternity" [IX. viii. 17]) and to what *he* can give birth ("whatever my soul may bring to birth" [IX. viii. 17), which includes the *Confessiones,* his other writings, and their immense heritages. Now, in the scene to which he turns, there is just mother and son, albeit a son who has already styled himself as a mother. Like all the *Confessiones,* the passage is addressed to God, and the reader is placed in the awkward position of overhearing someone else's prayer. What do we hear when we listen in to Augustine's prayer? We pick up his testimony of significant events in his life, and in this paragraph we apprehend two entwined testimonies, one about his mother's death and another about his long desired ascent to God who, he has come to realize, is the God of Jesus Christ:

> The day was imminent when she was to depart [*erat exitura*] this life (the day which you knew [*tu noveras*] and we did not). It came about, as I believe by your providence through your hidden ways, that she and I [*ego et ipsa soli*] were standing leaning out of a window overlooking a garden. It was at the house where we were staying at Ostia on the Tiber, where, far removed from the crowds, after the exhaustion of a long journey, we were recovering our strength for the voyage [*ubi*

remoti a turbis post longi itineris laborem instaurabamus nos navigationi]. (IX. x. 23)

At least three journeys are mentioned here, with two others in play, one of which will soon become the focus of the narrative.

Two journeys have already taken place, one is anticipated, and another was not known at the time being recalled. God knew it then, as Augustine freely acknowledges, and Augustine knows it now as he dictates his story, preparing to give it his full attention. Monica and Augustine have traveled to Ostia from Milan, where he had been baptized, and so we are quietly reminded of an earlier journey, Augustine's conversion from Manichaeism to Catholicism (which itself bespeaks a difficult journey from pride to humility). Now mother and son are waiting in Ostia, the port of Rome, before returning to their home in northern Africa where they intend to work for the Church. ("We looked for a place where we could be of most use in your service; all of us agreed on a move back to Africa" [IX.viii.17].) That voyage across the Mediterranean will not take place for Monica, for she will depart on another journey, from this life to the next, and before she does so she and her son will take another path, one that centuries later Bonaventure will call *itinerarium mentis in deum*, the mind's journey into God.[8]

Augustine credits God with arranging for Monica and him to meet alone (Chadwick does not translate *soli* here), apparently by chance, in their house by a window that overlooks a garden. The location is significant: If the window suggests light streaming in, the garden discreetly evokes paradise. Having leisure, and being undisturbed, they are free to talk as delicately prompted by the connotation of window and garden, and as led by the Holy Spirit:

> Alone with each other, we talked very intimately [*conloquebamur ergo soli valde dulciter*]. "Forgetting the past and reaching forward to what lies ahead" (Phil. 3:13) [*praeterita obliviscentes in ea quae ante sunt extenti*], we were searching together [*inter nos*] in the presence of the truth which is you yourself. (IX.x.23)

---

[8] See Bonaventure, *Itinerarium mentis in deum*, trans. and intro. Philotheus Boehner, Works of Saint Bonaventure, II (Saint Bonaventure, NY: The Franciscan Institute, 1956).

Again Augustine stresses that he and his mother are alone: this time *soli* is translated. This is a scene of searching, though we are not permitted to examine it closely, as we are in, say, Gregory of Nyssa's dialogue with his sister Macrina, *On the Soul and the Resurrection*.[9] There we see a Christian Platonic dialogue that recalls Plato's *Phaedo*.[10] The conversation between mother and son begins in the presence of God, now lauded as "the truth," and who serves in the narrative as the guarantor that they will not stray into error. Augustine alludes to Paul's recognition of his imperfection and his desire to be perfect, his single-minded focus on stretching into the future: "forgetting those things which are behind, and reaching forth unto those things which are before" [τὰ μὲν ὀπίσω ἐπιλανθανόμενος τοῖς δὲ ἔμπροσθεν ἐπεκτεινόμενος] (Phil. 3:13b). The prize Paul seeks is "the high calling of God in Christ Jesus" (Phil. 3:14b). We tend to associate this "reaching forth" with Gregory of Nyssa, especially with his homilies on the Canticle, yet it is also central here for Augustine.[11] Both Monica and he have put their pasts behind them, and strain towards what is to come: Less the journey to Africa, and their anticipated work for the Church, than for being eternally with God in Kingdom come. Their intimacy is only an index of a greater closeness to come with God and so with one another as well.

Already in their conversation they have crossed from life to death or, better, from earthly life to eternal life. Twice born, Augustine anticipates coming into the fullness of his second birth. It is an active expectation, requiring intense mental concentration:

> We asked what quality [*qualis*] of life the eternal life of the saints [*vita aeterna sanctorum*] will have, a life which "neither eye has seen nor ear heard, nor has it entered into the heart of man" (1 Cor. 2:9). But with the mouth of the heart wide open,

---

[9] See Gregory of Nyssa, *On the Soul and the Resurrection*, trans. and intro. Catharine P. Roth (Crestwood, NY: St Vladimir's Seminary Press, 2002).

[10] Of course, Augustine also inherited from Plato in this regard. See in particular *De magister*.

[11] See Gregory of Nyssa, *Commentary on the Song of Songs*, trans. and intro. Casimir McCambley, pref. Panagiotes Chrestou (Brookline, MA: Hellenic College Press, 1987).

we drank in the waters flowing from your spring on high, "the spring of life" (Ps. 35:10) which is with you [*sed inhiabamus ore cordis in superna fluenta fontis tui, fontis vitae, qui est apul te*]. Sprinkled with this dew to the limit of our capacity, our minds attempted in some degree to reflect on so great a reality [*ut inde pro captu nostro aspersi quoquo modo rem tantam cogitaremus*]. (IX.x.23)

Mother and son are engaged in a conversation, one apparently oriented by question and answer in lieu of an exchange of opinions, about the nature of eternal life with God (and not about the immortality of the soul such as was conducted by Gregory and Macrina), yet as reported the discussion immediately touches a limit. Nothing about the life of the saints in heaven has been revealed, as Paul points out in his first letter to the Corinthians. We do not know if the Scripture was quoted in the conversation or was added in the report of the colloquy. (Augustine says a little later about a related topic, "I said something like this, even if not in just this way," which inclines us to minimize the difference between event and report.)[12] Certainly Augustine and Monica drink the waters of life in order to reflect on the great reality: the *ut*-clause gets lost in the translation. But if Scripture is part of their conversation, it is not rooted in it. No attention is given to what Jesus says in the Gospels about heaven. In fact he says very little about what the life of the saints is like; his concern is how to live now so as to bring on the Kingdom and please God and not what life will be like with God. Yet Augustine and his mother do not begin by gathering what Scripture says about heaven as a place of joy and reward (Matt. 25:13-30), a Kingdom of justice (Luke 16:19-31), and a community without marriage (Luke 20:35). No reference is made to Jesus's powerful saying, "In my Father's house are many mansions: if [it were] not [so], I would have told you. I go to prepare a place for you" (John 14:2). Nor do they start by citing any Scripture about the general resurrection.

---

[12] Augustine, *Confessions*, IX.x.26. O'Donnell maintains that the Scriptural quotations are "adduced as commentary ex post facto," although he gives no warrant for this view. See O'Donnell, *Confessions*, III, 124.

Instead of beginning with revealed Scripture, or even with the nature of sanctity, Monica and Augustine go in search of *idipsum*, Itself or Selfsame, which Henry Chadwick translates a little too boldly as "eternal being itself," words that carry more freight than the Latin will bear alone, as we shall see. *Idipsum* bears some relation with the One of Plotinus that is beyond all categories and consequently unable to be described. It is this general Neo-Platonic orientation that suggests that the son takes charge of the conversation, using Neo-Platonism as the vehicle of Christian truth, but we are to remember how in *De Ordine* (386-87) Augustine encourages Monica to take part in philosophical discussions, saying first to her "There were plenty of philosopher-women in ancient times, and I rather like *your* philosophy" and then, later, to the reader, "no other person seemed to me fitter for true philosophy."[13] In their conversation they become receptive to the "spring of life [*fons vitae*]"which is with God.[14] Here sprinkling does not allude to the rite of asperges in which, outside Eastertide, during the principal Sunday mass, the altar, priests and congregation are sprinkled with holy water while part of Psalm 51 (50) is intoned (*Asperges me, Domine, hyssopo et mundabor*). That ritual was developed no earlier than the eighth century. Yet reciting the psalm at the foot of the altar before mass is a tradition that Augustine probably knew, and in his exegesis of Psalm 51 (50), written a decade after the *Confessiones*, he interprets hyssop as humility. "You will be sprinkled with hyssop, because the humility of Christ will cleanse you."[15] There is a difference between the human power of reasoning and the humility of Christ, and the conversation between Augustine and Monica falls between the Neo-Platonic and the ecclesial by virtue of Augustine's newfound humility and purity after his baptism. Humility and cognition are not opposed to one another. "Sprinked with this dew . . . our minds attempted in some degree to reflect on so great a reality [*tantam cogitaremus*]."Mother and son are actively trying to understand:

---

[13] Augustine, *On Order*, trans. and intro. Silvano Borruso (South Bend, IN: St Augustine's Press, 2007), I. xi.31, II.i.1.

[14] On the spring of life, also see Augustine, "Exposition of Psalm 41," 2, in *Expositions of the Psalms 33-50*, and *The Literal Meaning of Genesis*, XII.xxvi.54.

[15] Augustine, *Exposition of the Psalms 33-50*, ed. John E. Rotelle, trans. and notes Maria Boulding, The Works of Saint Augustine III/16 (Hyde Park, NY: New City Press, 2000), 420.

cogitaremus is the first-person plural imperfect active subjunctive of *cogito*.

Augustine underlines that the event befalling him and his mother is conducted by way of a conversation, one that seems to have a teleology running through it:

> The conversation led us towards the conclusion [*Cumque ad eum finem sermo perduceretur*] that the pleasure of the bodily senses, however delightful in the radiant light of this physical world, is seen by comparison with the life of eternity to be not even worth considering. Our minds were lifted up [the Latin, however, is *erigentes*] by an ardent affection towards eternal being itself [*nos ardentiore affectu in idipsum*]. Step by step [*perambulavimus gradium*] we climbed beyond all corporeal objects and the heaven itself, where sun, moon, and stars shed light on the earth. We ascended [*ascendebamus:* imperfect] even further [*adhuc:* to that point] by internal reflection and dialogue and wonder at your works [*ascendebamus interius cogitando et loquendo et mirando opera tua*] (IX.x.24)

This ascent is not simply intellectual, for their minds are raised by affection for God, here seen by way of *idipsum* rather than truth or beauty. It is orderly and gradual; they rise "step by step," and their wonder if what they have seen in their ascent (and not, as Chadwick's translation suggests, at the heavenly beings, which have been surpassed).

This is not the usual way in which contemplation takes place, since it does not characteristically occur by way of conversation or—as it seems in the report of the conversation—so quickly. Robert Grosseteste tells us that mystical theology is "the most secret talking with God," yet here we have a conversation that is in principle at least entirely public.[16] Also we should not think of "step by step" recapitulating the seven levels of the soul as elaborated in *De quantitate animæ*, written in Rome after Monica's

---

[16] See Robert Grosseteste, "Commentary on *De Mystica Theologia*," in *Mystical Theology: The Glosses by Thomas Gallus and the Commentary of Robert Grosseteste on "De Mystica Theologia*," ed., trans. and intro. James McEvoy (Leuven: Peeters, 2003), 65.

death, as well as in *De vera religion* and *De musica*.[17] If anything, the two already have reached stages four and five, self-purification and possession of purity, and so begin the ascent with the sixth stage, "the ardent desire to understand truth and perfection."[18] It seems that the dialogue facilitates the speed of ascent, and perhaps it indicates that neither partner dominates the colloquy. The intimacy of mother and son, the dynamic between a modestly educated woman of deep faith and a richly educated convert, along with the humility of both mother and son, appear to be conducive to the rapidity with which they climb beyond the stars.

The passage invites comparison with one in Book VII of the *Confessiones*. There Augustine tells God that "you brought under my eye some books of the Platonists [*quosdam platonicorum libros*], translated from Greek into Latin" (VII.ix.13), most likely including some writings by Porphyry, Iamblichus and a handful of Plotinus's *Enneads* translated into Latin by Marius Victorinus.[19] Shortly after, we find Augustine in Milan attempting ascents by way of Neo-Platonic reflection, passing from the visible to the invisible:

> I asked myself why I approved of the beauty of bodies, whether celestial or terrestrial, and what justification I had for giving an unqualified judgement on mutable things, saying 'This ought to be thus, and that ought not to be thus'. In the course of this inquiry why I made such value judgements as I was making, I found the unchangeable and authentic eternity of truth to transcend my mutable mind. And so step by step [*atque ita gradatim*] I ascended from bodies to the soul which perceives through the body, and from there to its inward force, to which bodily senses report external sensations, this being as high as the beasts go. From there I ascended to the power of reasoning to which is to be attributed the power of judging the deliverances of the bodily senses. This power, which in myself I found to be

---

[17] It is worth noting that Bonaventure comments on the seven steps in his *Itinerarium mentis in deum*, intro., trans. and commentary Philotheus Boehner, Works of Saint Bonaventure (Saint Bonaventure, NY: The Franciscan Institute, 1956), II. 10.

[18] Augustine, *The Greatness of the Soul*, XXXIII.lxxv.

[19] See Augustine, *City of God*, vol. III, trans. David S. Wiesen, VIII.xii.

mutable, raised itself to the level of its own intelligence, and led my thinking out of the ruts of habit. It withdrew itself from the contradictory swarms of imaginative fantasies, so as to discover the light by which it was flooded [*ut inveniret quo lumine aspergeretur*]. At that point it had no hesitation in declaring that the unchangeable is preferable to the changeable, and that on this ground it can know the unchangeable, since, unless it could somehow know this, there would be no certainty in preferring it to the mutable. So in the flash of a trembling glance it attained to that which is [*et pervenit ad id quod est in ictu trepidantis aspectus*]. (VII.xvi.23)

By philosophical questioning conducted in solitude Augustine raises himself to a momentary gaze at "that which is" [*id quod est*]. Plainly, Plotinus's *Enneads,* I.vi ("On Beauty") is a touchstone here. "But about the beauties beyond," Plotinus writes, "which it is no more the part of sense to see, but the soul sees them and speaks of them without instruments—we must go up to them and contemplate them and leave sense to stay below" (*Enneads,* I. vi. 4).[20] *Enneads,* V.i.4 may also be an inspiration: "If someone admires this perceptible universe, observing its size and beauty and the order of its everlasting course . . . let him ascend to its archetypal and truer reality and there see them all intelligible and eternal in it."[21] Equally likely to have had an effect on Augustine is Porphyry's advice "to fly from the body" in his letter to his wife, Marcella.[22]

Yet, as Augustine says, "I did not possess the strength to keep my vision fixed. My weakness reasserted itself, and I returned to my customary condition" (VII.xvi.23). It is intellectual ascent without the aid of divine grace to keep him safe in his weakness. Indeed, we have been warned of this failure. With hindsight,

---

[20] A. H. Armstrong, ed., *Plotinus,* 6 vols. (Cambridge, MA: Harvard University Press, 1966), vol. 1, *Enneads,* I.vi.4.

[21] Armstrong, *Plotinus,* vol. 5 (Cambridge, MA: Harvard University Press, 1984), *Enneads,* V.i.4.

[22] See Alice Zimmern, ed. and trans., *Porphyry, the Philosopher, to his Wife, Marcella,* pref. Richard Garnett (London: George Redway, 1896), 10. For a discussion of the likely influence of Porphyry on Augustine that considers earlier arguments on the issue, see Pierre Hadot, "Citations de Porphyre à propos d'une recente ouvrage," *Revue des Études Augustinniennes,* 2 (1960), 204-44.

Augustine found that the books of the Platonists came with a shadow cast over them: "First you wanted to show me how you 'resist the proud and give grace to the humble' (I Pet. 5:5), and with what mercy you have shown humanity the way of humility in that your 'Word was made flesh and dwelt among' men (John 1:14)" (VII.ix.13). Even more to the point is the probing question he asks of himself, "Where was the charity which builds on the foundation of humility which is Christ Jesus?" (VII.xx.26). And, finally, he tells God (and us) what is *not* in the Platonic books: "Those pages do not contain the face of this devotion, tears of confession, your sacrifice, a troubled spirit, a contrite and humble spirit (Ps. 50:19), the guarantee of your Holy Spirit (2 Cor. 5:5), the cup of our redemption" (VII.xxi.27). Despite all these caveats, though, Augustine acknowledges that the Christian God led him to the Platonic books: "With you as my guide . . . ," he writes (VII.x.16).

Similarities between the event at Milan and the description of what happened at Ostia will be perceived, especially the use of *aspergeretur* and the "trembling glance" at that which is, which will interest us later. The ascent at Ostia, however, is fundamentally of a different complexion than the events at Milan. It is Christian, oriented to love of God and neighbor, life in the Kingdom, not purely intellectual speculation. As late as *De civitate Dei* Augustine tells us of the Neo-Platonists, "they have declared that the light that illumines the intellects of men in all things that may be learned is this selfsame God [*ipsum Deum*] by whom all things were made."[23] Differences between Ostia and Milan include the fact that the former is a *conversation* (and that Monica's lifelong faith is needed for Augustine to encounter God as life and love), the *theme* of the conversation (sanctity and *idipsum*), and that Augustine has a newfound *humility, purity and love* after baptism, that act of dying into Christ.

If affect impels the ascent, the two participants are taken to the highest levels by "internal reflection," "dialogue," and "wonder." The dialogue is the medium of the ascent; it triggers internal reflection that is fuelled by wonder at creation, and its alternation of question and answer doubtless provides the steps and accounts for how Augustine knows of his mother's internal reflection. If we are reminded of the ascent evoked in the

---

[23] Augustine, *City of God*, VIII.vii.

Symposium, 210a-212b and of Plotinus's flight to the One (*Enneads,* VI.ix.9), we are also checked to think that, unlike the mystical tradition spawned by Socrates's friend, the seer Diotima, and the solitude of Plotinus's ecstasy, Augustine's model of ascent involves two people, not just an isolated soul enraptured by God. It will generate a tradition of dialogic mystical treatises, in which Love and Reason (among other couples) ascend to God through discussion.[24] We may not know how this dialogue between mother and son is conducted, but we know in advance that it will be one of Monica's last, and that it is pivotal for Augustine's remaining life. Does Monica have any inkling of her coming end, or does the fever come quite out of the blue and carry her away without any prior symptoms? We do not know. All that we know is that this is one of the mother and son's last conversations, which adds to the pathos of the scene.

In the sentence that follows the evocation of reflection, dialogue and wonder, the Latin is more dramatic than Chadwick's elegant English translation; the entry into the mind and an immediate transcendence of human cognition is put in the one sentence:

> . . . and we entered our own minds. We moved up beyond them [*et venimus in mentes nostras et transcendimus eas*] so as to attain to the region of inexhaustible abundance where you feed Israel eternally with truth for food [*in aeternum veritate pabulo*]. There life is the wisdom by which all creatures come into being, both things which were and which will be. But wisdom itself is not brought into being but is as it was and always will be. Furthermore, in this wisdom there is no past and future, but only being, since it is eternal. For to exist in the past or in the future is no property of the eternal [*nam fuisse et futurum esse non est aeternum*]. (IX.x.24)

Mother and son mentally climb beyond the heavens, ascend "even further," and so enter their own minds only to transcend them. After so many centuries since the *Confessiones* was dictated this remains an arresting sequence of thought, and its peculiarity is not

---

[24] See, for example, *A Mirror for Simple Souls,* trans. Charles Crawford (London: Gill and Macmillan, 1981).

softened by the young Augustine's belief, shared with Plotinus, that "we have God inside" and his co-ordinate injunction, "Return within yourself. In the inward man dwells truth."[25] When one goes past the planets and the stars by way of thought one truly enters into oneself: There is only mind that remains, it seems. But no, for one can be raised higher than mind and attain to the divine realm. It is as though one must find the eye of the soul in one's mind before one can see God. Yet none of this ascending to the heights is attained individually; throughout, Augustine is plain that it is achieved mutually, and in doing so he registers his distance from Plato and Plotinus and also, unknowingly, marks a difference in advance from Christian mystics to come. As though to underline the difference between his experience and those of the pagan philosophers, Augustine turns to a biblical image, the feeding of Israel: "I will feed them in a good pasture, and upon the high mountains of Israel shall their fold be: there shall they lie in a good fold, and [in] a fat pasture shall they feed upon the mountains of Israel" (Ezech. 34:14). Over a decade later, in 414, Augustine will pause in a sermon to make a stylistic flourish around this verse, "This is feeding Christ, this is feeding for Christ, this is feeding in Christ, not feeding oneself apart from Christ" [*Illoc est Christo pascere, hoc est in Christo pascere, et cum Christo pascere, praeter Christum sibi non pascere*].[26]

The eternal is not stretched across time from past to future but is beyond all temporal determinations. Once again, Augustine distinguishes the insight that he and his mother share from the speculations of Greek philosophers. Christianity gives the hope of eternal life (a quality) and not immortality (a duration), such as one finds discussed so movingly in the *Phaedo*.[27] God transcends his creation, including its temporal reach. This divine transcendence fiercely attracts mother and son:

---

[25] Augustine, *De Musica liber VI*, ed. and intro. Martin Jacobson (Stockholm: Almqvist and Wiksell International, 2002), 99, and "Of True Religion," in *Augustine: Earlier Writings*, ed. and trans. John H. S. Burleigh, The Library of Christian Classics, VI (London: SCM Press), 262. Also see Plotinus, *Enneads,* I.vi.9.

[26] Augustine, *Sermons,* II: *(20-50) On the Old Testament,* trans. and notes Edmund Hill, ed. John E. Rotelle, The Works of Saint Augustine III/2 (Brooklyn, NY: New City Press, 1990), 46. 30.

[27] See Plato, *Phaedo,* 69e-72d, 72e-73a, 82d-85b, 100c-104c.

And while we talked and panted after it, we touched it in some small degree by a moment of total concentration of the heart [*attingimus eam modice toto ictu cordis*]. And we sighed and left behind us "the firstfruits of the Spirit" (Rom. 8:23) bound to that higher world, as we returned to the noise of our human speech where a sentence has both a beginning and an ending. But what is to be compared with your word, Lord of our lives? It dwells in you without growing old and gives renewal to all things. (IX.x.24)

It will be noticed that the episode, which for ease of discussion I have divided into two, begins with an emphasis on mind (*venimus in mentes nostras*), just like the ascent we have considered in Book VII, and yet it ends with a stress on the heart (*ictu cordis*). There has been a qualitative change in orientation. The Christian God calls forth love, not only reason. It will also be noticed how Augustine conceives God, simply and barely as *id ipsum*. The man who found himself not long before in "the region of dissimilarity [*in regione dissimilitudinis*]" (VII.x.16) seeks salvation in the Selfsame. In calling God *id ipsum*, nothing is predicated of him, and certainly there is no metaphysical sense of being in play here, such as is suggested by Chadwick's translation as "eternal being itself."[28] The statement is apophatic, concerned only with the deity's nature being eternally beyond all change, and so worlds away from the dynamic conception of God that Aquinas will develop in concert with divine immutability, namely, God as event.[29] In Aquinas's words, God is *ipsum esse subsistens omnibus modis indeterminatum,*

---

[28] Maria Boulding renders the expression "*That Which Is*," which is preferable to Chadwick's translation. See Augustine, *The Confessions*, trans., intro. and notes Maria Boulding, ed. John E. Rotelle, The Works of Saint Augustine I/1 (Hyde Park, NY: New City Press, 1997), 227. William Watts is a reliable translator in this regard: he renders *id ipsum* as "Self-same." See Augustine, *Confessions, Books IX-XIII*, trans. William Watts (Cambridge, MA: Harvard University Press, 1912), 49. The same is true of E. B. Pusey's version. See his *The Confessions of S. Augustine*, rev. from a former translation, Library of Fathers of the Holy Catholic Church (Oxford: John Henry Parker, 1838), 173.

[29] Thomas Aquinas, *Summa theologiæ*, 1a q. 9.

15

wholly undetermined self-subsistent being (in the verbal sense of the word).[30]

Not that Augustine is always shy of associating God and being. In *Confessiones* VII we have already read, "And you cried from far away: 'Now, I am who I am' (Exod. 3:14) [*immo vero ego sum qui sum*]" (VII.x.16). A more explicit linking of *idipsum* and *sum qui sum* may be found in Augustine's exegesis of Psalm 121:

> What is Being-Itself? That which always exists unchangingly, which is not now one thing, now another. What is Being-Itself, Absolute Being, the Self-Same? That Which Is. What is That Which Is? The eternal, for anything that is constantly changing does not truly exist, because it does not abide—not that it is entirely nonexistent, but it does not exist in the highest sense. And what is That Which Is if not he who, when he wished to give Moses his mission, said to him, *I AM WHO AM* (Ex. 3:14)? What is That Which Is if not he who, when his servant objected. *So you are sending me. But what shall I say to the sons of Israel if they challenge me. Who sent you to us?* (Ex. 3:14), refused to give himself any other name than *I AM WHO AM*? He reiterated, *Thus shall you say to the children of Israel, HE WHO IS has sent me to you* (Ex. 3:14). This is Being-Iself, the Self-same: *I AM WHO AM. HE WHO IS has sent me to you.*[31]

> Quid est *idipsum?* Quod semper eodem modo est; quod non modo aliud, et modo aliud est. Quid est ergo *idipsum,* nisi, quod est? Quid est quod est? Quod aeternum est. Nam quod semper aliter atque aliter est, non est, quia non manet: non omnino non est, sed non summe est. Et quid est quod est, nisi ille qui quando mittebat Moysen, dixit illi: *Ego sum qui sum?* Quid est hoc, nisi ille qui cum diceret famulus ejus, *Ecce mittis me: si dixerit mihi populus, Quis te misit? quid dicam ei?* nomen

---

[30] Aquinas, *Summa theologiæ*, 1a, q. 11, art. 4, *responsio*. On Augustine's use of *id ipsum*, see Marion, *In the Self's Place,* ch. 7.

[31] Augustine, *Exposition of the Psalms, 121-150*, trans. and notes Maria Boulding, ed. Boniface Ramsey, The Works of Saint Augustine III/20 (Hyde Park, NY: New City Press, 2004), 18.

suum noluit aliud dicere, quam, *Ego sum qui sum;* et adjecit et ait, *Dices itaque filiis Israel, Qui est, misit me ad vos.* Ecce *idipsum, Ego sum qui sum, Qui est, misit me ad vos.*

Here the deictic *idipsum* is quickly coded to what Étienne Gilson called "the metaphysics of Exodus": God's self-revelation to Moses of himself as unconditioned being, *Qui est.*[32] Note, in particular, the rhetorical question, *Quid est ergo* idipsum, *nisi, quod est?,* which we may render in English as "What therefore is Itself unless I AM WHO I AM?" And consider also his remarks on naming God in *De Trinitate* VII:

> . . . it is impious to say that God subsists to and underlies his goodness, and that goodness is not his substance, or rather his being, nor is God his goodness, but it is in him as in an underlying subject. So it is clear that God is improperly called substance, in order to signify being by a more usual word. He is called being truly and properly in such a way that perhaps only God ought to be called being [*unde manifestum est Deum abusive substantiam vocari, ut nomine usitatiore intelligatur essentia, quod vere ac proprie dicitur; ita ut fortasse solum Deum dici oporteat essentiam*]. He alone truly is, because he is unchanging [*Est enim vere solus, quia incommutabilis est*], and he gave this as his name to his servant Moses when he said *I am who am,* and, *You will say to them, He who is sent me to you* (Ex. 3:14). But in any case, whether he is called being, which he is called properly, or substance, which he is called improperly, either word is predicated with reference to self, not by way of relationship with reference to something else. So for God to be is the same as to subsist, and therefore if the trinity is one being, it is also one substance [*Sed tamen sive essentia dicatur quod proprie dicitur, sive substantia quod abusive; utrumque ad se dicitur, non relative ad aliquid. Unde hoc est Deo esse quod subsistere, et ideo si una essentia Trinitas, una etiam substantia*].[33]

---

[32] See Étienne Gilson, *The Spirit of Medieval Philosophy,* trans. A. H. C. Downes (Notre Dame: University of Notre Dame Press, 1991), 51-52.
[33] Augustine, *The Trinity,* VII. iii.10.

God is not a substance, since that would mean there is a difference between his goodness and his being. No, God is an essence; and this is to say a good deal more than that God is *idipsum*. The ascent at Ostia appears not to be guided by a metaphysical notion of being, though Augustine's reflection on it, and his later theological insights into the divine essence, are touched by metaphysics, even if it is not the substance metaphysics of modern philosophy.[34]

Let us return to the text under discussion. In Latin one says *ictu oculi* to mean "in the blink of an eye," and one should keep in mind in this passage short and impulsive acts such as a stroke, blow or thrust when thinking of how the heart reaches the divine. Both mother and son are enabled to touch the divine, apparently as one. *Attingimus*: it is the first person plural present active indicative of *attingo*, from *ad* + *tango* ("touch"). Mother and son touch or reach out to make contact with the divine. Indeed, *attingo* can signify "taste" when put in the context of eating and drinking. Much of the western tradition of "mystical experience" will follow Augustine here, preferring the lexicon of touching and tasting to that of seeing, even though sight is a "theoretical sense," as Hegel says, and thereby gives us access to knowledge.[35] In contrast, touch and taste give us experience that is pre-theoretical. Monica and Augustine have momentarily reached outside or beyond time and space, have touched the divine word, and now return to the time of ordinary words, including those remembered in the *Confessiones*. They do not return entirely the same, however: they are partly bound in their higher nature to the Kingdom.

Yet the allusion to Paul's expression "the firstfruits of the Spirit" is not straightforward and needs to be read in the context of Paul's letter to the Romans:

> For we know that the whole creation groaneth and travaileth in pain together until now. And not only [they], but ourselves also, which have the firstfruits of the Spirit [ἀπαρχὴν τοῦ πνεύματος], even we ourselves groan

---

[34] For Marion, by contrast, Augustine is not engaged in metaphysics at all; indeed, metaphysics is a modern discourse, with an onto-theio-logical structure as diagnosed by Martin Heidegger. See his *In the Self's Place*, ch. 7.

[35] See G. W. F. Hegel, *Aesthetics: Lectures on Fine Art*, trans. T. M. Knox, 2 vols. (Oxford: Clarendon Press, 1975), I, 38.

within ourselves, waiting for the adoption, [to wit], the redemption of our body. For we are saved by hope: but hope that is seen is not hope: for what a man seeth, why doth he yet hope for? But if we hope for that we see not, [then] do we with patience wait for [it]. Likewise, the Spirit also helpeth our infirmities: for we know not what we should pray for as we ought: but the Spirit itself maketh intercession for us with groanings which cannot be uttered. (Rom. 8:22-26, KJV)

Even here, as Origen points out in his commentary on Romans, we have several options to weigh. "Firstfruits of the Spirit" could mean having the Holy Spirit, as distinct from ministering spirits, or it could mean having the highest gifts of the Holy Spirit, or it could mean Christ himself.[36] When he comes to comment on Rom. 8:23 in his *Propositions from the Epistle to the Romans* Augustine will focus on the resurrection: "For this adoption, already established for those who have believed, was accomplished only spiritually, not physically. For the body has not yet been remade by that heavenly transformation, as the spirit has already been changed through the reconciliation of faith, having turned from its errors to God. Therefore, even those who believe still await that manifestation to come at the resurrection of the body."[37] This gloss comes years later than the *Confessiones*, to be sure, and it converges with the eschatological emphasis of *De videndo Deo*. Monica and Augustine have been adopted spiritually but not yet physically; each awaits the resurrection from the dead, and we know, even if Augustine

---

[36] See Origen, *Commentary on the Epistle to the Romans*, 2 vols., trans. Thomas P. Scheck, The Fathers of the Church, vol. 104 (Washington, DC: The Catholic University of America Press, 2002), II, 74-76. It is worth mentioning that for Aquinas the "first fruits of the Spirit" refers to the Apostles, because they had "the Holy Spirit before others and more abundantly than others, just as earthly fruit which ripens earlier is richer and more delicious," *Commentary on the Letter of Saint Paul to the Romans*, trans. F. R. Larcher, ed. J. Mortensen and E. Alarcón (Lander, Wyoming: Aquinas Institute for the Study of Sacred Doctrine, 2012), 225.

[37] Paula Fredriksen Landes, ed., "Propositions from the Epistle to the Romans," 53, in *Augustine on Romans: Propositions from the Epistle to the Romans, Unfinished Commentary on the Epistle to the Romans* (Chico, CA: Scholar's Press, 1982).

and Monica in Ostia do not, that Monica has a shorter time to wait than her son.

Mother and son stretch beyond themselves, if only for a moment, when they touch *idipsum*. (Inevitably, we recall Phil. 3:13, the tutelary spirit of the passage, while acknowledging that we pass from ἐπέκτασις to ἔκστασις.) Stretched out beyond themselves, separating senses and soul, as Plotinus says, they have a foretaste of eternal life; it is a death of sorts, though one that is transitory, before eternal life, and before any resurrection. While Augustine evokes other moments of bliss in the *Confessiones* ("an extraordinary depth of feeling marked by a strange sweetness") he never again speaks of such things in the first person, except, in all likelihood, to reflect on this event.[38] He may well have been recalling the event when he defined "ecstasy" in *De Genesi ad litteram*, "When, however, the attention of the mind is totally turned aside and snatched away from the senses of the body, then you have what is more usually called ecstasy. Then whatever bodies may be there in front of the subject, even with his eyes wide open he simply does not see them at all, or of course hear any words spoken aloud."[39] Certainly the conversation seems to stop for a while–they fall silent and then both sigh–before returning to talk, of all things, about silence, which, because they speak in sentences, requires that they follow a temporal structure. (Distention, the temporal stretching of the soul, which is the contrary of ἐπέκτασις and ἔκστασις alike, will become an important motif of *Confessiones*, XI.) It is the twin traits of touching God and ecstasy that have made *Confessiones*, IX.x.23-25 a primary reference point for Christian mysticism, even though its dialogic nature makes it eccentric within that corpus.

Who or what do they touch? What is *idipsum*? If at first sight it seems to be only a Latin version of the rather chilly Neo-Platonic One, we should think twice. Like Augustine, we should read the Psalms in the Vulgate (that is, the *Iuxta Septuaginta* and not the *Iuxta Hebraicum*): *in pace in id ipsum dormiam et requiescam* ["In peace in the self same I will sleep, and I will rest"](Ps. 4:9). It might be said by way of objection that a biblical allusion from one of Augustine's favorite psalms–see *Confessiones*, IX.iv.8-11–could well have been added here, as elsewhere, when composing the text, while the experience itself could have been Neo-Platonic. This is

---

[38] Augustine, *Confessions*, X. xl. 65. Also see Plotinus, *Enneads*, I.vi.4.

[39] Augustine, *The Literal Meaning of Genesis*, xii.12.

possible in theory, though it is anachronistic to distinguish Neo-Platonism and Christianity so strictly in this age. To do so would render Gregory of Nyssa, for one, quite unintelligible. Augustine has changed before the ascent at Ostia: He has been baptized and approaches the ascent with newfound humility, purity and love. In reacting to this suggestion, it will be critically observed that if *idipsum* is understood to be the Christian God there is nothing said by Augustine by way of confessing the triune nature of this God. The experience would not be fully Christianized in its telling. We may readily concede that there are aspects of the text that leave no doubt about its Neo-Platonic provenance, even if one does not agree with Paul Henry that the entire conversation is "unquestionably Plotinian in mentality."[40] For we may reasonably ask "Whose mentality?" Augustine's would be only part of an answer, since the ascent occurs by way of a conversation and may well have been enabled by it; and while Augustine had probably read several of the *Enneads* his mother had not. We do not hear the conversation, for like Henry Mayhew's reports of conversations in *London Labour and the London Poor* (1851) we are given only a digest of it by the author, and Monica's voice is occluded. It is easy to conceive her having a Christian experience brought about by piety and next to impossible to imagine her having a Neo-Platonic experience spurred by the desire for intellectual ascent. Yet the experience of mother and son as related is one and the same. I shall return to this issue in a moment; the concept of "experience" in play here needs closer attention.

Augustine, we must remember, had sought Neo-Platonic ascent twice or thrice by himself in Milan and had found it frustrating because he was not converted to a better life by it. He fell back into old habits. There is no good theological reason why

---

[40] See Henry, *The Path to Transcendence*, 29. Also see Mandouze, *Saint Augustin: L'Aventure de la raison et de la grâce*, 697. O'Donnell argues that the ascent at Ostia was "not different, not uniquely better, not a denial of the excellence of Platonic mysticism, but better," *Confessions*, III, 128. I think this judgment misses the role of Monica in the ascent and also fails to take into account the newfound humility and love of Augustine associated with baptism. Martha Nussbaum is closer to the mark when she stresses the difference between the Neo-Platonic and the Christian ascents. See her "Augustine and Dante on the Ascent of Love," *The Augustinian Tradition*, ed. Gareth B. Matthews (Berkeley: University of California Press, 1999), 61-90.

he cannot ascend to God by way of beauty in preference to being or truth. Plotinus understands that they are co-ordinate, and neither the medieval nor the modern Church would disagree with him.[41] However, it must be acknowledged that at Ostia Augustine approaches God with affect transformed by humility, purity and love, having been baptized into Christ, and touches him as the unchanging Selfsame rather than as beauty or truth. Perhaps the hope of eternal life with the unchanging Word of God gave him the ardor that he needed and that he could not find any longer in *Enneads*, I:6. So we should take care not to think of *idipsum* too dryly; Augustine and Monica are concerned with the quality of *life* with God, the Kingdom itself, and the ascent is cued by Augustine's rebirth as a Catholic and Monica's vivid sense of a new start for her son. At any rate, the Neo-Platonic books, it seems, do not supply the content that Augustine needs and only provide an intellectual impetus for ascent. They are themselves a step on the way.

The intellectual interest of the Platonic books is testified in the *Contra Academicos* (386-87) written at Cassiciacum, a text that is closer to the date of Augustine's conversion than the *Confessiones* (397-401). In the passage of *Contra Academicos* that chiefly interests me, the newly converted Augustine exhorts his benefactor Romanianus to remember that when he left his son, Licentius, and friends after a visit to Milan they still yearned after philosophy, though perhaps not as enthusiastically as they might have done. This is φιλοσοφία, of course, and not "philosophy" in the modern sense of the word that bespeaks one or more contrasts with "religion" or "theology." In the ancient world φιλοσοφία and its Latin translation *philosophia* was precisely the love of wisdom, and it converged on many questions that we would now call religious. Augustine burned for this love on reading Cicero's now lost *Hortensius* as he tells us in *Confessiones* III and VIII.[42] When Plotinus writes on the One he is doing φιλοσοφία, and when the young Augustine wishes to devote himself to writing on all the *artes liberales* as a Christian he proposes to spend his life engaged in *philosophia.*[43]

---

[41] See Plotinus, *Enneads*, I.vi.6.
[42] See Augustine, *Confessions*, III.iv.8 and VIII.vii.17.
[43] See Augustine, *The Retractations*, trans. Mary Inez Bogan, The Fathers of the Church, 60 (Washington, DC: Catholic University of America Press,

Let us stay with *Contra Academicos* for a moment longer. Burning only with a moderate flame after Romanianus's departure, the young men around Augustine nonetheless continued their studies:

> But lo! when certain books full to the brim, as Celsinus says, had wafted to us good things of Arabia, when they had let a very few drops of most precious unguent fall upon that meager flame, they stirred up an incredible conflagration–incredible, Romanianus, incredible, and perhaps beyond even what you would believe of me– what more shall I say?–beyond even what I would believe of myself . . . Swiftly did I begin to return entirely to myself [*Prorsus totus in me cursim redibam*]. Actually, all that I did–let me admit it–was to look back from the end of a journey, as it were, to that religion which is implanted in us in our childhood days and bound up in the marrow of our bones. But she indeed was drawing me unknowing to herself. Therefore, stumbling, hastening, yet with hesitation I seized the Apostle Paul. For truly, I say to myself, those men would never have been able to do such great things, nor would they have lived as they evidently did live, if their writings and doctrines were opposed to this so great a good [*huic tanto bono*]. I read through all of it with the greatest attention and care.[44]

So we hear of another journey, one going back in time, from adulthood to childhood. A reading of the Neo-Platonic books leads Augustine to the Catholicism of his childhood, but not without a reservation. Does Christianity cohere with the insights of Plotinus and Porphyry, which he takes to be "so great a good"? He checks by reading Paul's letters with care and finds that the Christians and the Neo-Platonists essentially agree.[45] In fact Christianity magnifies the truth apparent in the Platonic books: "And then, indeed,

---

1968), I.v.6. Also see Augustine's estimation of the value of the liberal arts, *On Order*, II.ix.26.

[44] Augustine, *Against the Academics*, trans. John J. O'Meara, Ancient Christian Writers (New York: Newman Press, 1951), 69-70.

[45] Cf. Augustine, *Confessions*, VII.ix.14.

whatever had been the little radiance that had surrounded the face of philosophy before then, she now appeared so great" that it would astonish even Romanianus's adversary (whoever he may have been) and turn him to philosophy.[46] Accordingly, Augustine seeks to have Romanianus study philosophy in *Contra Academicos* and then, in *De vera religione* (390-91), urges him to become a Christian. The persuasion was successful: He converted to the faith in 396.

Later, in *Confessiones* VII.xxi.27, Augustine will rebel against the books of the Platonists, and even later, in *De civitate Dei* (413-27), he will give a more nuanced view of the Platonists who led him to read Paul with attention. For while the Platonists hold that there is the one true God they also mistakenly affirm that there are other gods who merit worship.[47] In the *Confessiones*, however, the emphasis is on the congruence of Neo-Platonism and Catholicism with regard to essentials: An entirely characteristic "Christian Platonism" of the day.[48] To say whether the experience at Ostia is Neo-Platonic or Christian is to sever something that cannot be neatly divided, although, to be sure, there are distinctions that can and should be drawn, including that between pride and humility, impurity and purity, as already noted more than once. One of the most important of these distinctions turns on the very idea of "experience" in this context. In what sense, if any, does the ascent at Ostia result in an "experience"? It appears, as we have seen, that it is a shared event, and no attention is given to any significant disparity between what the mother and the son undergo. Plainly, the encounter cannot be an empirical experience of any sort, and Augustine is clear that he and his mother stretch out from space and time in order to touch the deity.

As early as *De Ordine* Augustine had pondered the encounter with God, though then it was in terms of vision. "Great God, how will those eyes be!" he exclaims there.[49] Vision characterizes the ascents in Milan. Now, in Ostia, the experience is registered by way of hearing. The soul has ears as well as eyes. We think of Plotinus: "we must let perceptible sounds go (except in so far as we

---

[46] Augustine, *Against the Academics*, II.ii.6.
[47] See Augustine, *City of God*, VIII.xii-xiii.
[48] See, for example, R. Arnou, "Platonisme des Pères," *Dictionnaire de théologie catholique*, XIII, 2258-2392.
[49] Augustine, *On Order*, II.ii.51.

must listen to them) and keep the soul's power of apprehension pure and ready to hear the voices from on high."[50] Yet we also think of faith, recalling Paul, "So then faith [cometh] by hearing" (Rom. 10:17). Augustine reflects on the linguistic consequences of this extreme situation of hearing God at Ostia in a paragraph that is a sentence of 183 words, a *tour de force* of Latin prose. It begins:

> Therefore we said: If to anyone the tumult of the flesh has fallen silent, if the images of earth, water, and air are quiescent, if the heavens themselves are shut out and the very soul itself is making no sound and is surpassing itself by no longer thinking about itself, if all dreams and visions in the imagination are excluded, if all language and every sign and everything transitory is silence–for if anyone could hear them, this is what all of them would be saying, "We did not make ourselves, we were made by him who abides for eternity [*qui manet in aeternum*]" (Ps. 79:3, 5)–if after this declaration they were to keep silence, having directed our ears to him that made them, then he alone would speak not through them but through himself. (IX.x.25)[51]

Only if there is complete silence in all possible modes can one hear God speak directly and not through creation. But what is this divine speech?

> We would hear his word [*ut audiamus verbum*], not through the tongue of the flesh, nor through the voice of an angel, nor through the sound of thunder, not through the obscurity of a symbolic utterance. Him who in these things we love we would hear in person without their mediation [*ipsum sine his audiamus*] (IX.x.25)

---

[50] Armstrong, ed., *Enneads,* V.i.12.

[51] Proper ascription of Scriptural allusions in the *Confessiones* is a difficult business. Chadwick is not always in line with what scholarly commentators (especially O'Donnell) indicate. It is important to note, for instance, that *qui manet in aeternum* is a quotation of Sirach 18: 1, a key proof text for the Creation in patristic Christianity.

We are told how we would *not* hear God's word but not how we *would* hear it, despite the profound silence that makes it possible to hear it.

Yet Augustine has already heard this voice in his soul, in the understanding, as he goes on to say, not mentioning any of the senses:

> This is how it was when at that moment we extended our reach and in a flash of mental energy attained the eternal wisdom which abides beyond all things [*sicut nunc extendimus nos et rapida cognitatione attingimus aeternam sapientiam super omnia manentem*]. (IX.x.25)

We have passed from *attingimus eam modice toto ictu cordis* to *rapida cognitatione attingimus*, from the heart to the mind, though we should not suppose that Augustine is claiming a theoretical knowledge of God in the latter remark. Of course we remember the Neo-Platonic ascent from earthly beauty to the beautiful of book VII with its conclusion: "So in the flash of a trembling glance it attained to that which is [*et pervenit ad id quod est in ictu trepidantis aspectus*]." Yet there is no trembling in the Christian ascent, despite the warning that rings in Christian ears, "It is a fearful thing to fall into the hands of the living God" (Heb. 10:31, KJV). Needless to say, there is no mention of hearing anything, either through the senses or the "spiritual senses," and in fact that would be impossible, for Augustine has stretched beyond space and time in order mentally to touch God. His experience of the divine is strictly an experience without world. What could this possibly be?

We find the word *experientia* very rarely in Augustine, yet it orders his testimony and his theology from just behind the text.[52] Often enough in the *Confessiones* he reflects on experiences he has *had* (stealing pears, for example), but here in Ostia he tells us of an experience that he *cannot have* in the sense of retain it on its own terms. This is not to say that he and Monica are not active at the critical moment: "we extended our reach," he writes. Instead, it is to emphasize that the experience cannot be contained in their minds. They approach the deity in a sudden thought that takes

---

[52] See Hans Urs von Balthasar, *The Glory of the Lord: A Theological Aesthetics*, 7 vols., I: *Seeing the Form*, trans. Erasmo Leiva-Merikakis, ed. Joseph Fessio and John Riches (San Francisco: Ignatius Press, 1982), 284.

them outside space and time, yet this "flash" cannot be brought back fully with them and cannot be put into words. (They cannot bring *themselves* fully back.) To borrow a suggestive distinction drawn by Claude Romano, it is *événemential*, not *événementiel*: it *"illuminates its own context, rather than in any way receiving its meaning from it."*[53] This context is precisely "eternal life," the promised Kingdom.[54] Augustine reflects on his experience without experience:

> If only it could last, and other visions of a vastly inferior kind could be withdrawn! Then this alone could ravish and absorb and enfold in inward joys the person granted the vision [*si continuetur hoc et subtrahantur aliae visiones longe imparis generis et haec una rapiat et absorbeat et recondat in interiora gaudia spectatorem suum*]. So too eternal life [*sempiterna vita*] is of the quality of that moment of understanding [*momentum intellegentiae*] after which we sighed. Is not this the meaning of 'Enter into the joy of your Lord' (Matt. 25:21)? And when is that to be? Surely it is when 'we all rise again, but are not all changed' (1 Cor. 15:51). (IX.x.25)

Three things need to be heeded in these few lines. First, we need to see that we have shifted from hearing to seeing, though remaining "inward." The senses of the soul allow ready passage from the one to the other. Second, we have passed from the eternal to the sempiternal, from *aeternum* to *sempiterna*, which perhaps may be no more than an elegant stylistic variation, since *sempiternitas* means the everlasting or eternal and need not imply temporal duration. Yet the choice of words may also indicate an uncertainty about the role of the resurrected flesh in eternal life with God. In their movement from stretching to ecstasy, Augustine and Monica have separated body and soul and, as already observed, in effect have died without being resurrected. Their joy is "a moment of understanding" of the quality of life the saints enjoy with God before their resurrection in the flesh. Yet this resurrection will come, and an unanswered question in the text is how the

---

[53] Claude Romano, *Event and World*, trans. Shane Mackinlay (New York: Fordham University Press, 2009), 38.
[54] See Augustine, *City of God*, XX.9.

27

resurrected body can be eternal. Does it take up space and time? Or is it entirely mental? Whatever Neo-Platonic dimension runs through the ascent at Ostia for Augustine (though presumably not for Monica), it is modified by a belief in the resurrection. Yet this belief is not easy to align with his experience of the eternal. By the time he was concluding *De civitate Dei* he maintained, as he had done at times in earlier years, that the saints "are going to see God in the body itself," though exactly what this body is he cannot say.[55] The mind may be absorbed into the eternal, though a resurrected body, it seems, may need duration of some sort. One participates in eternal life through the Grace of God, and this need not be in contradiction with having a physical body that needs to experience duration. Third, it is significant that the event, being *événemential*, cannot be ascribed a cause within mundane existence. Only God can allow an ascent to him, and no amount of mental energy or even longing for God can guarantee that one can touch the divine.

"We asked what quality of life the eternal life of the saints will have": Such was the prompt for the event that has been described. And the answer is given in the dazzling "moment of understanding" which consists of "inward joys." The context that is illuminated cannot be articulated, for there has been no *conversio ad phantasma*, as Aquinas will say centuries later.[56] He would also say that Augustine and Monica received the *donum intellectus*, the gift of understanding, which lifts their cognitive abilities beyond their mortal limits. They are not given new knowledge of the deity but now they "know the same things more penetratingly and above the human mode."[57] The "vision" has not been an experience in any usual sense of the world; it has been an eschatological event that has changed both mother and son, giving them pre-thetic understanding of the quality of eternal life, and even a sense perhaps of resurrected life. Following Jean-Luc Marion, we might say that Augustine and Monica touched *idipsum* in a counter-

---

[55] Augustine, *City of God*, XXII. xxix. For a survey of Augustine's views of the resurrected body, see Brian E. Daley's fine article, "Resurrection," in *Augustine through the Ages: An Encyclopedia*, gen. ed., Allan D. Fitzgerald, foreword Jaroslav Pelikan (Grand Rapids: William B. Eerdmans Pub. Co., 1999), 722-23.

[56] See Aquinas, *Summa theologiae*, 1a q. 84 art. 7.

[57] Aquinas, *Commentary on Saint Paul's Epistle to the Galatians*, trans. F. R. Larcher, intro. Richard T. A. Murphy (Albany: Magi Books, 1966), 179.

experience, one that "resists the conditions of objectification," for
the God they encounter is certainly no object, not a being or a
phenomenon.[58] What is mentally touched abides beyond time and
space; the contact brings forth intense joy and also frustration by
dint of its brevity and the need to return to mundane life. The
Ostia "audition" is indeed saturated to the second degree, as
Marion would say: *idipsum* was unable to be aimed at, could not be
borne, evaded any analogy with experience, and could not be
looked at.[59]

Dom Cuthbert will tell us that the event at Ostia is a "mystical
experience" *par excellence.* "The claim consistently and
unequivocally made by the whole line of great mystics found,
perhaps, its simplest and most arresting expression in these words
of St Augustine: 'My mind in the flash of a trembling glance came
to Absolute Being – That Which Is.'"[60] He will do so because he
speaks from a modern tradition that has come to figure religion by
way of experience and that, in the wake of several important works
on "mysticism," now speaks of "mystical experience."[61] I am
thinking, in particular, of William James's *The Varieties of Religious
Experience* (1902), Friedrich von Hügel's *The Mystical Element of
Religion* (1908), Evelyn Underhill's *Mysticism* (1911), and Rudolf
Otto's *The Idea of the Holy* (1917). One of the reasons to study the
writings of the mystics, Dom Cuthbert says in his Prologue, is "for
the sake of their mysticism, itself, as a religious experience."[62] To
be sure, Dom Cuthbert is in some ways seeking to correct this
tradition by placing a steady emphasis on contemplation. He draws
from Auguste Saudreau and Augustin Poulin, among others, who
are concerned with interior prayer rather than experiences in a
narrow sense, and who know very well that spiritual consolations
are not usual features of mental prayer.[63] As he says,

---

[58] See Marion, *Being Given: Toward a Phenomenology of Givenness*, trans.
Jeffrey L. Kosky (Stanford: Stanford University Press, 2002), 215.
[59] See Marion, *Being Given*, § 24.
[60] Butler, *Western Mysticism*, 4.
[61] See my essay, "Religious Experience and the Phenomenality of God,"
Between Philosophy and Theology: Contemporary Interpretations of Christianity,
ed. Lieven Boeve and Christophe Brabant (Farnham: Ashgate, 2010), 127-
46.
[62] Butler, *Western Mysticism*, 3.
[63] See Auguste Saudreau, *The Degrees of the Spiritual Life: A Method of
Directing Souls According to their Progress in Virtue*, trans. Dom Bede Camm, 2

"'contemplation' is the word that will be met with in St Augustine, St Gregory, and St Bernard, to designate what is now commonly called 'the mystical experience'" (4). Yet is "mystical experience" simply a modern translation of "contemplation," one that leaves no remainder? Dom Cuthbert himself gives a reason for saying no when he writes of "experiences" that seem to take place only in the "higher kinds of contemplation," and of "frequent phases of prayer and contemplation . . . from which such experience is absent."[64] That great taxonomist of the contemplative life, Giovanni Scaramelli, would agree with him.[65] Contemplation does not always end in mystical experience, nor does "mystical experience" serve as a proper translation of *contemplatio*.

At Ostia Augustine and Monica followed Christian *contemplatio* in a manner that was peculiar and was to remain so throughout the tradition, except for treatises on mystical experience that took the form of dialogues. Not everyone can follow the Prince, Dom Cuthbert might say. If the son drew on Neo-Platonism as a vehicle for the ascent, the mother almost certainly did not, even though she is hailed as a wise woman and a true philosopher, and yet they both touched the unsayable God of Christianity. If we call this flash of insight an "experience," we must do so with many caveats; for it was a moment of understanding, one that took place outside space and time, one that strictly could not be objectified, and one that could not be communicated. What struck Augustine and his mother was not a unity with divine being but rather attaining ineffable contact with that which is above and beyond all change. The event at Ostia organizes the whole of the *Confessiones* from the vantage point of Book IX. We fully understand the most memorable line on its first page only when we have grasped the significance of the Christian ascent: "our heart is restless until it rests in you" [*inquietum est cor*

---

vols. (London: R. and T. Washbourne, 1907), and *The Life of Union with God, and the Means of Attaining It According to the Great Masters of Spirituality*, trans. E. J. Strickland (London: Burns Oates and Washbourne Ltd., 1927), esp. 12, and A. Poulain, *The Graces of Interior Prayer: A Treatise on Mystical Theology*, trans. Leonora L. Yorke Smith, pref. D. Considine (London: Kegan Paul, Trench, Trubner and Co., 1921).

[64] Butler, *Western Mysticism*, lviii.

[65] See G. B. Scaramelli, *A Handbook of Mystical Theology*, trans. D. H. S. Nicholson, intro. Allan Armstrong (Berwick, Maine: Ibis Press, 2005), ch. 3, 4.

nostrum donec requiescat in te] (I.i.1). Peace could only be found for Augustine after the *ictu cordis* at Ostia, in a journey passing from the region of dissimilarity to the Selfsame, from the world to the Kingdom.

Kevin Hart is Edwin B. Kyle Professor of Christian Studies at the University of Virginia where he also holds courtesy professorships in the Departments of English and French. He also holds the Eric D'Arcy Chair of Philosophy at the Australian Catholic University. His most recent scholarly work is an edition of Jean-Luc Marion's *The Essential Writings* (Fordham UP), and his most recent book of poetry is *Morning Knowledge* (Notre Dame UP).

ABANDONMENT: GIVING VOICE IN THE DESERT

Ron Broglio

> Stage Directions: "*As the scene opens, a dog is barking in the distance, alone in the silence a cow is lowing. The dog will bark again two or three times during the course of this piece. Another animal, a donkey, for example, will perhaps wander across the stage.*"[1]

> Every voice cries out in the desert, like the voice of the prophet. And it's in the desert of deserted existence, prey both to lack *and* to absence, that voice first makes itself heard.[2]

Nancy's essay "Vox Clamans in Deserto" is a disputation on the ecstatic nature of being in the world. Or more correctly, it is not a disputation but a performance: it is a matter of style and comportment in which its way of presenting a state of affairs is itself a model for the state of affairs. So, here at the outset we are set upon by several problems: what is this ecstatic nature of being in the world and why is Nancy writing a work as if it were to be a play performed by voices? Following these problems come others–how is this a mystical text and why in such a text do animals walk across its stage?

This text- or voice-play is centered around and encircles the Biblical passage in which John the Baptist is a voice crying out in the desert.[3] For Nancy we are all voices in the desert of deserted existence. In other words, our very existence, our being-in-the world is comportment in a desert. Such an environment is sparse

---

[1] Jean-Luc Nancy, "Vox Clamans in Deserto," *Multiple Arts: The Muse II* (Stanford, CA: Stanford University Press, 2006), 38. Unless otherwise noted, all references to Nancy are from this text.
[2] Nancy, 41.
[3] See John 1:23 and Isaiah 40:3.

and unforgiving. There is enough here to sustain, but no lush overabundance of life. Much like the dark night of the soul, the desert gives little comfort, almost nothing. There is a scarcity which just barely supports life. This almost nothing is also just enough, a desert which will sustain and transform life upon it. It is in this sense that John of the Cross can say that the mystic arrives at "a remarkably deep and vast wilderness unattainable by any human creature, into an immense unbounded desert, the more delightful, savorous, and loving, the deeper, vaster, and more solitary it is."[4] The desert weans us from corporeal joys and points us beyond ourselves to a "dark night" in which a beyond holds little hope of providing any light, insight, or revelation. "Deserted existence" is an existence abandoned, deserted, left with a promised companionship which will not come. It is a place where one is "prey both to lack *and* to absence." To be deserted is not to be alone but to be alone with the thought that it could be otherwise. It is this otherwise that will be an impetus for voicing, for calling out– to which I will return. Deserted and in an environment that feels inhuman, scarcity provides a lack, and absence by which we feel vulnerable and exposed.

Welcome to the vale of tears. Here we find what Heidegger called eksistence–the state of alienated self-awareness of our throwness in the world. In short, we find ourselves eccentric as if the spinning axis of our self were off center. We are the center of our world but feel decentered and out of place or as if standing outside ourselves:

> . . . the human being has a reflective attitude towards its experiences and towards itself. This is why human beings are eccentric, because they live beyond the limits set for them by nature by taking up a distance from their immediate experience. In living outside itself in its reflective activity, the human being achieves a break with nature.[5]

Heidegger re-centers humans through the task of worlding which aligns building, dwelling, and thinking into a whole or unity which

---

[4] John of the Cross, *Dark Night of the Soul* (New York: Harper Collins, 1993), II 17:6

[5] Simon Critchley, *Infinitely Demanding* (New York: Verso, 2008), 86.

will be the Way for a People (*Volk*). This is a grand History of a historically fashioned people whose narrative led to a wreckage. We live in the wake of this wreck. In this wake, Simon Critchley sees a fundamental divide in the human that cannot be smoothed over by building or dwelling or thinking. For him, there is no authentic dwelling. All dwelling is a bit off kilter. In the desert, we are never quite at home and there is no orientation by which to point elsewhere in order to find, to make or "to return" home. The desert provides the figure for Deleuze and Guattari's smooth space, the space of the nomad whose home is a homelessness. "Deserted existence" is also desert-ed existence, one whose very way of life is that of a desert. And yet, we have not yet given voice; we have not yet opened unto the desert. So far, we have dealt with the preliminaries, with a foundational (dis)placement that exercises what it means to be human.

> [I live in Tempe, Arizona and only a few miles from deep and isolating deserts. The Superstition Mountains overlook this Valley of the Sun and in those desert mountains tens of people die each year from sun and heat exposure and lack of water. You are invited to come visit me in the desert. This is a formal invitation–a voice crying out to readers, perhaps–and while I can offer hospitality, it is an inhospitable region where living is at its limits.]

Giving voice, crying out in the desert, is a rupture and event. Nancy characterizes the phenomenology of this event using Kristeva's voice which wanders onto the stage of his work. Here is Kristeva as written or "vocalized" by Nancy:

> The voice responds to the missing breast . . . The vocal cords stretch and vibrate in order to fill the emptiness of the mouth and the digestive track (a response to hunger) . . . The voice will take over the void . . . Muscular, gastric, and sphincter contractions reject, sometimes at the same time, air, food, waste. The voice springs from this rejection of air and nutritive or excremental matter; so as to be vocal, the first sonorous emissions not only have their origins in the glottis but are the audible mark of a complex phenomenon of muscular and rhythmic

contractions that is a rejection implicating the whole body.[6]

Voice begins with a dissatisfaction. Either we do not have that which would satisfy ("the missing breast") or we reject "air and nutritive" matter as not sufficient. The mystic in the desert is completely filled with a restlessness. One reads in mystic texts time and again a variant of the oft-repeated phrase: my heart is restless until it rests in Thee and as supplement, the Thee has receded, has disappeared, has abandoned the mystic in the desert.

For Nancy and Kristeva mystic restlessness is perpetual and the very site for human opening–"the first sonorous emissions not only have their origins in the glottis but are the audible mark of a complex phenomenon of muscular and rhythmic contractions." Being abandoned and abandoning the world (as not enough) puts us in a state of abandon. Only at such a moment would one risk exposure, vulnerability, and openness. In other words, only in abandon would one open the body and expose it to the inhuman desert. Such an opening is so violent to the body that it produces "a complex phenomenon of muscular and rhythmic contractions that is a rejection implicating the whole body."

> [To survive in the desert if caught with limited water, abandoned or disoriented and unsure how to get home, breathe through the nose. Do not open your mouth. Survival experts note that by breathing through the mouth you lose over twice as much water as breathing through the nose. Opening one's mouth in the desert is to expose oneself.][7]

This, then, is voice: abandonment in a desert. With such abandon we produce an audible mark of opening the body onto the world. Voice is a mark of the body–the opening of the mouth and glottis and the push of air by the diaphragm and through the lungs. Yet the voice is not body but that which is made possible by the body opening onto the world. It is the echo of the hollow center of the body. Like a fingerprint, each voice is unique: "Did you know that

---

[6] Nancy, 41.

[7] Take my word for this or consult desert survival guides: http://crisistimes.com/desert_water.php

vocal sounds are just about as singular as it gets, even more impossible to confuse than fingerprints, which are themselves unique?" Furthermore "it's not just we all have our own voices, but that all of us have several possible voices."[8] Voice embodies being singular-plural in which we are never an "interiority" but also already an outside onto the world. Voice gives voice to our eccentric nature of being both ourselves and beside ourselves.

Voice is a need and a gift. It is a need in as much as no object will satisfy nor make us feel complete. It is a gift in that while feeling incomplete and abandoned we do not turn inward but rather become even more vulnerable; we perform our vulnerability by opening outward, by giving voice–giving it like a gift from the very depths of our bodies. We give voice because although alone we somehow believe that it could be otherwise. Voice is the attempt to communicate, the desire to be other than abandoned. It is a utopic venture–the attempt to not be alone but rather to imagine community through communication. Far in the desert there is no guarantee of being heard nor if heard being understood.

> ['What is called thinking' is a call from elsewhere; it is the thought manifest in corporeal frictions, interlacings, and mixings.[9]]

Voice carries over a distance, across spaces. The flesh of the world makes possible the vibration of voice in the air. Distance which keeps us apart from one another and prevents contact is the very medium by which connection through voice is possible. Oh happy fault, this distance between us that brings an opening of the body and a guttural articulation across space. Nancy leverages this opening of the space between us:

> Voice wouldn't respond to the void . . . but would expose it, turn it toward the outside. Voice would be less the rejection than the ejection or the throw of an infinitely open void at the heart of singular being, at the heart of this abandoned being. What it would expose would be not a lack per se but a failure on the part of plenitude or presence that isn't actually a failing, since

---

[8] Nancy, 40.
[9] Avital Ronell, *Stupidity* (Chicago: University of Illinois Press, 2002), 179.

it's what constitutes what's proper to existence, what opens an always already open existence to what lies outside it.[10]

"What is proper to existence" is a spacing, a flesh of space where voice can resonate. In the desert we live an "always already open existence" which in voice opens to "what lies outside it."

This willingness to give oneself over to an outside through voice is part of Nancy's project to think "being-with" or *Mitsein*. As Ignaas Devisch explains: "What still has to be thought—and this is the reason the French philosopher wants to reopen Heidegger's crucial work—is the essentially plural structure of every *Dasein* or of every singularity."[11] Abandoned and in a state of abandon, *Dasein* for Nancy is necessarily a being-with. It is not a being-with that founds or grounds a homeland, a *Volk*. Rather it is a being-with that comes from exposure and vulnerability and that takes place in the distance or spacing of space.

While Heidegger introduces being-with, it remained secondary to a *Dasein* in its singularity and as part of a destiny of a people: "the same Heidegger also went astray with his vision of a people and a destiny conceived at least in part as a subject, which proves no doubt that *Dasein*'s 'being-toward-death' was never radically implicated in its being-with—in *Mitsein*—and it is this implication that remains to be thought."[12] Giving voice—as gift—is the role of the prophet in the desert, the one who calls out for a future "to come." Such a future is in the infinitive which is to say that it is in no particular temporal space of the past, present, nor future. It is a virtual space—an imagined community—that *authorizes* the voice as a calling out. We give voice because we imagine there is one who can hear. And it is the opening of oneself (who lives an "always already open existence") that *enables* voice. This community is at a distance—the spacing which allows a resonance

---

[10] Nancy, 42.

[11] Ignaas Devisch, "A Trembling Voice in the Desert: Jean-Luc Nancy's Rethinking of the Political Space," presented at Deconstruction Reading Politics conference University of Staffordshire, UK, 1999. http://ugent.academia.edu/IgnaasDevisch/Papers/258370/A_Trembling_Voice_In_the_Desert_Jean-Luc_Nancys_Rethinking_of_the_Space_of_the_Political

[12] Jean-Luc Nancy, *The Inoperative Community* (Minneapolis: Minnesota University Press, 1991), 14.

of voice–for all those who cry out in the desert of deserted existence.

This desert (and its imagined communities) has many sorts of voices. Voice is never a unity and each voice is already plural with its echoes and resonances and its eccentric qualities (as the voice is both within and outside the self).[13] But perhaps most radical in this multiplicity is Nancy's inclusion of nonhuman voices to the community of the desert. The text opens with stage directions worth ruminating upon:

> *a dog is barking in the distance, alone in the silence a cow is lowing. The dog will bark again two or three times during the course of this piece. Another animal, a donkey, for example, will perhaps wander across the stage.*

These stage directions are not the voices of the animals themselves but rather an invitation that we hear the others or the voices of the others. There is much at work in this moment. We may or may not see the other, but we hear its voice. We do not hear the other–as if there were a path to transparent communication–but rather we hear the voice of the other. To hear the voice includes hearing the corporeal opening of the body as sound resonates across it. These are bodies like or, in some instances, rather unlike our own and so produce inhuman voice.[14] Hearing the voice includes the capacities and dissonance of the spacing across distance, traversing distance, according to the capacity for projection.

["Cows have regional accents like humans, language specialists have suggested. They decided to examine the issue after dairy farmers noticed their cows had slightly different moos, depending on which herd they came from. John Wells, Professor of Phonetics at the

---

[13] Nancy, 44.

[14] I use the term "nonhuman" as a neutral description of animals other than humans. The term "inhuman" carries a different weight and potency as that which challenges the human. Voices emanating from nonhumans viscerally challenge humans: by dominating airwaves and marking space as other than human space, by troubling human intelligibility of the voice of the other, and by a sounds that humans strain to make or are unattainable by our bodies.

University of London, said regional twangs had been seen before in birds."][15]

While Nancy includes voices of many theorists–human theorists– throughout the text, the animals' voices are present only by directions rather than by textual transmission of voice by speech and language. The reader is given the note that animals are giving voice but the voices are not present. It may well be that language breaks down here. There is no human system of language capable of transmitting the voice of the animal. Nancy can gesture to animal voices but cannot provide the voices of the animals. As Nancy notes, voice proceeds language; voice is not of language but makes language possible. Between humans and animals there is not a common system of language but there is voice. As Wittgenstein famously said: "If a lion could talk, we could not understand him."[16] The lion problem is an issue of speech and meaning which is related to voice but different. In the lion problem the concern is social community, the discourse community in which language is fashioned to human (or nonhuman) experience of being-in-the-world or as Wittgenstein says "To imagine a language is to imagine a form of life." A lion's sense of being is different; so, its words, the meaning of the words, and its use of language would be different–even, as Wittgenstein says– unintelligible, baffling.

["The cries of a dog or of other animals aren't just noise. Every animal has a recognizable voice all its own."[17]

"Crickets in the meadows and cicadas in the trees, coyotes in the night hills, frogs in the ponds and whales in the oceans, birds in the skies make our planet continually resound with chant. Humans do not begin to sing, and do not sing, in dead silence. Our voices begin

---

[15] BBC News 23 August 2006 http://news.bbc.co.uk/2/hi/5277090.stm
[16] Ludwig Wittgenstein. *Philosophical Investigations.* New York, Macmillan, 1968. Pt. II, p. 223. See Cary Wolfe, *Animal Rites: American Culture, the Discourse of Species and Posthumanist Theory* (Chicago: University of Chicago Press, 2003), 44.
[17] Nancy, 38.

to purr, hum, and crescendo in the concerto and cacophony of nature and machines."][18]

Voice precedes speech and enables it. You might hear a familiar voice before you know what the person is saying. You identify the person by voice even before understanding the speech. As Nancy notes, humans are not alone in having voice: "Yes, there's no speech without voice, but there is such a thing as voice without speech. And not just for animals, but for us as well."[19] Nancy is trying to imagine a community that is larger than those who share a similar language. He is trying to imagine a community of humans and lions and yes, even aliens. Joining him in this experiment, let's ask: can we use the capacity of voice as a shared difference to address an alien/animal/other in an address that, admittedly, would be outside of a discourse community and outside of language? It would be an odd address, indeed, and Nancy hints at it throughout his essay where voices resonate and call out from one to an/other. Voice cannot hear but can voice; Voice can throw itself and articulates what it means to be bodily thrown into the world, to be a being who is situated in a world. Hearing voice transports the listener, possesses and intoxicates the listener who may well give voice in response.

Particularly odd in this stage direction is the absence of desert animals–the coyote, the quail, the gopher, the javelina. There is a dog, a cow, and "a donkey, for example" who wanders across the stage. All of them are domesticated animals. But can we not also imagine the nondomesticated–those that are farther afield in the alien space of the desert? Is the "for example" simply to say the list could go on further? And recall as well that "*The dog will bark again two or three times during the course of this piece.*"[20] The animal interrupts the human discourse to remind us there are others out there. Nancy does not write in these voices. The reader must imagine these (dis)placed voices. Nancy does not provide the interruptions–since to do so would be to schedule them and space them to his convenience. Rather, the interruption, to be an actual displacement, hovers over the text or haunts the text from within

---

[18] Alphonso Lingis, "Bestiality," *symploke* 6.1 (1998), 56-71, 59.
[19] Nancy, 38.
[20] Nancy, 38.

as the radical nature of voice which proceeds language and the noise of inhuman voice that disrupts the system of language.

> ["'we' are always radically other, already in- or ahuman in our very being–not just in the evolutionary, biological, and zoological fact of our physical vulnerability and mortality (which we share with other animals), our mammalian existence, of course, but also in our subjection to and constitution in the materiality and technicity of a language that is always on the scene before we are, as a precondition of our subjectivity."][21]

Even within us, voice feels both ours and alien–it is air from the outside and from within. It is sound within us but pushed beyond the boundary of our bodies. The technicity of voice–vocal chords, larynx, mouth–is our "own" but determined for us biologically prior to our arrival on the scene. In addressing voice, Nancy is concerned with a technicity prior to language. Animals give voice and each in its own way with unique vibration registering the breath moving across the opening of the body. Each eating and breathing body is equipped with the capacity for voice. The technicity is not a universal but rather is manifest and is utilized differently for each and all. Voice is a particular technicity we (as a community at a distance or a community to come) hold in common differently.

If Nancy's project is to imagine a *Mitsein*, a being-with, that radically defines *Dasein*, then the community of nonhumans remains a challenge to the prophetic voices in the desert. In the inhuman world of the desert, the desert of deserted existence, can we be with the voices that are not human? And what would such a radical being-with look like?

Tekeli-li! Tekeli-li! Is the haunting sound of alien voices in H. P. Lovecraft's masterwork *At the Mountains of Madness*.[22] In this novella, Antarctic explorers at the farthest reaches of extreme environment find a mountain-sized alien city built millions of years

---

[21] Cary Wolfe, "Exposures," S. Cavell, C. Diamond, J. McDowell, I. Hacking and C. Wolfe, *Philosophy and Animal Life* (New York: Columbia UP, 2009), 1-41, 27.
[22] H. P. Lovecraft, *At The Mountains of Madness* (New York: Random House, 2005), 93.

ago. While exploring the labyrinth ruins, the humans encounter a variety of alien life and then try to escape with their lives. From the depths of the inhuman world, the shape-shifting alien things cry "*Tekeli-li! Tekeli-li!*"[23] Lovecraft borrowed the sound from Edger Alan Poe's rambling tale of sea adventures *The Narrative of Arthur Gordon Pym of Nantucket*, where "Tekeli-li!" is the sound of a strange white bird, and "Tekeli-li" is the sound made by the natives who see anything white brought on their island, which itself is devoid of whiteness excepting the birds.[24] Tekeli-li becomes a figure for what cannot be understood and has no proper place within the culture. It is a vocalization, a voice of this otherness.

Lovecraft's aliens and Poe's birds offer alien voice–they give a voice of otherness. John Cunningham Lilly found in dolphins "genuine alien intelligences with which humans can interact in strange and mysterious ways."[25] Lilly's breakthrough moment in hearing the voice of the dolphin–actually hearing with ears that can hear (as the Bible dictates)–was when he had a dolphin on an operating table and while experimenting on its body the animal gave voice in what according to Lilly was the dolphin desperately trying to echo the voices of humans in the operating room. It wanted to communicate its own plight and could only penetrate the thick anthropocentricism of Lilly and his fellow scientists by throwing its voice in a modulation like that of the human. At this moment, Lilly realized the power of voice and its primacy beyond language. Lilly changed all his research to establish communication with dolphins. His work was in part funded by NASA and his former student Diana Reiss funded some of her PhD research in the 1980s through SETI (Search for Extra Terrestrial Intelligence). As Reiss and Lilly explain: if you want to understand what it is like to communicate with aliens, dolphins are the place to start. Animals and aliens offer us voices crying in the desert and remind us that *Mitsein* is a state of being(with) beyond the human. In doing so, these voices too are prophetic.

---

[23] In conversation Nicola Masciandaro has mentioned to me that such voices are doubly alien in that the cry of Shoggoth mimick with "no voice save the imitated accents of their bygone masters," so rather than alien voice it is also really the alienness of a voicelessness.

[24] China Miéville, "Introduction" to H. P. Lovecraft, *At the Mountains of Madness* (New York: Random House, 2005), xvii.

[25] Francis Jeffrey and John Cunningham Lilly. *John Lilly So far . . .* (Los Angels: Jeremy P. Tarcher, 1990), 239.

Language has been used as a uniquely marker of humans; language works to immunize us from our own animality. It marks the distinction between the humans and the nonhuman animals. But voice is not the property of humans alone. As nonhumans give voice, they mark a space which we cannot enter by language–a space that is not intelligible to us and yet as animals we participate in by hearing and giving voice in return. Voice and Nancy's essay on voice cannot function without this necessary supplement of animals. It is by them that the marker of not-language-but-voice is possible. Nancy turns his essay toward its conclusion by explaining that with voice

> the other is summoned at the point where there is neither subject nor signification. That is what I want to call the desert of *jouissance* or of joy. Arid, maybe, but never desolate. Neither desolate nor consoled, beyond either laughter or tears.

Voice does not give us the scaffolding for subject-object relations, "neither subject nor signification." Voice is an ephemeral event; it is a scarcity that cannot be grasped, nor seen, nor made to signify within the hermeneutic circle of language. It is the very little, almost nothing of bodies opened unto the desert. This is *Mitsein* which Heidegger could not think but has been the ongoing task for Nancy.

And so we return to the animals . . . they have not stopped walking across the stage and "interrupting" intelligible discourse with lowing and barking. They have haunted the scene of Nancy's performance since its beginnings. Karl Steel in his reflection on animal voices in the apocalyptic end of days explains that "we attend to the incomprehensibility of animal speech, not as a lacuna in the tradition's explanatory capability, but rather as a gap deliberately left open, a space that has not been stuffed with human meaning."[26] Voice is outside of time or at least a human time as there are voices before and after us. As such, voice bears witness to a nonhuman time and the time of the inhuman. If the Desert

---

26 Karl Steel, "Woofing and weeping with animals in the last days." Postmedieval: a journal of medieval cultural studies (2010) 1, 187–193. http://www.palgrave-journals.com/pmed/journal/v1/n1/full/pmed201024a.html

Fathers bear witness to animal voices, it is only because they are attuned to the nonhuman time and the radical elsewhere from which the these voices call. St. Anthony must share the desert with the wild animals who do not heed human dominion. He does not live in a human domain, a striated space, but rather the smooth and open terrain open to human and nonhumans alike. Unlike the cultural hermeneutic circle in which we might ask for whom the bell tolls, we would do well to ask for whom the voices call. They come from elsewhere and point us to a beyond "that has not been stuffed with human meaning" yet nevertheless these voices reside among us.

Ron Broglio is an associate professor in the Department of English at Arizona State University and Senior Scholar at the university's Global Institute of Sustainability. His research focuses on how philosophy and aesthetics can help us rethink the relationship between humans and the environment. He is author of *Surface Encounters: Thinking with Animals and Art* and *Technologies of the Picturesque.* He is currently working on an artistic and theoretical treatise on posthumanism and animal studies called *Animal Revolutions: Event to Come.*

COMMENTARIAL NOTHINGNESS

Daniel Colucciello Barber

> They live eternally with God, directly close to God, not
> beneath or above.
>
> —Meister Eckhart[1]

EQUAL TO NOTHING

Eckhart, when speaking of those who live directly close to
God, poses a question regarding their identity: "Who are they who
are thus equal?" He answers himself by commenting, "Those who
are equal to nothing, they alone are equal to God."[2] To be equal to
God is to be equal to nothing. These sermonic remarks provide a
commentary on the beginning of the Gospel of John,[3] which itself

---

[1] Meister Eckhart, *Meister Eckhart: The Essential Sermons, Commentaries,
Treatises, and Defense*, ed. and trans. Edmund Colledge and Bernard
McGinn (Mahwah, NJ: Paulist Press, 1981), Sermon 6, p. 187. I have
refrained from repeating the inverted commas that are found, in the
translation of this text, around "with God." They are interpolations, and
the reason I do not repeat them is my suspicion that the aim motivating
them—namely that of "clarifying" the text's meaning—serves to dissolve the
force of Eckhart's speech. It is erroneous, in my mind, to presume that
Eckhart's statement is in need of clarification, given that the sort of
distinctions on which clarity depends are precisely what Eckhart
repeatedly seeks to undermine, often quite explicitly and even more often
by way of performance. As Michael Sells has remarked, "Such
interpolations and the widespread acceptance they have received are
indicative of a pervasive modern dis-ease with the kind of mystical
language composed by Eckhart." See *Mystical Languages of Unsaying*
(Chicago: University of Chicago Press, 1994), 1.
[2] Eckhart, Sermon 6, p. 187.
[3] In order to add further complexity to this series, it should be observed
that sermon from which these remarks are taken, and in which the text
from John is referenced is a commentary on the Book of Wisdom,
specifically its statement that "The just will live forever" (Ws. 5:16). Ibid.,
p. 185.

is a commentary on the beginning of the Book of Genesis. The remarks thus emerge within a series of commentarial repetition that we might trace, moving backwards, from Eckhart to John to Genesis. On what is Genesis a commentary? We will answer this question, but not now. Our attention presently turns away from the "origins" of this commentarial series—hence holding in abeyance the problem of commenting on something prior to commentary—and toward the commentarial repetition taking place here in this commentary on Eckhart.

Our commentary on Eckhart's commentary commences with his strange assertion of an equality to God that is simultaneously and necessarily an equality to nothing. How should we understand this assertion? One way would be to emphasize the distinction of God from all things—that is, the difference between God's being and the being of all other beings. Foregrounding this distinction, we might read Eckhart's comment as follows: "God is absolutely distinct from all other things, and so the one who is equal to God must likewise be absolutely distinct from all things; to become equal to God is to become equal to no thing, for no thing can be equal to God." Such an interpretation—rather orthodox in its reliance on an account of God's distinction—revolves around the supposed irreducibility of all beings to God's being. The former beings participate in the being of the latter, but such participation does not alter the reality of distinction—in fact, participation is *required* by the unquestionability of this distinction.[4] Participation does not threaten to undermine the reality of distinction, on the contrary it is the effect of distinction's reality, which is to say that it is conceived in order to redeem, or to keep alive, the possibility that the actual difference (between God's being and all other beings) does not utterly foreclose the affirmative relation between the differentiated. This is the dialectic of distinction and participation, and it will be found in any interpretation of Eckhart's comment that relies on God's distinction. It is because of this presence of the dialectic that any such interpretation must be rejected.

To interpret Eckhart's comment by relying on a dialectic is to miss its meaning, and this is because there is no dialectic without

---

[4] Of course, one may already wonder whether one can "participate" in equality? Does not participation require a kind of inequality between participant and participated?

duality, which Eckhart explicitly refuses. It is easy enough to see why dialectic requires duality, for its movement depends on an opposition of two terms. Even if the dialectic resolves its opposition through a unitary term, this unity must be composite—as the result of two—rather than simple.[5] Thus dialectic cannot escape duality, but what still needs to be comprehended is the nature of Eckhart's *antagonism* toward duality. For this we can turn to another of Eckhart's sermons, wherein we find him commenting on the love of God. When we love God, what should we love God *as*, or in what *way* should we love God? It is not hard to imagine this question, posed "rhetorically" by Eckhart to himself, as a repetition of–a commentary on–Augustine's own rhetorical question: "But what do I love when I love my God?"[6] Augustine does eventually settle on an answer, but only after saying quite often what this beloved, or this God, is "not." Eckhart's commentarial repetition of Augustine's question picks up on this tendency toward divine indistinguishability; it seems to draw out of Augustine's text the failure of thought's ability to answer. Such failure, of course, is not really a failure. We could say that it is *actually* a failure, or more precisely that it is a failure *of actuality*, yet in saying this we observe that actual failure preserves the possibility of not answering.[7] And it is this possibility of not answering (the question of what is loved in and through the name of God) that Eckhart makes determinative: "You should love him as he is a non-God."[8]

---

[5] And if, perhaps, the dialectic does not want to compose its resolution, it will still find itself invoking something–perhaps a third term–that would function to resolve the duality, such that the resolution, while not necessarily composite, must be valorized against the background of duality.

[6] Augustine, *Confessions*, trans. R.S. Pine-Coffin (New York: Penguin Books, 1961), p. 213.

[7] In speaking affirmatively of a possibility of not answering, of not giving way to the divisions bound up in actuality, I have in mind Giorgio Agamben's (by now widespread) re-reading of the Aristotelian account of potentiality (or "possibility") and actuality. "Contrary to the traditional idea of potentiality that is annulled in actuality," he calls for a potentiality that "survives actuality and, in this way, *gives itself to itself*." See his *Potentialities*, trans. Daniel Heller-Roazen (Palo Alto, CA: Stanford UP, 1999), p. 184.

[8] Eckhart, Sermon 83, p. 208.

The problem with naming the beloved as God is that it divides the lover from the beloved, it makes divine love into a duality, whereas divine love is simple. It is love according to the One. Thus, when Eckhart says that we ought to love non-God, he continues by saying that we ought to love the One: we love him "as he is a pure, unmixed, bright 'One,' separated from all duality."[9] This allows us to see that non-God is not the opposite of God. After all, such a determination would create yet another duality, a duality no longer of God and all other beings, but still of God and non-God. Therefore non-God is not the opposite of God, it is the intensification or excess of God according to the One. This One precludes duality, but it is not *opposed* to duality—for this too would introduce a duality, namely between the One and duality. It is "separated from all duality." Non-God is thus the emergence of the One, from the One, which is indifferent to the difference of duality.

If Eckhart speaks of a One that is without duality and without mixture, then a dialectically mediated interpretation of his comment (on equality to God as equality to nothing) must be put out of play. Yet this returns us to the problem of grasping why it is that being equal to nothing is the condition of possibility for being equal to God. Clarity emerges when we look at the next line from Eckhart: "The divine being is equal to nothing."[10] This line significantly inflects the direction of our commentary. The interpretation we have already considered, and rejected, assumed an inverse relation between God and all other things, such that to become equal to God is to deny equality to all that which is not God. According to such an assumption, nothing becomes the intermediary between two poles of the given, namely God and anything that is different from God. Yet with this line Eckhart tells us that God, the "divine being," is likewise "equal to nothing." If God, like the soul, is equal to nothing, then nothing can no longer function within the conceptual division between God and all other things. Nothing is "separated from" all distinction, including God's.

---

[9] Ibid. In this sentence we are especially able to see the influence of Eckhart on various ideas found in the thought of François Laruelle, such as "vision-in-One," "unilateral duality," and the critique of mixture, as well as on Laruelle's reliance on the prefix "non-." As a way of developing this link, I have—in the previous sentence and elsewhere—used Laruelle's phrase, "according to," in order to articulate Eckhart's account of the One.

[10] Ibid., Sermon 6, p. 187.

The connection of "equality to nothing" with "equality to God" thus precludes the assumption that we must see all other beings as nothing *in relation to* the being of God. It is not a matter of opposition between God and the becoming nothing of all other beings, for God too is equal to nothing. Equality to nothing is the soul's condition for equality to God because equality to nothing likewise conditions God; equality to nothing is not what brings the soul toward God, it is what the soul and God already have *in common.* The upshot of all this is that nothingness ceases to be that which must be "crossed" in order to reach God. Nothingness, as Eckhart articulates it, is not what separates us from God, it is what identifies us with God. Such a shift in sensibility with regard to nothingness is, we might conjecture, the point at which Eckhart's thought departs from orthodoxy. In other words, what makes Eckhart heretical is not his mere discussion of or even emphasis on nothingness, it is more precisely the conceptual priority he grants it over the distinction between God and all other beings. We should not overlook the capacity of orthodox Christian theology to accommodate, and at times even to encourage, "mystical" discourses about nothingness. To name but one instance, Pseudo-Dionysius's powerful account of "divine darkness" did not divorce him from orthodox affirmation.[11] Yet the capacity for convergence between his writings and the norms of orthodoxy was a result of the absence, within the former, of anything approaching the explicitness with which Eckhart insists on a "commonality" or univocity of nothingness. It remains possible to write a commentary on Pseudo-Dionysius that does not threaten orthodoxy insofar as the nothingness of divine darkness is able to be interpreted as something like the interval between God and all other beings. Eckhart is thus separated from Pseudo-Dionysius insofar as his articulation of nothingness resists the work performed by orthodoxy, which is to preserve distinction (and especially the distinction between creator and creature).

Those familiar with the record will observe that Eckhart's thought, in spite of the heretical nature I am attributing to it, was not completely separated–in a historical sense–from Christian orthodoxy. Eckhart did not exactly affirm the status of his thought

---

[11] On "divine darkness," see Pseudo-Dionysius (the Aeropagite), *Pseudo-Dionysius: The Complete Works*, trans. Colm Luibheid (Mahwah, NJ: Paulist Press, 1987), pp. 135-137.

as "separated" from orthodoxy's dualities; he instead defended himself against heresy charges.[12] There is clearly something a bit opportunistic[13] in this defense, and its relative success can certainly be taken as indication that, even amidst the radicality of his account of nothingness, a path for its incorporation into orthodoxy remained. But this just raises the stakes of commentary. In other words, the capacity to incorporate Eckhart's thought, to chasten and disavow its separateness, depends on the availability of a commentary that would mute its heretical character; similarly, the capacity to express his thought's heretical character depends on the availability of a commentary that would affirm this character (while muting its orthodoxy). Does this demand for commentarial determination imply that there is something peculiar to Eckhart's thought, something that would not be found elsewhere?

There is in fact a sense in which Eckhart peculiarly demands commentary, it is just that this demand comes from language rather than from Eckhart. That is, the demand peculiarly present in Eckhart is the demand of language as such. If it is peculiarly present in Eckhart, then this is because Eckhart, unlike many others, does not block the demand that is already there. We block language's demand for commentary by dividing language up in some manner or another, by subjecting language to a duality—perhaps between original and derivative meanings, or between the sensical and the nonsensical, or above all between the fixed and the commented on. To do this to language is to dampen the cry of its polysemic infinitude,[14] which intrinsically demands commentary and makes commentary proper to all language, such that language is nothing but commentary upon commentary; to do this to language is to divert attention away from its essential potentiality and toward the regulation of the arbitrary division between the

---

[12] For a summation of the historical record, see Colledge, "Historical Data," in Eckhart, pp. 5-23.

[13] Far be it from me to blame him for this decision! Having said that, it is no doubt interesting to compare his response to charges of heresy with that of Marguerite Porete.

[14] Though one might "equally" describe this polysemic infinitude in terms of its failure to have a meaning. The point is that the commentarial nature of language refuses the divisions between right and wrong meaning, and between meaning and its lack. It may do so polysemically, by meaning too much, but it may just as well do so annihilatively, by meaning nothing at all.

meaningful and the unmeaningful, or the right meaning and the wrong meaning. What is accidental is not commentary, it is the division between the originally given and the act of commentary. In this regard, it is incredibly apt that many of the claims by which Eckhart brought himself trouble were associated with his vernacular sermons, which generally proceeded according to the form of biblical commentary and sought, throughout this commentary, to express these authoritative texts such that they would "make sense" in popular terms. This meant, among other things, that the meaning of the sacred became inseparable from the risks of translation and rephrasing that vernacular expression–with its exteriority to the "proper" language of the sacred–demanded.[15] It is as if Eckhart's heretical character consisted not just in its denial of orthodoxy but also its free exercise of speech, its affirmation of language as such, wherever it takes place.[16]

Once one makes this affirmation one is already heretical, irreducibly so, for one understands language *in its separation from*

---

[15] Colledge, in "Historical Data," p. 12, notes that the condemnation written against Eckhart "does not, as it seems to do, distinguish, as critics today commonly do, between his learned treatises and his popular vernacular sermons." My point, however, is not that the charges against Eckhart were neatly divided along this distinction, but rather that the *fact* of Eckhart's vernacular freedom of speech was seen–not just in its content but also, or moreso, in its performativity–as threatening to orthodoxy. This point is bolstered by Colledge's observation that the condemnation lists propositions that, though taken from Eckhart's Latin treatises, are attributed to his German sermons. It is as if heretical propositions, even when they are known to have come from "proper" Latin, are imagined as *necessarily* vernacular. I have, in this commentary on Eckhart, limited myself to his sermons in order to play along with this sense of the vernacular's force (though this is not to say such force is absent from his "learned treatises").

[16] As Nicola Masciandaro, discussing the taking place of language as such, or language as the taking place of the world as such, remarks: "the ground of language, its very possibility, is the *unity of life*. This unity is not something transcendent or outside the world, but rather constitutes the world as such, that is, it is of a piece with the plural fact of our being here in the first place, our topos. Language thus belongs to the originary goodness of world, to the goodness of its taking place . . . Language, like being, is not a thing, but a belonging, a participation in the innermost exteriority of the world's taking place." See "Falling Out of Language, Animally," *Whiskey & Fox* 4 (2010): 22-27, at 23-24.

the duality of orthodoxy and heterodoxy. One then understands language as intrinsically commentarial, or as separated from the duality of original truth and derivative commentary on that truth. This, I am wagering in the commentary that I write, here and now, is the way to interpret the meaning of Eckhart's own sermonic, vernacular commentaries. That Eckhart sought to de-hereticize his thought is no matter, for the heretical force remains, and so it needs only a commentary that would attend to its force, without duality. To do this—that is, to comment upon Eckhart without duality—requires that we conceive commentary as taking place without being a commentary *on* something. As long as commentary is commentary on something else, then duality remains. What is therefore necessary is a commentary on nothing.

BLESSED IS THE REFUSAL OF WORK

In order to elaborate the way in which we can see Eckhart providing a commentary on nothing, let us return to his discussion of the connection between equality to God and equality to nothing. What must be made explicit is the way that nothing functions as the third term in virtue of which God and the soul are equal. A basic account of relation imagines that two related things involve a third thing, namely the relation. To speak of equality between the soul and God, then, is to raise the question of what that third thing is—that is, it raises the question of the nature of their equality. On an orthodox theological account, such equality belongs to God, so that the soul's equality to God is conditioned by God's equality to Godself. In this sense, equality is always asymmetrical, for the soul's equality to God is dependent on God's auto-equality, whereas God's equality to the soul does not depend on the soul's auto-equality. If one wished to avoid such asymmetry—and a genuinely equal relation *should* be free of asymmetry—then one might try to imagine the third term, the relation, as a medium between God and the soul. The difficulty with this strategy, however, is that it does not completely abolish asymmetry. For even if one imagines the equality of God and the soul in terms of something in between them—in terms of their middle, or medium— the initial assumption of inequality between God and the soul (as the greater and the lesser) remains. A relation based on a middle point between two unequal beings moderates inequality but does not remove it. The equality of God and the soul here amounts to the mediation of a prior inequality.

54

It is for this reason that Eckhart, when attempting to think rigorously the equality of God and the soul, refuses to admit a third term. As long as there is a third term, inequality remains, and so the thought of equality precludes any thing in virtue of which these two are related. Hence the soul that is equal to God is equal to nothing, *just as* God is equal to nothing. The soul is like God not because it shares something with God, but because it, like God, does not make itself equal to anything. The soul, equal *to* God in that it, equally like God, is equal to nothing, can be said to be equal *with* God, in nothing. A strange equality thus emerges, namely one that cannot be named, one that refuses any identification. Yet grammar remains, even amidst this attempt to wriggle out of it by dint of nothingness–which is to say that even as Eckhart pronounces an equality without any third term, he must express this equality in such a way that the problem of a third term appears. As soon as one says that X and Y are equal, one finds oneself thinking and asking about the shared quality (which can be neither X nor Y) that renders them equivalent. The habit of linguistic practice tends toward that which Eckhart's logic refuses, and it is in order to respond to this dilemma that Eckhart speaks of "nothing." The nothing here invoked lacks the qualities that would allow it to be a thing, yet it is more real than any mediating thing– in fact, its reality stems precisely from this *inability* to be something. If one expresses nothing, then one has already contravened this nothing through the act of expression. It is enough to note–without getting fixated on–the obvious difficulty this involves. More worthy of attention is the way that Eckhart negotiates this difficulty. He does not refuse to address the tendency of linguistic practice when it presses toward a third term in virtue of which two terms are equal. As we have just noted, when he feels this pressure to speak of the commonality between God and the soul he does not stop speaking, rather he assumes the pressure in order to subvert its resolution by saying that equality is found in nothing. This indicates Eckhart's willingness to acknowledge the habit of linguistic practice even as he wants to reveal the limit of such practice when it comes to thinking radical equality. Such equality, by its very nature, cannot be divided, and so we cannot speak in a manner that would divide equality between equalized terms and the term that equalizes. The term that equalizes, and that would thus divide equality, is not there, it is nothing. What we can see is that nothing, for Eckhart, does not refer so much as *perform*: his

55

concern is not to speak of a nothing that, because it is nothing, cannot be expressed; it is, more exactly, to show the radical equality of things, to express this equality in such a way that the equality is not divided in the act of expression. Nothing, for Eckhart, is a way of expressing equality without division. Nothingness emerges in language as a way of undermining the habit of divisively practicing language; nothingness emerges as the commentary of language on itself.

Language, when subjected to the habit of division, tends to subject equality *to* something, and so Eckhart's expression of nothing serves to return language to itself, to free it from its habitual duality. This tendency toward divisiveness is present not only in habits of linguistic use, but also in habits of temporal narration. Just as there is a habit of dividing language between what is expressed and its expression,[17] so there is a habit of dividing time into what has taken place and what has yet to take place. History, we might say, is merely the confused effect of this last division–though Eckhart frames the division of time in terms not of history but of "working." It is the notion of performing a work, he says, that falsely turns time into a duality–that is, the duality of a state of affairs prior to the work and of a state of affairs that would be achieved as a result of the work's completion. No "fruit" can genuinely be born in such a duality, for the temporality of the soul's equality with God is subjected to the strictures of the work. To put oneself to work is to divide oneself from God, for works are "attachments," i.e. conditions that obscure the unconditioned equality of the soul with God. As Eckhart comments: "Every attachment to every work deprives one of the freedom to wait upon God in the present and to follow him alone . . . free and renewed in every present moment, as if this were all that you had ever had or wanted or could do."[18] The desire to achieve something through labor is what must be refused, for the moment one assumes this frame of mind one must see one's value

---

[17] Here I have in mind Gilles Deleuze's commentary on Spinozian immanence, such that it revolves around a notion of expression in which "what is expressed" and "that which expresses" are immanent to one another–neither is allowed to transcend the other. This, he says, is "the double immanence of expression in what expresses itself, and of what is expressed in its expression." See *Expressionism in Philosophy: Spinoza*, trans. Martin Joughin (New York: Zone Books, 1992).

[18] Eckhart, Sermon 2, p. 178.

as exterior to oneself. Even if one is confident that one can complete the work, or even if one does in fact complete the work, the problem still remains, for the value achieved is a value that depends on the division of time: the value achieved will never have meaning without contrast to its prior lack. Such is the logic of achievement, which puts one to work in the name of a future state of affairs that is promised to be superior to the prior state of affairs. What is lost in this attachment to work is time, or freedom, or oneself, or God–all are lost, and they are lost simultaneously for they are equal to one another. We have already commented on the equality of the self (or soul) with God, but we can now see that this equality appears temporally in the present moment, or more precisely in "every" present moment. It is in the moment that one is perfectly free, for the moment names time without the duality of past and future; the moment cannot be put to work, for work emerges only through the contrast between past and future. To refuse work and to remain in the present is to remain in equality with God, which is lost through the division of time just as much as it is lost through the distinction between God's being and all other beings. Eckhart, when commenting elsewhere about "blessedness," in which the soul is equal with God, remarks that it "has neither before nor after, and it is not waiting for anything that is to come, for it can neither gain nor lose."[19] When it comes to the equality of the soul with God, the "with" takes place in a moment, such that the division of this moment into before and after, into what has been and what is to come, effects a division between the soul and God–or, simply put, it effects the loss of blessedness.

The lesson of this commentary on the connection between temporality and radical equality is that the division of the former occludes the reality of the latter. Or, we could say that the reality of the latter makes the division of the former unnecessary, revealing it as a miscomprehension of what one already is. The same sort of lesson is expressed by Spinoza when he says, in the last proposition of the *Ethics*, that, "Blessedness is not the reward of virtue, but virtue itself." We are mistaken, he continues, when we think that "we enjoy [blessedness] because we restrain our lusts; on the contrary, because we enjoy it, we are able to restrain them."[20] The

---

[19] Ibid., Sermon 52, p. 201.

[20] Benedict de Spinoza, *Ethics*, trans. Edwin Curley (New York: Penguin Books, 1996), p. 180. It is wrong to presume–as we all too often do–that

point that here joins Spinoza to Eckhart is the priority of blessedness to any kind of labor. It has sometimes been imagined that Spinoza's concern is proto-Kantian, i.e. that one should pursue virtue for its own sake rather than for any reward. Yet the point is more radical. Obviously, the pursuit of virtue as a work that aims to yield some gain is precluded by Spinoza, but the problem with such a pursuit is not merely that it seeks gain *rather than* virtue itself–no, the problem with this pursuit is that it *is* a pursuit, that it seeks anything at all. The enjoyment of blessedness is prior to all work, and so the problem with work, at base, is that it denies the "already thereness" of blessedness, it exteriorizes it from oneself as something to be gained in the future, something to be achieved.[21]

For Spinoza, then, the loss of blessedness stems from the idea that one ought to gain something. This is once again an echo of Eckhart, who we have already seen connecting the logic of "neither before nor after" to the logic of "neither gain nor loss." The division of time may be escaped through the escape from work, which may be escaped by realizing that there is neither gain nor loss: there is no need to attach oneself to work because the aim of work is to gain, or to prevent an imagined loss, and neither of these (nor even their duality) can emerge, given that one is equal with God. The question Eckhart thus poses, if only implicitly, is: Why do you work when you do not need to work? Why do you not refuse the supposition that work is necessary? And it is in the same sense that he poses another, more explicit question regarding prayer: Why do you look for prayer from the outside when you do not need anything? Noting that people often ask him for prayer, Eckhart tells us that he responds by thinking, "Why do you not stay in yourself and hold on to your own good? After all, you are carrying all truth in you in an essential manner."[22] Prayer, like work, puts the self in a situation of lack, it makes the self into

---

Spinoza belongs to modernity that has purportedly broken with what historically preceded. Such historical *narratives*–note that these are not the same as "historicizations" or critical genealogies–easily fall prey to the sort of divisiveness that Eckhart, and Spinoza, refuse. This same point may be kept in mind with regard to my commentary, later in this essay, on Kafka.

[21] In this sense, it is unsurprising that a figure such as Antonio Negri, for whom the Autonomist strategy of "refusal of work" was central, eventually found himself drawn to the writings of Spinoza.

[22] Eckhart, Sermon 5b, p. 184.

something that begins by being divided from what it wills, and thus prayer too is precluded by the self's equality with God.

This critique of prayer holds not just when one asks for it from another self, but also when one turns to God. It is because of one's equality with God–"God and I, we are one"[23]–that one cannot address God as something exterior. And to pray to God for something is to imagine God as exterior, it is to deny equality. "If a man obtains or accepts something from outside himself, he is in this wrong. One should not accept or esteem God as being outside oneself, but as one's own and as what is within one; nor should one serve or labor for any recompense."[24] What is striking in this comment is not just the refusal of prayer, but more so the connection between this refusal and the refusal of work. Both amount to petitions for what one does not need, they divide the petitioner or laborer from that for which one petitions or labors. Furthermore, they subject equality to the duality of servant and master: "if I were accepting anything from God, I should be subject to him as a servant, and he in giving would be as a master."[25] Such a situation contravenes one's equality with God, and so prayer, like work, must be refused. Radical equality is posed against any dialectic of servant and master, or of worker and compensator–even when the master or compensator is God–and it is posed as what is already there, in the present moment, prior to any relation to exteriority.

COMMENTARY: CLOSE BESIDE AND UNDIVIDABLE FROM ITSELF

The implications of this insistence on radical equality, including antagonism toward Hegelian dialectics, certain forms of Marxism, and analogical or transcendent ontologies, is not hard to identify. What I want to attend to, however, are the implications that such radical equality has for Christianity, at least in its theologically orthodox form. The two features of Christian orthodoxy that here interest me are: its Christological claims, according to which humanity has a problematic (or at least incomplete) relation to God that demands a mediatic solution; and its sense of distinctiveness with regard to other religions, or to its

---

[23] Ibid., Sermon 6, p. 188.
[24] Ibid.
[25] Ibid.

others that it names as religions. Both of these, I want to show, are undermined by Eckhart's thought.

Eckhart's writing makes clear that the first of these features is dissolved. We have already glimpsed this in his claim that one ought not imagine one's relation to God in terms of prayer's mediation. However, because he remains true to his insistence on the refusal of duality, he does not set up his thought as something that is divided from Christianity. On the contrary, he makes use of the material claimed by Christianity in order to show that it cannot support Christianity's theologically orthodox commitment to mediation. For example, the comment regarding the soul's equality to God, with which my own commentary began, is situated as a commentary on the Christian Bible's claim that, "The Word was with God" (Jn. 1:1). Eckhart, drawing on a spatial metaphor, contends that this proclamation about the "wholly equal" means that the Word "was close beside, not beneath there or above there, but just equal."[26] It is as a consequence of this equality between Word and God that he comments on the equality between the soul and God: "So should the just soul be equal with God and close beside God, equal beside him, not beneath or above."[27] Of course, orthodox theology refuses to draw this consequence–that is, it affirms equality between the Word and God, but it does not likewise affirm equality between the soul and God. The latter may in some sense be *achieved,* but only through the successful mediation of the soul by the Word, who took on human form in the person of Christ. Christian orthodoxy thus draws on a variety of assumptions that Eckhart, as a result of his account of radical equality, refuses to give place, most notably: the distinction between God and all other beings, which is not altered by the Word's incarnation, since the Word is equal with God by nature and all other beings are not; and the centrality of work, which is the means by which all other beings are able to achieve the equality that they lack by nature and that the Word, through its salvific mediation, enables them to gain.

Eckhart, regardless of his historical attempt to evade heresy charges, provides a heretical commentary, for he clearly expresses that Christ has nothing to do with mediating to all other beings something that they lack. Take, for instance, his commentary on a

---

[26] Ibid., p. 187.
[27] Ibid.

story that he tells in which a king gives his daughter to the son of a poor man. Obviously, Eckhart comments, the son benefits from this event. But does, say, the brother of that poor man likewise benefit? Eckhart feints in the affirmative–yes, he says, it would seem that, "All who were of that [poor] man's family would be ennobled and honored" by this event. Having said this, however, Eckhart provides his ultimate response, by way of a cutting pair of questions: "How would it help me if I had a brother who was a rich man, if I still remained poor? How would it help me if I had a brother who was a wise man, if I still remained a fool?"[28] Of course, it would not be much help. Similarly, it would not be much help if Christ, or the incarnate Word, is equal to God while we lack this equality by nature. In other words, the point of his commentary on this story is that what is said of Christ, if it is of any help at all, must be said of us in the same sense that it is said of Christ. It does not suffice to imagine oneself as affiliated to Christ in an extrinsic manner, for that would correspond to the brother who is affiliated to the king by marriage, i.e. through an intermediary. What Christ brings is not something that can be applied to us from outside; Christ is not exterior to the self. In fact, Christ does not bring us anything at all, for to imagine such a scenario would be to imagine that Christ arrives for our gain, that Christ gives us something that we did not already have.

As long as we hold on to this image, we remain family by marriage, or in-laws of the divine, which is to say that we turn ourselves into beings who imagine themselves in terms of a before and an after (marriage's mediation). So what, then, does Christ bring? Nothing. But if Christ does not bring us anything, then why should he be seen as having any significance? Eckhart has anticipated this question, which he phrases as follows: "Since in this nature I have everything that Christ according to his humanity can attain, how is it that we exalt and honor Christ as our Lord and our God?"[29] He answers by redefining–quite substantively–the meaning of Christ's exaltation. Christ is not the mediator between an already distinguished God and humanity, he is instead a messenger who proclaims to humanity, and against humanity's divisive denials, that humanity and God are One. The equality of the Word with God is not something attributed to humanity, for

---

[28] Ibid., Sermon 5b, p. 182.
[29] Ibid.

there is nothing to be attributed, and equality is to nothing, not even to the Mediator. Such, we may recall, was the meaning of blessedness, and so we find Eckhart commenting that Christ is exalted precisely because "he became a messenger from God to us and brought us our blessedness."[30] But if he "brought us" our blessedness, then is this not something gained? The potential confusion, however, is removed when Eckhart continues by saying that this "brought" blessedness was not exterior in the first place, that it only seemed so as a result of our denial. "The blessedness that he brought us was ours." Indeed, "Everything good that all the saints have possessed, and Mary the mother of God, and Christ in his humanity, all that is my own in this human nature."[31] Every supposed mediator is no mediator at all, what they are supposed to mediate is not in need of mediation, for it is one's "own."[32] There can be no mediation, for the mediators are equal to one's own nature–and it makes no difference whether the mediator is a saint (who is supposed to have moved from humanity toward God) or Christ (who is supposed to have moved from God toward humanity). So why, once again, is Christ exalted? It is not because of what he brought but because of what he refused to divide, namely the equality with God that we already possessed. What he brought us, then, was nothing.[33]

We thus see how the first feature of orthodox Christianity mentioned above, i.e. the notion of Christ as mediatic resolution of humanity's division from God, is undermined by Eckhart's writing.

---

[30] Ibid.

[31] Ibid. In fact, we might imagine Eckhart's general insistence on equality–for instance, his concern to emphasize God's equal nearness to all that is created–as an indication of the transhuman.

[32] For a fuller account of the nature of mediation in Eckhart, see Eugene Thacker, "The Wayless Abyss: Mysticism and Mediation," in *Postmedieval* 3.1 (2012): 80-96.

[33] Eckhart at one point speaks of Christ's performance as "messenger" in terms of a story about a wife who, having lost an eye, feared that her husband would no longer love her. The husband, in order to aid her belief in his love, also "gouged out" one of his eyes. What is of interest, Eckhart makes clear, is that the bond of love between husband and wife–i.e., between God and humanity–was not *achieved* by this gouging, for it was never lost in the first place. The love was always there; what was at risk was the wife's belief in this love. The husband's gouging–i.e., the incarnation of the Word–serves not to mediate the bond but rather to undermine the wife's denial of the bond. See Eckhart, Sermon 22, p. 193.

But what about the second feature, that of Christianity's self-proclaimed distinctiveness from (and superiority to) other religions? This too has been rendered inviable: if Christ does not bring anything to humanity, then there is nothing on the basis of which a religion stemming from Christ could distinguish itself from others. In other words, Eckhart's heretical account of Christ does not just undermine the orthodox notion of mediation, it likewise undermines the notion that Christianity is distinct from its supposed rivals. Yet what still needs to be addressed is the precise nature of Eckhart's heresy with regard to Christianity.

We might assume that Eckhart's writing constitutes a heretical position. Yet this may be saying too much–not because the writing is not heretical, but because it remains questionable whether it should constitute a "position." If Eckhart's heresy resides in his commentarial expression, then to imagine this expression as a commentary *on* or *about* a position is already to dilute the force of that expression. It is to make commentary into commentary on something–Christianity, or God, for instance–to divide commentary into expression and what expression expresses. We have seen, however, that it is possible to understand Eckhart's commentary as revolving around nothing. Even as it twists about, saying one thing, qualifying that saying, then saying another thing–and in this manner accumulating and expanding its expressivity–it remains undividable from itself, it never points to something but always calls for the erasure of anything that it may appear to have installed. Commentarial nothingness becomes contagious, it affects even the reader, undermining his ability to move from commentary's expression to what the commentary is supposed to be about.

All of this holds for the relation between Eckhart's heresy and Christianity. In other words, if Eckhart's commentary refuses to reduce expression to something that is expressed, if his commentary ultimately revolves around nothingness, then the fact that his commentary bears a relation to Christian material cannot be made determinative. This is not to deny the Christian character of his commentary, but it is to refuse to make Christianity prior to commentary. The commentary emerges in relation to Christianity, yet in doing so it refuses to be about Christianity, much less any thing at all.

Along these lines, the force of Eckhart's well noted invocation, to "pray to God that we may be free of God," cannot

be to distinguish a true God from a false God.[34] Some will insist–
no doubt in an attempt to inoculate themselves against
commentarial nothingness–that this distinction does obtain, for
God is addressed even amidst the invocation of freedom from
God, and so God remains as that in virtue of which such freedom
is able to arise. But why must this be the case? Why could not the
aim be to render nonsensical–through commentarial
performance–the very notion of prayer to God? Eckhart's
invocation is, in fact, nonsensical, at least as long as one thinks that
the commentary revolves around something outside of it, as long
as one divides the commentary between its expression and what it
expresses. How, after all, can Eckhart pray to something while
simultaneously calling for freedom from that something? Or how
can one speak in terms of Christianity while simultaneously calling
for freedom from Christian terms of determination? Such questions
remain irresolvable–and Eckhart's simultaneous use of and
departure from Christian terms remains nonsensical–only insofar
as one assumes that Eckhart's invocation must be an expression of
something.

It is, in fact, precisely in order to evade such irresolvability
and nonsensicality that the inverted commas are deployed.
Specifically, inverted commas are imposed on the God from which
we seek freedom, but not on the God to which we pray for
freedom. God, and Eckhart's expression, are subjected to the
duality of exteriority's punctuation. If those marks are not imposed,
if no distinction is introduced from outside of Eckhart's expression,
then the expression undermines itself, it seeks freedom from the
same thing to which it prays. If such expressive tension is not
resolved, then what is expressed will continue to be undermined
by itself, which means that commentary will call for more
commentary, and that every commentarial performance will lead
to nothing, nothing but more commentary. *Commentarial
nothingness.* This, precisely, is the heresy of Eckhart: not to take a
heretical position on something called Christianity, but to
comment on Christianity in such a manner that the commentary
ceases to belong to Christianity, or that the commentary takes
Christianity as occasion for departure. Eckhart's heresy takes place

---

[34] Ibid., Sermon 52, p. 202. I have followed my earlier mentioned practice
of refusing to include the interpolated inverted commas, which surround
the second instance of "God."

within Christianity, yet because it emerges by way of commentarial nothingness it does not need to remain in that place, nor does it need to remain opposed to commentarial nothingness occasioned outside of Christianity. Commentarial nothingness is able to go wherever.

WHEREVER

Commentarial nothingness, as it is expressed in Eckhart– though this is already an infelicitous expression, given that commentarial nothingness simply *is* Eckhart's expression–emerges simultaneously as coiling and uncoiling, annihilating and expanding, and this is because it plays on the tension of an equality so radical that it can be nothing other than One, and so undividable that it can only be expressed as nothing. His commentary expresses a "with" of all souls and God that does not admit division, and yet the act of expression constantly runs up against the impossibility of mirroring such a One, for expression is irrepressibly composite. Expression is necessarily composed, but its composition expresses the One. Accordingly, it must refuse the tendency toward composition, or toward composition that gestures *to* a One that would be dualistically opposed to the act of composition, and it does so by insisting that the commentary is about nothing. There is nothing other than the One, but since this One cannot be composed, and since expression is nothing if not composition, then nothingness recurs.[35] Commentary here denotes writing that is involved in the experience of the One/nothing: commentarially expressing the One, in its unlimitedness, requires spatiotemporal expansion, but the commentary that satisfies this requirement is simultaneously annihilated by the nothingness that emerges in its composition.

As a means of further exemplifying this logic of commentarial nothingness, we may return to my remark, at the outset of this

---

[35] This simultaneity of the One and nothing can also be pursued by way of the simultaneity of Eckhart's notions of possession and poverty. He will emphasize that we already possess all truth and thus are without need of an outside, but also that we should become poor, so that we do not imagine ourselves as things in relation exterior things. There is an evident commonality between these emphases–namely the refusal of division–but it should be noted that this refusal occurs, simultaneously, from both directions. It is according to the One that we possesses everything, whereas it is according to nothingness that we are poor.

essay, that the commentary emerging in this essay, here and now, can be seen as yet another in a series of commentaries: this is a commentary on Eckhart's commentary on the book of John, which is a commentary on the book of Genesis, which is a commentary on the beginning of what we call creation. Our focus thus shifts "backward" by looking at the *Zohar's* commentary on Genesis. Of course, there can be no origin of commentary, insofar as the term "origin" carries with it connotations of something that would be there, prior to commentary's commencement. The aim is thus to see how commentary, even when it addresses its supposed origin, still refuses division.

The very first verse of the Hebrew Bible, speaking of the origin of the universe, is rendered by the *Zohar* as, "With Beginning, _____ created *Elohim*" (Gen. 1:1).[36] Let us note that "*Elohim*," which here indicates God, is positioned so as to be the effect of the act of creation. In Hebrew, the verse reads, "Bereshit bara Elohim." What concerns us, specifically, is the order of the last two words. "Bara," uncontroversially translated by way of the verb, "to create," is prior to "Elohim." In this commentarial translation, then, the words are left in their exact order: God is said only after creation is said. To translate in this manner, however, is to frustrate grammar, as well as received connotations of God as creator, or as the origin of all creation. In fact, it is precisely so as to avoid such frustrations that we will often find translations switching the order, such that they are able to tell us that "God created." Yet this is an imposition on the text, and it is to the credit of the *Zohar's* commentary on Genesis's commentary on creation that it allows the apparent nonsensicality of the text to remain, such that it can provoke more commentary. If it is through Genesis's commentarial expression that we know about God, then why should we insist on shifting this expression so that it conforms to a God that has no basis in the expression? The *Zohar's* refusal to change the word order can therefore be seen as a refusal to divide commentary into expression and what is expressed. Yet the problem remains: if Genesis's text is read directly, then how should we respond to the phrase, "created God"? If God is not the cause but rather the effect of creation, then what is the cause? If God is not the creator, then what created God?

---

[36] *Zohar: The Book of Enlightenment*, trans. Daniel Chanan Matt (Mahwah, NJ: Paulist Press, 1983), 50.

The *Zohar's* response to this line of questioning is to introduce _____. In other words, it acknowledges the force of the problem that the reader encounters, or the problem of grammar's tendency to look for a creator whenever an act of creation is indicated. However, it refuses to deny the text, or to blunt the force of its expressive nonsensicality. That is, it refuses to turn God, which appears after the verb, into that which was there prior to the verb. But what, then, was there before the verb? The text does not say. Yet if the text were left as "created God," then the tendency of the reader may very well lead him to imaginatively reverse the word order and reduce the problematic "created God" to the more sensical "God created." In order to avoid this imaginative resolution, to prevent the dissolution of the text's intrinsic problematicity, the *Zohar* comments that "_____ created God." This is not a resolution of so much as an insistence on the problematic force of the text, for it makes impossible the division between the text's expression and the text's meaning. If the origin is expressed as _____, then there can be no origin. But what can commentary be about, if it is not about God? And from whence does expression emerge, if even God is an expression that emerges . . . from what? There is no answer–and what is more, the fact that there is no answer *is* expressed, as _____. The *Zohar* refuses to divide expression from God, and it furthermore refuses to divide expression from what might be imagined as prior to God, for even that which is supposed to be prior to God is neither outside of commentary (for it is commentarially expressed) nor a composite part within the commentary (for it, unlike God, does not appear as something, only as _____). We could say, in fact, that _____ is a commentary on commentary, within the commentary, which always demands more commentary.

This commentarial demand to always express _____, while simultaneously expressing that such expression is _____–a tension not unlike the coiling, uncoiling, and recoiling that emerges in Eckhart's tension between the One and nothing–is expressed elsewhere in the *Zohar*. For instance, we find it commenting, within the same passage, that God is "hidden, concealed, transcendent, beyond, beyond," but also that "God is known and grasped."[37] How can this be the case? The *Zohar* tells us that when God is known and grasped, it is "to the degree that

---

[37] Ibid., 65-66.

one opens the gates of imagination!"[38] In other words, God is known through imagination, which we can understand as commentarial expression. If one imagines God, then one's imagination provides a commentary that opens something of the divine. Yet this something must then be erased as if it were nothing, for the divine is not something that *correlates to* expression–how could there be any correlation if there can be no division in the first place? Thus the *Zohar*, after posing the question of whether God is "known as He really is," responds by commenting, "No one has ever been able to attain such knowledge of Him." God is thus "known and unknown."[39] The demand is to continually comment, but in doing so to comment that such commentary has not given way to the something about which the commentary may be imagined to speak. Commentary simultaneously speaks of something and marks that this something is never spoken *about* by commentary, for commentary is undividable from itself. Commentary never leaves itself, but its expression remains open; it opens precisely by never ceasing to comment, for by remaining commentary it remains within the expressive opening _____.

In terms of space, commentary expresses a divinity that is simultaneously everywhere and nowhere. It is an exile that remains One with that from which it is supposed to be exiled; exile expresses that God is "unknown," that it can never be identified with the something of a place, but also that every place is an opening of the divine, such that the places of exile are simultaneously gates through which God is "known." As Kafka– who no doubt received and commentarially expressed, through novel means, the Kabbalistic tradition–put it: the human "is a free and secure citizen of the world, for he is fettered to a chain which is long enough to give him the freedom of all earthly space, and yet only so long that nothing can drag him past the frontiers of the world."[40] We are bound to a space that expresses our freedom–that is, we find in every place a freedom that is bound to one place or another. We cannot get outside the space of these places, yet this space freely expresses the divine, for, as Kafka continues to say, the

---

[38] Ibid., 66.

[39] Ibid.

[40] Franz Kafka, "Paradise," in *Parables and Paradoxes*, trans. Willa and Edwin Muir (New York: Schocken Books, 1975), p. 31.

human "simultaneously . . . is a free and secure citizen of Heaven as well." The resulting dynamic is as follows: "if he heads, say, for the earth, his heavenly collar throttles him, and if he heads for Heaven, his earthly one does the same."[41]

Kafka's remarks can thus be understood as a commentary on the *Zohar's* expression of simultaneous knowing and unknowing of the divine, which is exilically expressed at every place on earth, in the gate of every place, but which can never be found in a distinct place outside of earth. _____ is everywhere. Or, to put it otherwise, exile is everywhere, as long as one understands that everywhere returns us from exile. This a tensional thought, one demanding commentary, a commentary that robs us of the peace that comes from being able to distinguish one place from another or earth (as the totality of all places) from heaven. Their supposed separations are precisely what are refused by Kafka's simultaneity of earthly and divine citizenship, by his commentary on the reality that there is no composite world, but only _____. Thus he remarks that "the whole visible world is perhaps nothing more than the rationalization of a man who wants to find peace for a moment."[42] Places do not belong to a world distinct from the divine–such a world, in fact, is nothing more than a "rationalization"–they belong to a divinity that undermines the distinction of any place at the same time that it refuses to be thought as its own distinct place.

Eckhart comments, along similar lines, that one "should be so poor that he should not be or have any place in which God should work." Yet place is bound up not only with the logic of achievement, but also with that of division. Thus he continues by commenting that, "When man clings to place, he clings to distinction."[43] To identify oneself by *being* or *having* a place is to divide oneself from the equality with God that is already there. Accordingly, to imagine that one has a place is to imagine that God has a place, a place that is exterior to one's own. The problem with having a place is therefore inseparable from the problem of putting God in a place. At the same time, to *refuse* that one has a place is equally to refuse that God has a place, for it is to refuse the divisions between places. Those who are equal to no place, they

---

[41] Ibid.
[42] Ibid., p. 33.
[43] Eckhart, Sermon 52, p. 2.

alone are equal to God, for God is equal to no place. In fact, God's refusal of place can be worked through every imagined division. The *Zohar* observes that both "beings up above" and "creatures down below" mark, but initially fail to understand, God's refusal of place. "The ones below proclaim that He is above," while "the ones above proclaim that He is below."[44] Both thus grasp that God cannot be limited to the place where they find themselves, but at this point division remains, for God, though not imagined as being in one's own place, is still imagined as being in another place–if not below then above, and if not above then below. They fully grasp God's refusal of place only when they proclaim that, "He is unknowable," that there is no place where God can be located. Yet this refusal of any place is equal with an affirmation of all place, at least in the sense that God has nothing to do with the division of place. "Finally all of them, above and below, declare: 'Blessed be the presence of *YHVH* wherever He is.'"[45] There is no place for God, which means not only that God is not in one place or another, but also that God is not in a place beyond place–after all, this too would be a place. God has no place because God is nowhere, but nowhere is not another place, it is unplaceability, which is simultaneously the ability to be equal with any place whatever. God's nowhere is equal with God's wherever. Or as Deleuze and Guattari comment about utopia, it "refers not only to no-where but also to now-here."[46] And–to return to Eckhart in order to continue commenting, here and now, on his commentary on equality with God–let us say that he agrees with all of them, for wherever one is, one is equal with God, and so God is wherever.

In the beginning there is exile, or exile is what you get if you begin by locating yourself in relation to something that is there in the beginning. Yet what was there in the beginning is _____, and that is where you still are, here and now, namely the present moment, which does not admit a difference between a before and an after, much less a lost beginning and a culminating return. Thus the moment is exile, but it is the exile of _____. Exile is loss

---

[44] *Zohar*, p. 65.

[45] Ibid.

[46] Gilles Deleuze and Félix Guattari, *What is Philosophy?*, trans. Hugh Tomlinson and Graham Burchell (New York: Columbia UP, 1994), p. 100. Specifically, they are speaking of utopia as it is inflected by Samuel Butler's "Erehwon."

only if one divides it from something to which it is supposed to return, and such division is refused in the moment of the soul's equality with God, the moment here and now, in which one is free from relating a place to God because one is free wherever God is, equal wherever the place. Exile is commentarial expression, wherever.[47]

Daniel Colucciello Barber is a fellow at the ICI Berlin Institute for Cultural Inquiry. He is the author of *On Diaspora: Christianity, Religion, and Secularity* (Cascade, 2011), and *Deleuze and the Naming of God: The Novelty of Immanence* (Edinburgh University Press, forthcoming).

---

[47] I would like to thank the editors of this volume, Nicola Masciandaro and Eugene Thacker, for their very helpful remarks on this essay.

THINKING THE CHARNEL GROUND (THE CHARNEL GROUND THINKING): AUTO-COMMENTARY AND DEATH IN ESOTERIC BUDDHISM

Timothy Morton

to return to the quiescence of the inorganic world
– Sigmund Freud[1]

This essay has already begun to comment on itself. To repeat itself, folding into itself like a strand of DNA. Is this auto-commentary a mode of life, or a mode of death? Is it not rather an uncanny mode of undeath?

"We're angels of life / We're angels of death." Hawkwind sing psychedelic songs of sorrow and insight. But who or what is doing the singing? Esoteric traditions of mysticism, the kind that gives rise to proclamations like the lyrics of Hawkwind, are forms of speculative realism. Like speculative philosophy, mysticism wagers that humans can think what lies outside what Quentin Meillassoux calls the correlationist circle, or what mysticism calls ego.[2] What else can you say about one of the most repeatable experiments on Earth?[3] Take almost any human nervous system, subject it to

---

[1] Sigmund Freud, *Beyond the Pleasure Principle*, tr. James Strachey, intro. and notes Gregory Zilboorg (New York: Norton, 1961), 56.
[2] Quentin Meillassoux, *After Finitude: An Essay on the Necessity of Contingency* (Continuum, 2009), 5.
[3] A point made clear in the Shamatha Project, for instance. See Clifford Saron, et al., "Intensive Meditation Training Improves Perceptual Discrimination and Sustained Attention," *Psychological Science* 21.6 (2010): 829–839. See Donald Lopez, *Buddhism and Science: A Guide for the Perplexed* (Chicago: University of Chicago Press, 2008). James Austin, *Zen and the Brain: Towards an Understanding of Meditation and Consciousness* (Cambridge,

various processes—silence, contemplative practices of the mind and body such as yoga and meditation, devotional practices such as kirtan and prayer—and the humans start to say the same thing. New Age philosophy is built on the supposed truisms that Sufi and Tibetan yogi speak alike, what Aldous Huxley called the perennial philosophy.[4] But why throw out the speculative baby with the New Age bathwater? Is it possible that contemplative humans are reporting something true about experience? And that beyond this, that this truth speaks a truth about biological—or even physical—existence as such?

To put it in terms of this essay's very form: is it possible for skirt the perilous edge of New Age syncretism in the name of a darker, stranger form of speculation that accepts the discoveries of science—that wagers, indeed, that mysticism is a form of science? For mysticism is the science of quiescence: the pursuit of the philosopher's stone is the pursuit of how to become a stone. As such, mysticism is threatening to established religious institutions that demand respect for an all too human hierarchy. The first few centuries of Christianity were spent in an all out assault against "Gnosticism" that resulted in Jesus, who argued that we are all sons of God, being kicked upstairs into an exclusive club of one.[5] Recent philosophical attacks on contemplative spirituality, for instance by Slavoj Žižek, only perpetuate the all too human pursuits of the early Church Fathers. Yet they are right to fear contemplation. Contemplation places us outside the human, outside of life, in a universe of death.[6]

What does this have to do with the practice of commentary? The notion of commentary comes into play in very significant ways in estoteric Buddhist mysticism. Dzogchen tantric liturgies are renowned for *auto-commentary*: including the gloss within the text itself, rather than in the margin. For instance, Chögyam Trungpa's *Sadhana of Mahamudra* was written in 1968 in an attempt to "quell

---

MA: MIT Press, 1999). See also Sam Harris, *The End of Faith: Religion, Terror, and the Future of Reason* (New York: Norton, 2004), 204–221.

[4] Aldous Huxley, *The Perennial Philosophy* (London: Chatto and Windus, 1947).

[5] Elaine Pagels, *The Gnostic Gospels* (New York: Random House, 1989) 119–141.

[6] The most rigorous exploration of this to date has been Ray Brassier, *Nihil Unbound* (New York: Palgrave, 2007), 234–238.

the mighty warring of the three lords of materialism."[7] In this sadhana (a sadhana is a Tantric liturgy, involving a feast), the pracitioner reads out to herself exactly the experiential states at which the liturgy aims:

> In the state of nonmeditation all phenomena subside in that great graveyard in which lie buried the complexities of samsara and nirvana. This is the universal ground of everything; it is the basis of freedom and also the basis of confusion. Within it, the vajra anger, the flame of death, burns fiercely and consumes the fabric of dualistic thoughts. The black river of death, the vajra passion, turbulent with massive waves, destroys the raft of conceptualization to the roaring sound of the immeasurable void. The great poisonous wind of the vajra ignorance blows with all-pervading energy like an autumn storm and sweeps away all thoughts of possessiveness and self like a pile of dust.[8]

Trungpa's approach seems to be highly congruent with the view of Dzogchen, considered to be the highest of the six yanas or "vehicles" of esoteric Buddhism (Kriya, Upa, Yoga, Maha, Anu and Ati). The view is that the nature or essence of mind is already completely enlightened, requiring no further effort to realize anything, but simply an attunement to it.

Thus the mind can experience this basic profound enlightenment, and think and discourse at the very same time. There is no gap between immediate experience and its mediation. Auto-commentary becomes fully possible. Since conceptual thoughts are essentially expressions of the completely enlightened nature of mind, there is no problem in thinking per se, only in fixation on thinking and its products. Thus, it seems to follow from this that unlike other Buddhist liturgies, the Dzogchen tantras describe what they are doing while they are doing it, without dissonance.

---

[7] Chögyam Trungpa Rinpoche, *The Sadhana of Mahamudra which Quells the Mighty Warring of the Three Lords of Materialism and Brings Realization of the Ocean of Siddhas of the Practice Lineage* (Halifax, Nova Scotia: Nalanda Translation Committee, 1980).

[8] Trungpa, *Sadhana of Mahamudra*, 8.

It seems radical to think that a marginal gloss could embody the sacred as much as the central text. The very idea undoes the difference between center and edge that underwrites the difference between commentary and main text. This is in keeping with the Dzogchen idea that reality as such is already a perfect, spontaneously arranged mandala that lacks a center or an edge. As the *Sadhana of Mahamudra* puts it: "This is the mandala which is never arranged but is always complete."[9] The term *commentary* stems from the Latin roots *cum* and *mens*, implying that in commentary one mixes one's mind with the text. A commentary is a collection of memoranda, things to be held in mind; or a memoir, aids to personal recollection.[10] But perhaps there is a deeper reason why commentary seems appropriate for thinking the mystical text. For esoteric Buddhism, the mind of the teacher who transmitted the teachings is an expression of the nature of mind totally intimate with the practitioner. Thus commentary implies mixing one's mind with the guru's mind, the essence of the teachings, refuting by example Plato's distinction between written and oral memory.[11] This bond between textuality and immediacy was considered dangerous and to be kept secret from those who had not done sufficient preparation.

Why? Because of a disturbing *intimacy*, I shall argue, that exists beyond being and not-being. Martin Hägglund argues no sentient being whatsoever can logically desire fullness. This would mean to desire to have one's desire erased, and to have things that are only constituted in and as lack made suddenly present, which would amount to their vanishing from the face of things.[12] Such an argument has often been leveled by Western philosophy against Buddhism. Millions of humans do desire Nirvana, which at least on Hägglund's view is "absolute death."[13] Yet these humans do not experience their desire as meaningless, although this "absolute death" is equivalent to the desire for fullness, on Hägglund's view.

---

[9] Trungpa, *Sadhana of Mahamudra*, 7.
[10] *Oxford English Dictionary*, "commentary," n.1.
[11] Plato, *Phaedrus*, tr. Alexander Nehamas and Paul Woodruff, in *Plato: Complete Works*, ed. John Cooper (Inianapolis: Hackett, 1997) 506–556 (541–553).
[12] Martin Hägglund, *Radical Atheism: Derrida and the Time of Life* (Stanford: Stanford University Press, 2008), 11, 30, 117–118, 192–195, 198–204, 208.
[13] Hägglund, *Radical Atheism*, 8, 29, 32, 162, 229.

How might esoteric practice take on Hägglund? Perhaps the most effective way would be from the inside rather than from the outside. Let us grant that the world is (almost) as he says. How might the esoteric desire for fullness might work alongside rather than against a deconstructive view of identity, that is along with the "desire for survival" that Hägglund argues is intrinsic to being an impermanent, mortal being? My opening suggestion would be to look to Bataille. Bataille argues that religion is not the search for something bigger than oneself, like a giant crowd in which to be lost (a fascistic notion), but the search for a lost intimacy.[14] With this model, we have several items on Hägglund's checklist, without having to endorse radical atheism. We have a nontotalizable reality, openness to the new and to the stranger, and a nonrealizable infinity of interrelation. What we have is *non-theism* rather than theism or atheism, if by "theism" we mean belief in some transcendent beyond, and if by "atheism" we mean simple denial of anything beyond the empirical.

To see the world only in terms of a vanishing trace structure is to see something true, but it is also to delimit the world in so doing. This delimited world cannot explain some of the basic facts of the larger world. The fact that a liturgy and its commentary can be exactly the same thing implies that the makers of the liturgy believe that one can surprise oneself. In other words, one is able to think rationally while undergoing "mystical" experiences, and vice versa, without the two canceling one another out. There is no spell to be broken. Thus writing–and things that bear the stigma of writing, such as commentary–is no longer a poison. The presence of the occult bond between writing and the real is reflected in Guru Yoga, a certain practice in which one prepares oneself to receive the sacred teachings by reciting a certain mantra 1.2 million times. In the preparatory practice of prostrations, one visualizes a wish-fulfilling tree, on the back branch of which is a vast collection of sacred texts. The texts are speaking themselves, in millions of

---

[14] Georges Bataille, *Theory of Religion*, tr. Robert Hurley (Cambridge, Mass.: MIT Press, 1992), 57. For the "something bigger" motif, see William James, *The Varieties of Religious Experience* (London: Penguin, 1985), 525–almost the last thing James says about religion in his concluding chapter. David Wood has stated a contrasting view: David Wood and J. Aaron Simmons, "Moments of Intense Presence: A Conversation with David Wood," *Journal For Cultural and Religious Theory* 10.1 (Winter 2009): 81–101.

syllables that mutter on the breeze. This disturbing sound is supposed to fill the space of the visualization, which may be thought as a channeling or attunement to a real entity that exists beyond the conceptual mind.

This essay will thus proceed by trying to think the unthinkable, the unthinkable that Dzogchen nevertheless suggests is well within the capacity of sentient beings to think and to experience, even to talk about, even while it is occurring, without breaking anything. The essay begins by arguing that for esoteric Buddhism, realization is not a mental state in the sense of a thought-about… held by a mind. Rather, realization is just physical reality as such, outside the echo chamber of mentation. How does the esoteric practitioner get there? The notion of commentary comes into play. Through a path laid out by what Freud calls the death drive, I shall focus some of this analysis on sentences that comment on themselves, yet negate themselves in the process. Self-replicating molecules are *physical auto-commentaries* that are attempting to solve their inner disequilibrium: to die.

ENLIGHTENMENT AS / IN PHYSICAL REALITY

Sigmund Freud's *Beyond the Pleasure Principle* speculates about what happens to a single-celled lifeform. The cell must take in nutrients to survive, so its boundary must be permeable (eros, the "life" drive). It must then absorb and digest what it takes in from the outside. It strives towards equilibrium, metabolizing what it absorbs (the death drive).[15] It develops a membrane that is quasi-inorganic, nonliving, to resist the intensity of the outside: a shield of death.[16] Famously—and beautifully in James Strachey's translation—Freud argues that the purpose of life is death, to return to an inorganic state, or as Strachey's translation puts it, "the quiescence of the inorganic world."[17] This search for quiescence Freud names the Nirvana principle, borrowing the term from another psychoanalyst.[18] Nirvana: extinction. What if this were not just a metaphor?

---

[15] Freud, *Beyond the Pleasure Principle*, 20–22.

[16] Freud, *Beyond the Pleasure Principle*, 21. See Brassier, *Nihil Unbound: Enlightenment and Extinction* (New York: Palgrave, 2010), 237–238.

[17] Freud, *Beyond the Pleasure Principle*, 56.

[18] Freud, *Beyond the Pleasure Principle*, 50. The psychoanalyst in question is Barbara Low.

What if, in other words–assuming again that mysticism is a form of speculative realism–nirvana as such, "extinction" (to use a provocative term of Ray Brassier's that is also the literal translation of nirvana) really were the goal of biological life?[19] When Buddhism talks about transcending desire and clinging, Western thinking often takes this to mean a bad suicidal drive. What if, however, this conclusion was actually accurate, even more accurate than nineteenth-century philosophers (Schopenhauer, Nietzsche, and a host of Buddhaphobes) reckoned?

We can proceed even further. What if nirvana really was a state of "quiescence," with all the participle-like, gerundive quality of that word: a form of awareness, an "-ence" as it were that happens to someone, or to something? In that case, awareness would not be a property of subjects, whether considered as emergent effects of biological processes or taken as supervenient facts that transcend or subtend the physical realm. Biology is already thinking cognition outside the supposed exigencies of having nerves and a brain.[20] As a matter of fact, awareness would not even be a function of living systems, since the ultimate conclusion here is that you can be "dead"–switched off, post-orgasm, floating in satisfaction–and still sentient. But what if you could be actually dead and still sentient? Philosophy has tended to balk at such questions.[21]

What if, just to push it even further, sentience was not some kind of soul or essence that survives death, but is in fact a default mode of existing at all, whether you are organic or not? Panpsychism thinks this thought.[22] But what if–concluding this long series of speculations–panpsychism had it upside down? So that sentience is not what every entity has in some sense, but that

---

[19] Ray Brassier, *Nihil Unbound*; "Extinction" is the final word of that text (239).
[20] Consider the study of quorum sensing in bacteria: http://www.nottingham.ac.uk/quorum/
[21] Reza Negarestani powerfully examines this paucity in "Drafting the Inhuman: Conjectures on Capitalism and Organic Necrocracy," in Levi Bryant, Nick Srnicek and Graham Harman, eds., *The Speculative Turn: Continental Materialism and Realism* (Melbourne: re.press, 2011), 182–201 (194–195 n.20).
[22] For a range of essays on panpsychism see David Skrbina, ed., *Mind that Abides: Panpsychism in the New Millennium* (Philadelphia: John Benjamins, 2009).

what sentience is resembles a mute object like a pencil, resting silently (perhaps "quiescently") on this table? "The third of the Fates alone, the silent Goddess of Death."[23] So that mystical practices of contemplation were about stripping away our illusions about the nature of sentience until we arrive at an object-like entity, an entity that precisely is not "us" but is far more intimately "there" than us? Our self as a decapitated corpse, to speak somewhat poetically? "Nearer than breathing, closer than hands and feet."[24]

This actual body then is precisely what becomes enlightened. Or rather, again using mystical language: the body is already enlightened. It's simply that we are confused about this. So our job is to strip away our confusion. At a deep enough level, this means stripping away us–then who is doing the stripping? Something is executing its own program.

Freud remarks that "the phenomena of heredity and the facts of embryology" demonstrate the reality of the compulsion to repeat, which he interprets as evidence of the death drive.[25] He gives the examples of how the ontogeny of the embryo recapitulates the phylogeny of lifeforms. Freud notes that this recapitulation is inefficient–why not just proceed directly to the required shape? We shall return to this point when we consider sex. But repetition in lifeforms lies far deeper than embryonic stages of living organisms. RNA and DNA molecules are in a state of irreducible disequilibrium. They are like Henkin sentences: "There is a version of me in system X." Viruses are capsules of RNA (mostly) that tell DNA to find a copy of itself in its system. Or viruses resemble Cretan liar paradoxes: "I am a Cretan; I am lying." That's how they kill you–they turn you into an infinitely looped virus factory. Just like a computer virus in fact. If you think a virus is alive, you must also think a computer virus is alive, in every meaningful sense of "alive." A virus is already a form of non-life, questioning in its very existence the rigid boundary between organic and inorganic worlds.[26] This is because DNA is also somewhere in this non-thin, non-rigid boundary, this edge that is

---

[23] Sigmund Freud, "The Theme of the Three Caskets," in Peter Gay, ed., *The Freud Reader* (New York: Norton, 1989), 514–522 (522).

[24] George Morrison, "The Reawakening of Mysticism," *The Weaving of Glory* (Grand Rapids, MI: Kregel Publications, 1994), 103–110 (106).

[25] Freud, *Beyond the Pleasure Principle*, 31.

[26] I use the term "non-life" to evoke the "non-philosophy" of François Laruelle.

no edge teeming with entities: plasmids, replicons, insertions, junk DNA, virions, viroids. All these entities exist because of self-replicators, which may have started with non-organic replicators such as a silicate crystal (how strange, a silicon based entity "before" life), to which RNA could attach itself.[27] In this sense, the death drive predates life itself. The silicate crystal accepts the RNA strand in order to "solve" the stain that is its existence, only to find itself ineluctably reproducing.

Why do replicators replicate? Isn't it because of some fundamental disequilibrium that the molecule is somehow "trying" to shake off? Isn't DNA also trying to "return to the quiescence of the inorganic world"? Isn't the death drive, then, far far lower down than single-celled organisms, relative newcomers on the four and a half billion-year-old scene? Wouldn't it be unsurprising then that if the death drive were installed at this fundamental level, all levels above it would manifest it in different ways, until we reach self-reflexive levels of consciousness and the meaning-saturated worlds humans and other life forms spin for themselves– civilization, in a word?

And isn't this the ironic thing about civilization, according to Freud: that the more of it you have, the more death you have? Because the death drive can't eradicate itself. It is the stain that is trying to get rid of itself, the anomaly that is trying to wipe itself out–through further anomalies. Quine sentences, of which the Cretan liar paradox is a potent example, try to swallow themselves:

IS NOT A COMPLETE SENTENCE
IS NOT A COMPLETE SENTENCE.

But in the process of trying to swallow themselves, they make more of themselves. Notice the similarity of this sentence to an auto-commentary. The sentence is a commentary on its truth status.

In the process of trying to solve its inner disequilibrium, DNA and other replicators do the only thing they do–replicate. The trouble is, the more you pursue it, the more *life* you live. The death

---

[27] This is Sol Spiegelman's "RNA World," a strange world that must have preexisted life, since DNA requires ribosomes, and ribosomes require DNA. In order to break the circle, Spiegelman posits RNA World: *The Ancestor's Tale: A Pilgrimage to the Dawn of Life* (London: Phoenix, 2005), 582–594.

drive is precisely this momentum to cancel oneself out, to erase the stain of existence. Death is the essence of life:

> The attributes of life were at some time evoked in inanimate matter by the action of a force of whose nature we can form no conception. It may perhaps have been a process similar in type to that which later caused the development of consciousness in a particular stratum of living matter. The tension which then arose in what had hitherto been an inanimate substance endeavoured to cancel itself out. In this way the first instinct came into being: the instinct to return to the inanimate state.[28]

DNA is involved in a noir plot in which the detective finds out that he is the killer. In attempting to solve the riddle of its existence, DNA redoubles existence.

Isn't this an elegant example of Buddhist samsara? By trying to solve your problem, you create another problem—because *you* *are* the problem. In this sense, anxiety, the bedrock emotion in Buddhism, existentialism and psychoanalysis is the default state of existing, not because of some special vitalist soul force, but because of the conundrum "experienced" by DNA itself, and molecules like it.[29] Anxiety courses through our being precisely because it is archaeological evidence of a deadlock that goes far, far, deeper than us, deeper even than life itself. In this the Buddhist Wheel of Life accords with Freud. Life is depicted as a never-ending wheel in which the snake (aggression) chases the pig (ignorance) chasing the chicken (passion), generating the six realms of existence: all this is enclosed in the jaws of Yama, the god of death. Sentient beings find themselves inside this vast entity, which elsewhere I call a *hyperobject*, as surely as they find themselves inside a twenty-sided capsule of protein (cold virus) or a capsule of skin (myself). Deleuze calls Freudian death a "transcendental principle."[30] But I claim that

---

[28] Freud, *Beyond the Pleasure Principle*, 32.

[29] Of course this argument is proposed via another route by Martin Heidegger in *Being and Time*, tr. Joan Stambaugh (Albany, N.Y: State University of New York Press, 1996), 316 and *passim*.

[30] Gilles Deleuze, *Difference and Repetition*, tr. Paul Patton (New York: Continuum, 2007), 18.

it only appears as a "principle" because we exist on its interior and so we can't alter it. It is better thought as a gigantic mouth. DNA "wants" to cancel itself out. In this sense DNA radicalizes Freud's sense of "organic," by which he surely means "alive," so that the "inorganic" is the world of what Wordsworth calls "rocks, and stones."[31] But by "organic" we now mean "carbon-based self-replicator"–a far wider definition that goes beyond the onto-theological boundaries of "life" towards an undead zone of non-life, a charnel ground (favored spot of tantric yogis) where zombies roam. Enlightenment, then, is zombification: making peace with the inner zombie. Far from transcending the world of material objects, meditation burrows down further into them, releasing subjective confusions such as the idea of a separate ego. One really does become like a stone, as is said in the Zen meditation manuals.[32] Surely this is why Vajrayana (esoteric, "diamond" or "thunderbolt" vehicle) Buddhism selects for people with intense emotional strife and high intelligence: because intense life is directly proportional to intense death. Placid, calm people tend not to get it at all. It's the people on the edge of a nervous breakdown who are most likely to awaken in one lifetime, or go mad in the attempt.

THE HORROR OF BLISS

Hence perhaps the role of ouroboric postures in yoga and meditation: turning yourself into a pretzel provides archaeological evidence of DNA disequilibrium, obvious in its double-helix form and its viral, infinite loopiness: Henkin sentences and Cretan liar paradoxes that viral code embodies are self-swallowing propositions. (It's tempting, in syncretistic fashion, to speculate on the significance of serpentine forms in esoteric spirituality, from the serpent guarding the tree in Genesis to the kundalini or serpent energy in a subtle channel parallel with the spine.) The evidence present in the images of self-swallowing, navel gazing contemplatives that so scared nineteenth-century philosophers is there precisely because of the physical disequilibrium that shatters

---

[31] William Wordsworth, "A Slumber Did My Spirit Seal," in *The Major Works: Including the Prelude*, ed. Stephen Gill (Oxford: Oxford University Press, 2008).
[32] Daisetz Teitaro Suzuki, *An Introduction to Zen Buddhism* (New York: Grove Press, 1964), 47.

the coherence of the levels above it.[33] To this extent, rather than being dismissed as narcissistic (only wounded narcissism dismisses itself thus), postures of meditation should be celebrated not because they are New Age symbols of balance and intertwining harmony–but because they aren't. And because enlightenment is indeed physical–it's a function of a substance that "poses" itself, that has a posture. As any experienced meditator will tell you, the physical posture is about eighty percent of the practice.

Hence also perhaps the role of stillness and silence in esoteric rituals: becoming physically still, ceasing speech, ceasing the motion of the prana through the body, bringing these flows into the central channel. These practices are supported by philosophical negations, such as those found in the apophatic traditions of Judaism and Christianity, and the Mahayana philosophy of emptiness (Nagarjuna, Chandrakirti): negation is the work of death, peeling away and rejecting, spitting out.[34] This philosophical work, from the esoteric point of view, leads to an ability to tolerate the already-there presence of intimate, physical reality (luminosity, in Buddhist terminology): philosophy as allergy medicine. What is being stripped away and expelled is confusion–but in a way that is congruent with intellectual processing speeds. Negation provides a toy version of the real thing to amuse the frog of intellect while it sits in the increasingly hot water of the real. But eventually the toy is put aside and the more direct work of silencing oneself begins. The real is unspeakable, like the taste of sugar to a mute person (the traditional analogy in the Dzogchen tradition of Tibetan Buddhism).

Freud argues that the death drive is silent: "[it is] a transcendental principle, whereas the pleasure principle is only psychological … [the death drive] not given in experience" (Deleuze).[35] In early Christian esotericism (Gnosticism), God is named "the Silence."[36] To attend to this silence is to shut down slightly, to turn inward slightly. The manuals say that bliss is

---

[33] See Timothy Morton, "Hegel on Buddhism," in Mark Lussier, ed., "Romanticism and Buddhism," *Romantic Praxis* (http://www.rc.umd.edu/praxis/buddhism/morton/morton.html).
[34] Sigmund Freud, "Negation," *The Standard Edition of the Complete Psychological Works of Sigmund Freud,* ed. and tr. James Strachey, 24 vols. (London: Hogarth Press, 1953), 9.233–240.
[35] Deleuze, *Difference and Repetition,* 18.
[36] Pagels, *Gnostic Gospels,* xvii, 50, 53–54, 59.

there.[37] Bliss is the little death, the orgasm that plays aikido with the life drive by disarming it with its own energy, and lays it out flat to rest in space. Bliss is evidence that the body is relieved that the ego has departed. Strictly speaking, then, it's the body that becomes enlightened. The manuals say that different parts of your body can have an orgasm, that our fixation on genital orgasm inhibits the flow of bliss. Why? Perhaps because it perpetuates a Cartesian illusion—here I am, "having" an orgasm. Bliss, when it flows throughout the body, erases the ego's (mis)identification with physical reality through an aikido-like extension of pleasure beyond its normal bounds: death erasing pleasure through its own force, taking us beyond the pleasure principle.

This explains why bliss is often felt as a disturbing, creeping sensation more akin to horror than something warm and fuzzy, and why mental hospitals are full of people who have spontaneous physical sensations of bliss outside their genitals.[38] Bliss is automatic: what is scary is that mysticism works—it summons bliss, a devouring, Cthulhu-like entity existing in some unspeakable higher-dimensional phase space.[39] (Literally: the sensation is surely a derivative of some kind of wave-like function of nervous energy.) "Hell was what he wanted: Hell was what he got."[40] These experiences, happening in people without religious training of any kind, are perfectly understandable if the speculative, mystical hypothesis that enlightenment happens in the body is correct. When mystics (and New Agers) talk about feeling insights "at a cellular level"–well, why not? Perhaps this is indeed the level at which such insights occur. And if it occurs there, why not also in nonsentient physical objects like toothbrushes and quasars?

Heterosexual reproduction is very expensive way of passing on DNA from a strictly utilitarian point of view. It's always better to be a clone. Perhaps this is precisely the point. Inherently inefficient heterosexual sex is an attempt by DNA to arrest its mad rush to replicate. Bliss would then be an experiential signal that

---

[37] So many traditions, so little time, so just a few will do: The Six Yogas of Naropa, Dzoghen, St. Theresa, St. John of the Cross, Rumi.

[38] Stanislav Grof, *Spiritual Emergency: When Personal Transformation Becomes a Crisis* (Los Angeles: Tarcher, 1989).

[39] Just as Cthulhu "sleeps" in a high-dimensional Gaussian (non-Euclidean) space far out in the Universe, but can be summoned with the right incantation.

[40] Tony Randell, dir., *Hellbound: Hellraiser 2* (New World Pictures, 1988).

some temporary equilibrium had been attained at some level of physical being. Heterosexual reproduction then is the pursuit of death, by death. (Poetry aside, perhaps this also explains why heterosexuality floats on top of a giant ocean of homosexuality and cloning.)[41] Bliss is the birthright of a lifeform, but also its deathright. A common refrain in esoteric religion is that bliss burns illusion. What remains after sex according to the tantric traditions, and basic common sense? Awareness. Is awareness then outside life, beyond life, in objects of all kinds? In substance as such? I'm not pushing panpsychism here, I'm actually arguing for the opposite: not that a stone has awareness, but that awareness is like a stone, just like they say in the Zen manuals.[42]

It's no accident that to reach this uncanny, even horrifying bliss one must pass through sunlit canyons of despair, strange vast chambers of slow motion sadness, abysses oozing with melancholic sweetness and darkness–the dark night of the, that is the soul, or what Nicola Masciandaro calls the sorrow of being.[43] The dark night of the soul is disturbing because melancholia, the default mode of being an ego, is holding on for dear life to nothing. Because the soul's essence is this very quiescence of the inorganic world, it must remember through this darkness that everything else is an illusion, a delusion that the soul matters, that reality is about it, for it–even the nothingness of melancholy self-reference is a delusion. How to let go? You have to tunnel further in–that's what every mystical text on the planet says.

Why? If we speculate here, it's because melancholia is a distorted photocopy of the truth of the charnel ground of existence. Depression is the rush of death-in-life decelerated by some psychic object that holds the mind in its jaws until we learn to hear its truth. Depression is frozen wisdom. Inside the ice is molten water. What replaces the delusion of melancholy is what is already the case–the simple coexistence of entities, "objects" to use Graham Harman's terminology. So spiritual depression doesn't exactly swing "back" to two-dimensional happiness, which has become an impossible

---

[41] Joan Roughgarden, *Evolution's Rainbow: Diversity, Gender, and Sexuality in Nature and People* (Berkeley: University of California Press, 2004), Dawkins, *Ancestor's Tale*, 626.

[42] Shunryu Suzuki, "Last Lecture of Sesshin," February 28, 1970 (http://www.shunryusuzuki.com/suzuki/index.cgi/700228Va180.html)

[43] Nicola Masciandaro, "The Sorrow of Being," *Qui Parle* 19.1 (Fall-Winter, 2010), 9–35.

escape route. Depression simply dissipates, like Arctic frost in the bright cold air. It enfolds itself back into the mute coexistence of things. Melancholy is supposed to be the pathological twin of mourning.[44] But the small print of mourning is that to pass through it we must dwell with melancholia. Melancholy is a lump in our throat, a rock in our stomach, a knot in our subtle body channels, an object-like entity that seems to stick in our being. It reminds us of the object world we strive to leave behind in our quest to compute the impossible. As such, the sorrow of being goes "deep down things" (to use Gerard Manley Hopkins's phrase).[45]

MYSTICISM AS SPECULATIVE REALISM

Again, mysticism is a form of speculative realism: the attempt to talk outside the ego, based on the fact that ego is only an illusion. In fact, from this point of view, what's perplexing is that confusion happens at all. What's perplexing is "this life," not what lies "beyond" life. It's perfectly "natural" that enlightenment happens all the time, because we don't have an ego, but we do have physical bodies. It's not some gift from above, but the spontaneity of what is below. Which is why esoteric traditions jealously guard their secrets: they can be abused because enlightenment is not difficult at all–it is in fact the default mode of existing, period. Armed with this information, which also makes you immune to normative standards of law and pathology, you could become a demonic ego, a being known as Rudra in Tantric Buddhism. Even Rudra is all right in the end, because enlightenment ultimately humiliates even this demonic state. The traditional story is that Buddha anally penetrates Rudra, shocking him into giving up. Vajrayana enjoins practitioners to visualize themselves as enlightened beings such as Green Tara or Manjushri–like emptiness philosophies, but working with bliss rather than intellect, this approach provides an allergy medicine against rejecting the object-like existence of mind essence.

---

[44] Sigmund Freud, *Mourning and Melancholia, The Standard Edition of the Complete Psychological Works of Sigmund Freud*, ed. and tr. James Strachey, 24 vols. (London: Hogarth Press, 1953), 14.237–258.

[45] Gerard Manley Hopkins, "The World is Charged with the Grandeur of God," *The Major Works*, ed. Catherine Phillips (Oxford: Oxford University Press, 2009).

These deities are often depicted trampling on the corpse of the Rudra of ego. Visualization (and mantra) has been described as an "enlightenment virus"–a sort of Henkin sentence that dismantles the ego through bliss.[46] Repetition is a feature of the death drive. Mantras are viral clones of sacred words, uttered millions of times. Preliminary practices for the Vajrayana include 1.2 million repetitions of the Guru Yoga mantra (*Om Ah Hung Vajra Guru Padma Siddhi Hung*), and 100 000 repetitions of the hundred-syllable Vajrasattva mantra, along with 100 000 prostrations. Meditation is a viral clone of attention. In basic shamatha you place your attention on an object (the breath, a statue, a visualization) over and over again, bringing your attention back when you get lost. In more advanced practices you remain undistracted in "nonmeditation," repeating the experience of letting go over and over again.

From standpoint of the kusulu, the "simple meditator," the entire universe is a charnel ground, a place teeming with dead objects, pieces of hair and fingers, some of them walking around with the brain still inside the skull ("alive"). The yogi is friendly with death, because death is more intimate than life, because there is "life after death"–as I argued a while back, what's harder to explain is the life "before" death, this apparently different state that humans so rigidly demarcate from everything around it in time and space. The esoteric meditation manuals of Mahamudra instruct you to meditate like a corpse. Could this be because a corpse is already meditating, in every meaningful sense? A Dzogchen yogi is a *kusulu*–three Tibetan words meaning "eat," "sleep" and "shit." Far from a demeaning term, this is the highest designation. It describes someone who knows what they are about. Such a yogi or yogini (the female form) experiences a charnel ground as a space of intimacy, not a cold, repellent place of terror, but a warm, loving place–not because she is suffering from the delusion that the corpses are really alive, but because she isn't. The ultimate funeral for such a yogini is sky burial, being chopped up to be eaten and shat out by vultures: the most ecological death imaginable, one that acknowledges the fact of coexistence that exists prior to thinking about it, and without the need for thinking about it.

---

[46] Tsoknyi Rinpoche, retreat, Crestone Colorado August 2006 (and frequently at other times and in other places).

NOWNESS OF DEATH

One of the most potent symbols of the dharmakaya in Dzogchen–the dharmakaya being the essence of reality–is a skull. The "second Buddha" who brought Buddhism to Tibet, Padmasmabhava, is often depicted holding a trident, upon which are impaled (in ascending order) a freshly decapitated human head, a rotting human head, and a skull. Dakinis–enlightened female beings–drink blood from skull cups. These cups (kapala) and the ritual drum (damaru) are best made from the skull of a baby. Tantric deities play drums made of human skin, the dead integument that "shield[s]" the living inside from the non-living outside.[47] This essay is arguing that these objects are not metaphorical. They are symbols in the Coleridgean sense: pieces of reality that have somehow made it into experience. Tantric Buddhism is a profound acknowledgment and acceptance of this reality. As one high Tibetan lama observes, "Spit into a cup. Now drink the spit. Why can't you do it? It was just in your mouth. You see? We have a problem."[48]

Why is it no accident that to reach the charnel ground you must pass through the valley of sorrow? Because the darkness is installed at the DNA level. DNA replication is a forgetting of the inorganic essence of DNA. Life cleaves to the delusion that life is why life lives. Yet DNA is also simply molecular physical form, "as it is," *thathata* (suchness): "emptiness is no other than form" (the Prajnaparamita Sutra of Mahayana Buddhism) because form itself, substance in the most cornily Aristotelian sense, if you like, is Buddha, directly, without needing any kind of transformation. Why? Could it be that when Buddhism refers to Buddha nature as *tathagatagharba*–enlightened seed, enlightened essence–it really means that the seed-like quality is what is enlightened? At least one teacher calls it *enlightened genes.*[49] What if genes actually were enlightened? In other words, what if what we call "awareness" is simply what for Heidegger is the "as-structure" of the way an object manifests to another object?

---

[47] Freud, *Beyond the Pleasure Principle*, 21.

[48] Tsoknyi Rinpoche, Empowerment Retreat, Crestone, Colorado, August 2009.

[49] Chögyam Trungpa: this is a literal translation of the Sanskrit term *tathagatagharba*.

In that case, a pencil resting on a table is doing exactly what my mind is doing when it rests on the pencil. Awareness according to this logic is an almost trivial, totally inescapable fact of existing at all. No wonder then that esoteric Buddhism calls it *ordinary mind.*[50] To this extent, esoteric means "secret" not because it's arcane or even because as just argued it's dangerous, but because it's self-concealingly obvious. Like an expert shoplifter who steals items right in front of the camera–because no one would believe that the crime is taking place before their eyes–this fundamental fact of reality hides in plain view.[51] It's difficult to see precisely because it's easy. The Artificial Intelligence (AI) and anti-AI philosophers are uncannily similar insofar as they both want to posit awareness as some kind of special feature, a bonus prize for having an organized nervous system, or for being highly evolved (an absurdly anti-Darwinian view for supposed reductionists), or "complex" (just ask a slime mold who's more complex, them or humans).[52] The panpsychicists are also in this camp since they posit consciousness as a supervenient fact, a special kind of reality beyond physical matter. In sharp contrast to AI, anti-AI and panpsychism, mysticism and speculative realism drastically *cheapen* the value of consciousness. In my view this makes it even more mysterious than before, and it opens up the universe as a plenum of unique, discrete entities, each apprehending things differently.

In this sense, life after death is the regular state of affairs. Tibetan Buddhism says that every phase of existence is a bardo, an in-between state. To that extent, at this moment, we are all in the position of Tim Robbins's character in *Jacob's Ladder*: we have no idea that we are already dead. Isn't this the basic plot of a certain form of noir, in which the reflecting subject realizes that she is the substance on which she is reflecting?[53] What requires explanation is *life before death.* To speculate further, after death states, also highly repeatable and remarkably similar, are indeed

---

[50] Chögyam Trungpa, *Cutting Through Spiritual Materialism* (Boston: Shambhala, 1973), 67–68.

[51] This is a constant theme in psychoanalysis, for instance in Jacques Lacan's analysis of Poe's story "The Purloined Letter," *Seminar on the Purloined Letter* (http://www.lacan.com/purloined.htm).

[52] Slime molds traverse three distinct states of being: amoeba, plasmodium, sporangium.

[53] The temptation to make this into a neat Hegelian symmetry is overwhelming, but mistaken.

"experiences" of entities that remain after the body has become a corpse. Thus near-death experiences, induced by accidents or suitably high doses of psychedelic drugs such as DMT, temporarily cancel out the illusions of life before death. But unlike some forms of nihilism, in which there is nothing outside the "manifest" reality that appears to human mentation, there is something–everything in fact, even mentation as such.[54] This is where I must part company with Ray Brassier. In his brilliant reading of *Beyond the Pleasure Principle* Brassier argues: "the trace of aboriginal death [the need for an "inorganic" membrane that shields the organism from the outside, like a coat of dead skin] harbours an impossible demand for organic life: it is the trace of a trauma that demands to be integrated into the psychic economy of the organism, but which cannot because it expresses the originary traumatic scission between organic and inorganic. The organism cannot live the death that gives rise to the difference between life and death." Thus "Extinction is real but not empirical."[55] To which the yogi replies, "Au contraire, Mister. I'm living it right now. So are you if you did but examine yourself." The yogi might even accuse the nihilist of chickening out at the last moment–by restricting experience to the "manifest," the nihilist is still caught in the circle of correlationism, that is, the circle of ego. If all that exists are objects that "experience" in any case, without some mysterious supervenient subject, then the "outside" is happening right now. You are holding it in your hands. You are reading it.

Though it sounds paradoxical to put it this way, remember that apprehension is a supremely default mode of existence: what pencils do to table tops. Slime molds can navigate around a maze: how come consciousness is restricted to having a nervous system, let alone to being "highly organized" or "complex"?[56] An object-oriented approach (a branch of speculative realism that I'm using here) provides a no-nonsense account of near-death experiences that, while not materialist, strictly speaking, is not idealist either. On this view, so-called near-death experience is a default mode that is happening all the time, but it's overwhelmed in lifeforms

---

[54] For the counterargument about the "manifest image," see Brassier, *Nihil Unbound*, chapter 1, especially 5–6, 25–26.

[55] Brassier, *Nihil Unbound*, 238.

[56] See Toshiyuki Nakagaki, "Smart behavior of true slime mold in a labyrinth," *Research in Microbiology* 152 (2001), 767–770.

with nervous systems by other signals. At the very least, an interpretation along these lines has the beneficial quality of being frighteningly straightforward and weirdly far-out simultaneously, for exactly the same reasons.

Doesn't this also mean that any attempt to undermine the logic of the death drive (and its sometime incarnation in theistic concepts such as god), through appeals to survival, are ultimately flimsy and, worse, self-defeating?[57] Even more seriously, aren't these attempts squarely on the side of idealizing "life before death" and thus not really materialist, though they claim to be? On the logic of the appeal to this kind of survival, life becomes a sad game of trying to avoid the inevitable. Far from being appeals to an atheism deeper than any possible theism (because god himself must be subject to the logic of self-preservation), these are the stereotypical reaction formations of modern utilitarianism par excellence, which doesn't even understand Darwin. The appeal to survival expresses a wish to return to a pre-Freudian universe, a wish to un-learn, to un-think, that perversely enacts the death drive in its very form, while denying the death drive in its content. The appeal has the form of a Cretan liar paradox. In starker terms, *the appeal is the death drive.* "Living on" is the very form of death in its most confusing, most anti-mystical guise.[58]

For a strict Darwinist, survival means passing on your DNA. What exactly survives here? A pattern, a form encoded in DNA. Not you, not your species—that's the lesson of Darwin even before DNA's discovery: there are no species and they have no origin.[59] Nothing "lives on." Survival means only that you didn't die before you had kids. Moreover, this "survival" is strictly a function of DNA's relentless drive to cancel itself out—so the death fish on the back of my car eats the survival fish on the back of Martin Hägglund's car.[60] DNA only reproduces to "solve" the problem of its inner disequilibrium. "The aim of life is death," quite literally,

---

[57] For instance in Hägglund, *Radical Atheism* (see above).

[58] Hägglund, *Radical Atheism*, 33, 129–130, 167, 202.

[59] Timothy Morton, *The Ecological Thought* (Cambridge, MA: Harvard University Press, 2010), 43–45, 60–68, 120.

[60] For a powerful opening statement in a similar counter-argument, see Adam Kotsko, "Something I find Questionable in Hägglund" (http://www.itself.wordpress.com/2011/02/12/something-i-find-questionable-in-hagglund/)

perhaps more literally than Freud himself meant when he penned this phrase.[61]

So when Buddhism teaches that the dharma is about how to die, it is speaking the honest truth.[62] To say that Buddhism can only ponder these issues because we care about living a day longer to ponder them is to assume that caring happens in a subject who emerges from, or is supervenient upon, some physical entity–an assumption that mysticism and speculative realism rule out, either because this subject is never constitutive of physical reality (the critique of correlationism), or because "caring" is a version of the Heideggerian as-strucure common to pencils, quasars and hanging chad.[63] There is scant but vivid evidence that this is the case. There are moments in art, for instance, such as *The Rime of the Ancient Mariner*, which have uncanniness without violence: sadness and horror, somehow combined. It's assumed that you can't combine them, because horror is an experience of a physical limit, and you have to have digested your trauma somewhat to have sadness. But if the after-death state is actually the default state of objects in the Universe, Buddhism is right to say that sadness and horror can be combined–compassion and renunciation, two major affective states for Buddhists, superimpose the one on the other precisely as ways of transcending the illusion of a rigidly separated zone of life as opposed to death. You can be horrified and soft at the same time, because your ego is only a construct–you give up the idea of merely surviving. The "transcendental fact" is the hyperobject of death's maw, the jaws of Yama. To think otherwise is to separate life from death rigidly, which is pure onto-theology. To claim that horror precludes sadness is to remain in dualism, tinged with a flavor of Burkean authoritarianism: the sublime becomes the terror to which you must submit.

Mysticism claims that there is indeed a life beyond death, and that we are living it right now. Esoteric Buddhism claims that the Buddhas–the actual Buddhas, not seeds, not ideas, not images– reside in your heart and in your brain, in your very flesh. When you die they manifest unclouded by the noise and confusion of

[61] Freud, *Beyond the Pleasure Principle*, 32.
[62] Sakyong Mipham Rinpoche, *Seminary Transcripts*, 1999 (Halifax, Nova Scotia: Vajradhatu, 1999).
[63] Graham Harman, *Tool-Being: Heidegger and the Metaphysics of Objects* (Peru, IL: Open Court, 2002), 8–9, 22, 32, 42, 45–47, 50, 60–61, 68–81.

samsaric existence, the crazy struggle of life to unlive itself. Enlightenment is nothing more nor less than objective, physical existence and coexistence. There is nothing to struggle against, only the quiescence of the inorganic world, the silence that filled Pascal with dread.[64] This nothing is curiously similar to the nothing found in mystical Christianity a nothing that is not simply the absence of something.[65] In Tantric Buddhism, mind essence is described as vajra nature, that is, as an indestructible object, literally a "diamond." The vajra nature is an indestructible object because it is made of nothing, "a nothing that is not negative." But it is indeed an object, a "sparkling stone" as the Flemish Christian mystic John Ruusbroec puts it. A stone that knows, however impossible to imagine that is in conventional philosophical terms.

In live performances of the song "Angels of Death" Dave Brock turns the terms "life . . . death" and around and around, as if death keeps on undercutting life, even as life keeps finding itself singing about itself, like a mirror being turned around and around to reflect, then not reflect, then to reflect again. This is the afterlife.[66] We are undead: "angels of life . . . angels of death . . . Born to erase / All of your days."

Rice University

---

[64] Blaise Pascal, *Pensées*, tr. A. J. Krailsheime (Harmondsworth: Penguin, 1995), 201.

[65] Eugene Thacker, "The Wayless Abyss: Mysticism and Mediation," *Postmedieval* 3.1, paragraph 23 (http://postmedievalcrowdreview.wordpress.com/papers/thacker/).

[66] See Eugene Thacker's very suggestive exploration of the limits of "life" in *After Life* (Chicago: University of Chicago Press, 2010), in particular 91–95, a discussion of how Islamic mysticism generates a "dark" concept of life.

WHEN DEATH BECAME A CREATURE: SAINT FRANCIS & SISTER DEATH

Beatrice Marovich

1.

Saint Francis–dressed in his rough and grizzled robes–reaches his hands into the air. He is destabilized, as though the ecstatic fervor coursing through his veins (pulsing just under the surface of his translucent skin) might set his lumbering and bony body to flight. He looks to the birds. He is fixated on the way their wings cut, knife-like, through the thick air. Creatures, each one of them, who do not seem to recall their point of departure. He is watching their small and tenacious eyes that glint like polished onyx. He is a madman in the marketplace: he has something to tell them. *I know*, he wants to say, *where this liberty to fly comes from.*

2.

Saint Francis–dressed in his rough and grizzled robes–reclines. His eyes are closed. His hood is carefully tucked around his head and covers his ears. There is the suggestion of a smile on his lips. Friars, on their knees, kiss at the soles of his dead feet. The *transitus* must have, already, begun. Or does the soup of his soul still keep him warm? A nobleman, in folds of silk, kneels by his side. The four fingers of his left hand are sunk into the sacred wound between Francis's ribs. Doubting, we are meant to think. But there is no blood. Into what other world does this gash lead? We cannot see the expression on the nobleman's face. But his fingers, frozen into this fresco by Giotto, have been there for hundreds of years–transfixed.

95

SAINT FRANCIS was a friend to all creatures. Or so the legend goes. He is now–by the writ of Pope John Paul II–patron saint of ecology. The historian Lynn White Jr., in his mythical condemnation of Christianity as a force of ecological destruction, made a hero of Francis. He was, White argued, a "left-wing" heretic–one who sought to "set up a democracy of all God's creatures."[1] Other Christian saints, says White, wanted "dominance over creatures."[2] But Francis, White felt, was something different.[3] Francis, instead, beckons us down the path to a harmonious sense of cosmic connection. Or so this particular story goes.

This is, when we skim over the surface, what we might immediately see in the *Laudes Creaturarum*–commonly translated as the "Praise of Creatures" or "Canticle of Brother Sun."[4] It is one of the few written texts properly attributed to Francis himself, a text that tantalizes with a glimpse into the sanctified mind. Francis addresses each of the elements (earth, wind, water, fire) as his brothers and sisters, evoking a sense of ancestral familiarity with the world itself. Francis even–through a turn of phrase–renders *death* a fellow creature. Death becomes a creature he can live in fellowship with, rather than fear. Is this Francis, the eco-warrior, who *liberates* death from a horrific state of abjection? Or is this Francis, the terrified human being, who seeks to *subject* death to a creaturely, mortal, condition?

Françoise Dastur argues that Christianity maintains a paradoxical relation to death: one that is simultaneously a recognition and a denial. The figure of a dying, wounded Christ on the cross places death at the heart of this faith. "The spectacle of the Passion of the Christ, which Christians constantly have before their eyes, endlessly enjoins them to remember that death is what

---

[1] Lynn White Jr., "The Historical Roots of Our Ecologic Crisis," *Science*, New Series, 155 (1967): 1203-1207, 1206.

[2] White Jr., "The Historical Roots," 1207.

[3] I will not, here, entertain the copious critiques of White's rather simplistic characterization of both Francis and Christianity. They are many. Suffice it to say that I use White's analysis here because I do find it–in spite of the polemics–indicative of a reading of Francis that pardons him from sins that even fellow saints have been accused of.

[4] All English translations of this poem are borrowed from: Alessandro Vettori, *Poets of Divine Love: Franciscan Mystical Poetry of the Thirteenth Century* (New York: Fordham University Press, 2004).

constitutes the very essence of their being. To live as a Christian is to live in the imminence of death."[5] And yet, central as death might be, it is only a passage. In the hierarchy of creation, death itself becomes more fleeting than God's eternity. Christianity, Dastur argues, relates to death in "the dialectical form of a recognition that is at the same time a denial."[6] Francis embraces Sister Death as a fellow creature, in recognition of some mutual mortality. But, in doing this, he rejects the power that death might otherwise have over him. Does he fall, neatly, into this pattern of paradoxical rejection and recognition that Dastur illuminates?

In this dynamic, Dastur argues, this Christian paradox of death continues to re-create death as the ultimate scandal. It continues to abject death. But is this, truly, the case with Francis's *lauda*? Does Francis's paradoxical relation to death ultimately resolve into a kind of violent synthesis, where death's ecological import is denied and rejected? Is Francis's kinship with death ultimately without camaraderie? Or does this patron saint of the ecological open a real space for death–as a creature–to live, move, and have a being?

Altissimu omnipotente, bon signore,	*Most high, omnipotent, and kindly Lord,*
tue so le laude, la gloria e l'onore et benedictione:	*yours are the praise, the glory, all blessings and all fame.*
ad te solu, altissimo, se confanno,	*To you alone, most High, do they belong*
et nullu homo ene dignu te mentovare.	*as there is here no man worthy to speak your name.*

The text opens with an invocation to the Most High. This song of praise is directed: its movement is ever upward, ever inward, ever intoxicated, ever disturbed by the elusive work of a Most High. The trajectory of this praise is not into the radical diversity of creaturely bodies. This song of praise is not meant to celebrate creatures *for the sake of* creatures. The bodies of creatures will light up in the following stanzas. But they are not illuminated

---

[5] Francoise Dastur, *How Are We to Confront Death?: An Introduction to Philosophy*, trans. Robert Vallier (New York: Fordham University Press, 2012), 33.
[6] Dastur, *How Are We*, 35.

for their own sake. They are illuminated for what they might otherwise obscure. They are praised for their roots, their origins, their beginnings, their ground, their superstructure. They are praised *not* because they are strange or particular. Rather, these strange and particular creatures are praised because they are shards of, instantiations of, a particularity that resounds in and around all creatures: the Most High. "Our age tends to regard Saint Francis romantically as a person who was kind to animals and friendly toward birds," Edward Armstrong wrote in the early 1970s. "But when emphasis on this aspect of his character involves failure to stress his complete devotion to his Lord and Master, the outcome is a very distorted picture of the man and his message."[7] Indeed, he is friend to all creatures–not only animals, but the force of the wind, the earth's elements. Their friendship, their kinship, is mediated by the Most High.

It is precisely this Most High that gives structure and shape to the complex world of creatures. The Most High brings unity to creaturely difference. Phillip Sheldrake argues that Duns Scotus's concept of the perfection of "the particular" was influenced, above all, by the tenor of Francis's canticle. "Francis experienced each particular element of creation," Sheldrake explains, "not merely Creation as an abstract whole."[8] It is precisely this dignity Francis grants to each particular creature that leads to Scotus's *haecceitas*–"thisness"–says Sheldrake. Thisness, Sheldrake intimates, obliges God to find a place "among the rejected garbage of this world."[9] Every particular thing *matters*. All matter, no matter how filthy, how useless, has a place. Not even in the furthest recesses of the landfill of creation is anything lost. And yet, this garbage is *perfect garbage*. It betrays a particular glow of the light. Because the Most High itself collapses into, decays into, the garbage of this world, we celebrate its thisness. The lights that flicker in the garbage piles of this world obey their hushed and almost incomprehensible command to glow.

There is, perhaps, a kind of immanent and topographical quality to this Most High. The structure that is imposed upon the

---

[7] Edward A. Armstrong, *Saint Francis: Nature Mystic* (Berkeley, Los Angeles & London: University of California Press, 1973), 6.
[8] Philip Sheldrake, "Human Identity and the Particularity of Place," *Spiritus: A Journal of Christian Spirituality* 1 (2001): 43-64.
[9] Sheldrake, "Human Identity," 60.

set of all creatures is that of a thisness that is seen less as *imposed from above* and more as a kind of installation of *aboveness* into each thing. As Giorgio Agamben describes Almaric of Bena's interpretation of the phrase "God is in all things", God does not so much "take place" or have a place. Rather, God becomes the "taking place of the entities." God becomes, "the being-worm of the worm, the being-stone of the stone."[10] So it is, perhaps, with the thisness of creatures in the wake of Francis's Most High.

It is the glow of this Most High, argues D.H.S. Nicholson, that makes Francis a mystic. Mysticism, as Nicholson describes it, carries as its sole end and aim "the necessity for the annihilation of self as precedent to that knowledge of God."[11] What happens after this annihilation, argues Nicholson, is not a dissolution but, instead, the discovery of a new thread that weaves the fabric of creation all over again. "There is thus a unity running through the mystic's life . . . a thread upon which his actions are strung which leads finally to Deity." It is upon the discovery of this thread, says Nicholson, that a mystic like Francis discovers he is, "supremely free, inasmuch as he can be confronted with no circumstances where God cannot be found."[12] It is this thin and elusive thread of the Most High that Francis invites us to take up (or to see as *already* woven into the fabric of our being) as we embark on this song of praise.

Laudato sie, mi Signore, cun tutte le tue creature, spezialmente messer lo frate Sole, lo quale è iorno, e allumini noi per lui. Ed ello è bello e radiante cun grande splendore: de te, Altissimo, porta significazione.	*Praised, O my Lord, with all your creatures be, most especially master brother sun, who dawns for us, and You through him give light: and fair he is and shining with mighty luminescence, And carries, O most High, a glimpse of what You are.*

---

[10] Giorgio Agamben, *The Coming Community*, trans. Michael Hardt (Minneapolis: University of Minnesota Press, 1993), 14.5.
[11] D.H.S. Nicholson, *The Mysticism of Saint Francis of Assisi* (Boston: Small, Maynard & Company, 1923), 23.
[12] Nicholson, *Mysticism of Saint Francis*, 315.

Praise is built, formally, into the body of the text itself. The *Laudes Creaturarum* is a formal echo of the Latin *lauda*, a liturgical prayer used at the morning mass. But this *lauda* was of the vernacular Italian variety—meant to be performed as minstrelsy, among the people, in the streets. The vernacular *lauda*, says Alessandro Vettori, had an "inelegant, rough quality" that made it appealing as a form of popular piety. This facilitated the transfer of high-church morality into new pockets in the social fabric. "What the mendicant movements did on a sociological level, the *lauda* did on a catechetical level."[13] There is, of course, a paucity of reliable information about this particular *lauda*. A number of hagiographers have testified to what Vettori calls the "melic nature" of the text— that its form indicates an intent to be sung. But particular details (the melody itself, for example) have been lost.[14] The sole element that, now, seems to give this *lauda* a rhythm of its own is the litanic structure carried through the repetition of the "Praised be" (*Laudato sì*). The repetition of praise shapes the text through the "sweet tyranny" of its litany.[15]

There has been controversy, among commentators, as to the correct translation of the Italian *per*. Should Francis be understood, here, to be praising God "for" creatures?[16] Or "through" creatures? To praise the divine *for* the creatures would be to take each creature as evidence of its creator's greatness. This is what Roger Sorrell describes as the "causal interpretation."[17] Each creature is a sign that points to its initial cause. Sorrell argues that the Italian *per* should function, here, more like the French *par* to be read as "by" or "through." God, in other words, would be praised *through* creatures, *via* creatures. The creature becomes more than a sign or a signal but, itself, a medium of transfer with agency. This, Sorrell

---

[13] Vettori, *Poets of Divine Love*, xv.

[14] Vettori, *Poets of Divine Love*, 65.

[15] The phrase "sweet tyranny" is pulled from Leo Spitzer's commentary on the text: Vettori, *Poets of Divine Love*, 74.

[16] It should be mentioned, perhaps, that the "per" we find in the Catholic Credo (when it reads, "per quem ómnia facta sunt") typically translates as, "by whom all things were made." This places the agency on the side of the creator figure. Following this logic, perhaps, the *per* that we read here would also carry the association of reading as such a "by" or "through."

[17] Roger D. Sorrell, *St. Francis of Assisi and Nature: Tradition and Innovation in Western Christian Attitudes toward the Environment* (New York & Oxford: Oxford University Press, 1988), 115.

argues, is more indicative of Francis's stance that reverence and praise for creatures also revealed "creation's autonomous beauty and worth."[18] I submit, however, that whatever autonomy creatures have in this schema, it is fragile. Creatures may be autonomous in relation to one another, for instance. The human creature might have few justifiable reasons to serve as tyrant of the created world. But this creaturely autonomy is always capped by the mutual subjection of creatures to the power of their god. To keep open the tension in this potentially ambiguous preposition is to keep that autonomy teetering on the high wire.

The stakes, here in the opening stanzas of the *lauda*, are indeed high. Which is to say that Francis welcomes us into the world of the text at the pinnacle of creation. We open with a reference to the Most High, and we descend into an invocation of the sun. We begin a tour of the hierarchy of creation. The sun earns the title of "master"–a figure of power and authority. The sun stands as, quite literally, a sign of the divine. To begin with a figure of light is to echo the creation story in the Genesis narrative: *let there be light,* God commands, and the sun snaps to attention. The sun was there at the beginning of the creation. The sun is quite nearly coeval with God himself. The sun might be the *logos*–the principle of life that twists and winds its way through the rest of the creation. The sun might be the Son–Christ, that Sun of God.

> *Laudato si, mi Signore, per sora* *Praised be, my Lord, for sister*
> *Luna a le Stelle:*   *moon and every star:*
> *in cielo l'hai formate clarite e*   *in heaven You made them*
> *preziose e belle.*   *precious and clear and fair.*

The sun is, moreover, a man. The sun–in this familial cosmos–is the brotherly element. Now we meet the woman who lives in the shadows of the sun: the moon, sister moon. In the *lauda*, says Edward Armstrong, "sun, fire, and weather are masculine because the qualities associated with them are power and robustness; the moon, water, and earth are praised for their gentleness and generosity, the moon for her charity, water for her cleanliness."[19] It is sex, gender–the old union of opposites–that makes this an active cosmos. The oscillation back and forth between the masculine and

---

[18] Sorrell, *St. Francis of Assisi and Nature*, 125.
[19] Armstrong, *Saint Francis: Nature Mystic*, 231.

the feminine elements will now give the *lauda* an additional rhythm, below that "sweet tyranny" of the litanical beat of praise. We alternate back and forth between power and virtue, they temper one another. And yet, however much they may harmonize, this pairing of sexual opposites also casts the text's subjections into sharper relief.

Vettori argues that this pairing of sexual opposites makes this a mystical text of sexual union. The binomial work of the male-female gendered pair is reminiscent, he says, of the Garden of Eden. We begin to sense, in the text, the aromas of this prelapsarian paradise. This is the almost saccharine perfume of melancholy. "The interactive structure of the two genders mirrors the love uniting mankind to divinity," argues Vettori.[20] There is the suggestion of a near completeness in this tension between gendered opposites. "The matrimonial union of two genders coincides with the inextricable bond of fraternity and sorority uniting all creation."[21] Francis seeks "the recovery of the harmony governing the universe at creation."[22] It is the bifurcation of the earth into gendered pairs that will, in part, help him to accomplish this.

His craving for a paradisiacal state may, in fact, *also* be apparent in Francis's deep kinship with animals (an element of the cosmos that is, in fact, conspicuously absent from this *lauda*.) Mircea Eliade argues that kinship with animals reveals an ecstatic desire to return to a prelapsarian state. This becomes, Eliade argues, especially apparent when we look at the example of Francis.[23] Eliade compares Francis to the shaman who, in trance, uses a secret language (sometimes referred to as the "language of the animals"[24]). In being *like* animals, in being uniquely capable of speaking their language the mystic (as shaman), is pulled "out of the general condition of 'fallen' humanity" and is somehow permitted "to re-enter the *illud tempus* described to us by the paradise myths." The ability to communicate with animals, in other

---

[20] Vettori, *Poets of Divine Love*, 41.

[21] Vettori, *Poets of Divine Love*, 55.

[22] Vettori, *Poets of Divine Love*, 59.

[23] Mircea Eliade, *Myths, Dreams, and Mysteries: The Encounter Between Contemporary Faiths and Archaic Realities*, trans. Philip Mairet (New York: Harper & Brothers Publishers, 1960).

[24] Eliade, *Myths, Dreams, and Mysteries*, 61.

words, is meant to be interpreted as a sign that the mystic has, "a spiritual life much richer than the merely human life of ordinary mortals."[25] Francis's sense of creaturely life, his understanding of the deep ancestral kinship at work in creaturely life (across the elemental spectrum), and its harmonies, might be read as a sign of his ecstasies, or his mystical aims.

But it is important–especially when we are, after all, talking about the animal bodies of creatures–not to let the sexual tones in this harmony be deafened, either. The sexual tensions of the poem become more apparent, perhaps, when we think of Francis as something like a courtly love poet. Francis steps into the role of Troubadour for God. The glorification of the female was a conceptual innovation of courtly love poetry that Francis mimicked in other contexts. This was, says Vettori, the nature of Francis's reverence for Lady Poverty. "Although earlier orders had viewed celibacy as a spiritual marriage to the Church, or to Christ, Franciscanism revises the concept by introducing the intermediary value of poverty and allegorizing her as a lady, a woman who preserves features and characteristics of distant and aloof courtly love ladies."[26] The Franciscan friars were offered the image of a woman who is dingy, without jewels, grown gaunt from a lack of food. But yet, their devotion "resembles the relation of male lover to female beloved in courtly love, in which subordination and service were absolute prerequisites for participating in the new way of loving."[27] In courtly love, in the reverence for Lady Poverty, the faint promise of sexual union (of an end to desire) is enough to justify the subordination of the male (the lover, the friar) to the female (holy poverty, or the feminine symbolic figurehead of feudal authority.) This is a rhetoric that drives sexual submission.

Here in the *lauda*, however, the female is passive. She is the moon: patient, quiet, hiding herself in cycles. Here, it is the female element who becomes submissive.

---

[25] Eliade, *Myths, Dreams, and Mysteries*, 63.

[26] Vettori, *Poets of Divine Love*, 47.

[27] Vettori, *Poets of Divine Love*, 47.

> Laudato si, mu Signore, per
>   frate Vento,
> a per Aere e Nubilo e Sereno e
>   onne tempo,
> per lo quale a le tue creature dai
>   sustentamento.

> Praised be, my Lord, for brother
>   wind,
> for the air and clouds and every
>   kind of weather
> by which You give your
>   creatures nourishment.

In spite of the fact that the masculine elements here are indeed those of power (wind, weather), submission is not to the male elements of the cosmos, either. The function of the turbulence of wind, air, or clouds, is not to demand obedience but rather to serve: to nourish. The harmony of the binomial pair (the male/female, the brother/sister, the sun/moon) is, together, subordinate to the power they should praise. In their union, in the pairing of sexual opposites, they are in the sway of a holy kind of back-and-forth. This is the paradisiacal pairing of the Garden. Together, the pair of opposites is to submit to a state of initial condition–in their mutuality, they both maintain an awareness of the condition of possibility for this mutuality (their creation). There is something, perhaps, more Trinitarian about this dynamic. The pair of opposites is not complete without the third–their condition of possibility, the unifying or synthesizing dynamic that continues to draw out and sustain the tensions between them.

> Laudato si, mi Signore, per sor
>   Aqua,
> la quale è molto utile e umile a
>   preziosa e casta.

> Praised be, my Lord, for our
>   sister water,
> which is so useful, humble, and
>   precious and pure.

The role, however, of the female elements is distinct. The metaphysical characteristics of these gendered elements are loaded with function and responsibility. The female elements of creation bear the weight of the virtues. While it is the responsibility of brother sun to fuel the elements of the universe, and the responsibility of brother wind to mix them up and nourish them into action, it is the responsibility of sister water to purify, to make virtuous. It is through sister water that humility and purity work their way into the cosmos.

The female factors in the cosmos appear to be responsible for actually living out (or embodying) the virtues themselves. What

Mary Daly called "phallic morality" was a celebration, or glorification, of the virtuous behaviors expected from the subordinate (such as, quintessentially, women): a sacrificial kind of love, deep and reverential humility.[28] Although the ideology of this "phallic morality" was to demand such virtuous behavior across the gender divide, this ethic came to be seen as quintessentially feminine, passive. To be virtuous was to be subordinate, passive, feminine. Here in the *lauda*, the female flow of water carries the silt of this virtue as she rushes on toward purification. But the glorification of passivity need not be aqueous. For Catherine of Genoa–a female mystic who found herself made pure only by the power of divine love–it was fire that purified. The "fire of God's love" that tears through the soul was designed, she suggested, to strip it of "imperfections" like "a dross."[29] As fire purifies metal by molting it, casting off the scum, God purifies the soul, she suggests.

Laudato si, mi Signore, per frate Foco,	*Praised be, my Lord, for brother fire*
per lo quale enn'allumini la nocte:	*through which you lend us luster through the night,*
ed ello è bello e iocondo e robusto e forte.	*and he is fair and merry, and vigorous and strong.*

In brother fire, however, we encounter strength and vigor. But the brotherhood that Francis invokes–this cosmic friendship between men–should not be likened to that of fraternal societies. Francis's obsession with brotherhood, argues G.K. Chesterton, "will be entirely misunderstood if it is understood in the sense of what is often called camaraderie; the back-slapping sort of brotherhood." What we see, here, is not power back-slapping with power–the kinship of fraternal order. The kind of brotherhood that we see in Francis is a folkloric variety that builds and develops in "that [same] fairy borderland" where he dreamt about flowers and animals. It was a brotherhood of pious politeness, argues

---

[28] See Mary Daly, *Beyond God the Father: Toward a Philosophy of Women's Liberation* (Boston: Beacon Press, 1973).
[29] Catherine of Genoa, *Purgation and Purgatory: The Spiritual Dialogue* (Mahwah, New Jersey: Paulist Press, 1979), 80.

Chesterton, which would have driven Francis to apologize to a cat for stepping on its tail.[30]

The tale of Francis's troubled encounter with brother fire, toward the end of his short life, reveals that Francis did not hope the fraternity to be unidirectional. It was not, merely, a courtesy that *he* extended to the other creatures of the world. As Chesterton describes it, Francis's diseased eyes were on the verge of blindness–to which the only remedy at the time seemed to have been to cauterize his eyes, without anesthetic. "In other words it was to burn his living eyeballs with a red-hot iron." When the iron was brought close to his face, threatening with its hot, hot heat, Francis reportedly "rose as with an urbane gesture and spoke as to an invisible presence: 'Brother Fire, God made you beautiful and strong and useful; I pray you to be courteous with me.'" It is a soft command–one that recognizes the superior power of the opponent, but attempts a domestication of that power nonetheless. Francis demands politeness from brother fire, much as he is willing to treat this brother with courtesy and respect. Chesterton charges that this moment was one of the "masterpieces" in the "art of life."[31] It is artful in its mythic, meticulous politeness. But I think it also reveals the extent to which Francis saw himself as something like God's circus trainer in the wilderness of the creaturely world. Francis was not a man at the mercy of the ravenous beauty of the creaturely world–he used tools that would allow him to discipline and punish, to control, to bring about the cold and fierce beauty of cosmic order.

His friendship with nonhuman creatures was often animated by forms of domestication. In the legend of the wolf of Gubbio, Francis was rumored to have traveled to the city of Gubbio, where a wolf was haunting the outskirts of the city. Citizens reportedly left their houses only when armed. Yet no one was able to chase the wolf away. Francis trekked out into the woods alone, making a sign of the cross at the wolf as it lunged for him. This drove the animal to fall at Francis's feet. Francis began to address him as "Brother Wolf" and proceeded to scold him for the crimes he'd perpetuated in the region. The two of them returned to the city, together, giving Francis cause to preach a sermon.

---

[30] G.K. Chesterton, *St. Francis of Assisi* (Garden City, New York: Doubleday, Doran & Company, Inc., 1924), 139.
[31] Chesterton, *St. Francis of Assisi*, 137.

What this story would seem to indicate, argues David Salter, is that Francis "would appear to have recognized that the creature was an autonomous being in his own right, who was entitled to be treated by humans with respect and understanding, and not simply as an inanimate object with no independent claim to life."[32] The wolf was not to be chased after with knives or arrows, in other words, but was to be reasoned with and treated courteously. Salter suggests, however, that this story does not present us with an example of Francis's democratic and egalitarian relationship with nonhuman creatures. Francis was condemning the wolf's "bestial" behavior and was civilizing him, humanizing him, domesticating him. This was a form of "moral censure" that insisted the wolf "curb his wolfish instincts" and seek to recover the prelapsarian state of innocence that Francis and his fellow Christians sought. What this looks like, argues Salter, is something more like the re-establishment of human dominion, rather than an egalitarian democracy of all creatures.[33] It looks, perhaps, like a demand that nonhuman creatures become subject to a world crafted by the humans. There is something of this, too, in the story of Francis's sermon to the birds. Commanding that the birds give praise to the creator who gave them such beauty in flight, Francis takes on the glimmer of a missionary evangelist to another continent. He speaks another language, he brings them–with a strangely intense delight–an alien god. It rings with the tone of a colonial enterprise.

Roger Sorrel has suggested that the Franciscan view of creation has much in common with the Cistercian view: both orders sought to celebrate the harmonic patterns woven into the creation. But Sorrell finds the sharpest point of distinction in the fact that the Cistercians were driven to "reconcile a deep reverence for creation with a need for technical domination of the environment for protection, security, and support." Sorrell's theory is that this is because the Cistercians were a settled, monastic community. The Franciscan approach, Sorrell argues, "arose from a more primitively organized social grouping very much attached to a life of wandering and individual meditative retreat."[34] Sorrell

---

[32] David Salter, *Holy and Noble Beasts: Encounters With Animals in Medieval Literature* (Woodbridge, Suffolk, U.K. ; Rochester, NY: D.S. Brewer, 2001), 29.

[33] Salter, *Holy and Noble Beasts*, 30.

[34] Sorrell, *Saint Francis of Assisi and Nature*, 37.

believes that this drove a more "humble intimacy with the natural environment."[35] Yet doesn't this make something of a noble savage of Francis himself? Nomadic life is not without its own forms of technical, environmental, domination. Certainly, Francis's techniques of control are subtle and abstract. But this does not mean they are nonexistent.

Francis's relationship with Brother Ass (his scornfully affectionate nickname for his own animal body) is both similar to, and different from, his treatment of nonhuman creatures. That is to say, Francis demands of his animal body the same sort of strict discipline and control that he expected of nonhuman animals. His animal body was, in a sense, another creature to control and civilize. But that he exercises this control on what is most intimate to him complicates the narrative that Francis was merely seeking a form of dominion and control that would serve to *please* the purely human.

Francis was an ascetic whose spirituality was dependent upon various forms of bodily subjection. The name "Brother Ass," of course, makes reference to a domesticated creature who was long notorious for its ability to patiently bear the weight of a load, and the crack of a whip.[36] It was also, however, an animal that was seen—in medieval culture—as able to bear its load with a certain amount of bliss. Control of the impulse of his own animal body was a necessity, for Francis. He was known for his resistance to satiate his body's needs—with either food or water. He resisted sufficiency. As a mendicant, he would force himself to eat the piles of domestic refuse that were made available to him. On the rare occasion that he was brought a delicious treat, he was rumored to mix the food with ashes.[37] To cultivate a love of poverty meant that his body would never experience the sensual pleasures of food. He was training himself, domesticating himself, into a life without

---

[35] Sorrell, *Saint Francis of Assisi and Nature*, 38.

[36] Francis's reference to the ass carries something of the jest in it, as well. The humor, certainly, was not lost on him. Medieval culture celebrated the ass as a symbol of folly. The medieval *asinaria festa* (the "feast of the ass") was accompanied by the "Orientis Partibus" (the "song of the ass") and congregants were invited to, "banish ill will and gloom". See Max Harris, *Sacred Folly: A New History of the Feast of Fools* (Ithaca, New York: Cornell University Press, 2011), 101.

[37] Nicholson, *Mysticism of Saint Francis*, 204.

gratifications. Yet, like an ass, he bore the burden of this discipline with a certain kind of joy.

The aim of Francis's bodily discipline, however, extended beyond the realm of gustatory delights. He was not merely training his animal body to grow wholly unaccustomed to the riches, the delight, of food. He was civilizing his own body, disciplining his own body, to be close to, respectful of, intimate with, bodies that were excluded from civilization proper. I am thinking, especially, of the story of Francis and the leper. In the European Middle Ages, of course, those inflicted with leprosy were quarantined–kept at a distance from the social order. Lepers were, in some locations, adorned with a bell that warned of their approach. In some local mythologies they were understood to hover indiscriminately between life and death–they were understood to be something like ghosts. This fear–of a body affected by leprosy–was shared by a younger Francis. His decision to embrace a leper is often pointed to as a crucial foothold in his spiritual path: a road to Damascus moment.[38] Nicholson argues that this was, "his first act of violent self-control"–an act that would shape his bodily practices for the rest of his life.[39] This was a form of corporeal domination that did not protect him but, instead, made him more vulnerable. It was a civilizing act that was set in contradistinction to the dominant societal injunctions: to keep the fabric of the social order clean, safe, free of disease.[40]

There are strange tensions at play in Francis's text. Creaturely bodies–the flesh of actually existing, real things–are important for what they reveal about Francis's mystical vision. Indeed, they are beautiful for the harmonious threads that weave them together– that reveal their interdependence. It is an interdependence that connects creaturely bodies to a strange ancestral web. And yet what is also revealed, upon closer examination, are the marks left

---

[38] See, for example (where this exact vocabulary is used) Paul M. Allen and Joan deRis Allen, *Francis of Assisi's Canticle of the Creatures: A Modern Spiritual Path* (New York: Continuum, 1996), 43.

[39] Nicholson, *Mysticism of Saint Francis*, 203.

[40] This can be complicated, somewhat, when we observe the fact that according to legend, the body of the actual leper disappears after Francis's embrace. That the leper was merely a miraculous instantiation, rather than an actual creaturely body, would suggest that Francis was never truly at risk anyhow. This makes the aim and effect of the narrative somewhat more ambiguous.

behind when this fine and fragile web pulls them together. When we look at what *happens* to creaturely bodies, in this mystical vision, we do not miss the subtle pain it inflicts upon them. We cannot quite cast a blind eye to the price they pay for harmony.

The body itself, argues Arnold Davidson, was important in the case of Francis for the way that it was able to "physicalize" his mysticism. In the event of miracles or mystical states, "it was all too easy to reinterpret psychologically these mystical states and to consider them as nothing more than excesses of the imagination."[41] Davidson sees this happening, especially, with Francis's stigmata. The stigmata, "marked, one could say, a new stage in the history of the miraculous."[42] It was able, Davidson suggests, to impart something more concrete about Francis's mysticism into the iconography of the saint. "The iconography of the stigmatization much more directly depicts the vision as a corporeal one. An imaginative vision, being produced in the beholder's imagination, could not be seen by other people. If more than one person sees the vision, then it must be a corporeal vision, whereby the object exists outside the people beholding it."[43] The creaturely body, in Francis's mysticism, was a stage that was being set—one that revealed evidence of the divine that any of us could reach out and touch. Does Francis's marshalling of the elements in this *lauda* not perform a similar function? *Revelation is everywhere, to be seen, everything we can touch,* it suggests. The divine is, everywhere, physicalized. The thread of the Most High is even woven into that which terrifies: the burn of the fire, the ravages of disease, a gaping wound. If we are unafraid to pull close, we begin to see how it ties us together. And how it pinches, when it does so.

Laudato si, mi Signore, per sora nostra matre Terra, la quale ne sostenta e governa,	*Praised be, my Lord, for our sister, mother earth, which does sustain and govern us,*
e prouce diversi fructi con coloriti fiore ed erba.	*and brings forth diverse fruits with colored buds and grass.*

---

[41] Arnold I. Davidson, "Miracles of Bodily Transformation, or How St. Francis Received the Stigmata," *Critical Inquiry* 35 (2009): 451-480, 477.
[42] Davidson, "Miracles of Bodily Transformation," 456.
[43] Davidson, "Miracles of Bodily Transformation," 475.

It may, as I have been suggesting, be unwise to pastoralize Francis. But as this stanza of his *lauda* makes clear–the language he uses makes it easy to do so. The Francis of legend was gaping with the sacred wounds of stigmata, revels in his own self-starvation, was driven to kiss lepers. But the tone of this comforting *lauda* is clean and bright. The "sweet tyranny" of the repetitive, liturgical scheme, gives the song its own sense of comfort. Beyond that, the imagery itself is pretty and perfumed–enough to pacify. The unsettling power, the potential terror of all that is fecund, is not articulated. It is not given imagery. But Francis's own linguistic pastorialization of the great big mother seems to be a form of sanitization.

Francis praises, here, the feminine "sister mother" he calls earth. Not only does she nurture and sustain, but he grants her a marginal degree of authority in his claim that she "governs" us. Yet this authority is also undermined by her very title. She is not *simply* a mother–she is not *enough* to be a mother. Instead, she is a "sister mother"–a title that undermines her motherliness by softening it with the fresh, young face of sisterliness. This is a sharp contrast with brother sun, who receives the title of "messer"–a title that is placed *before* the appellation "brother."

The abject, as I have suggested, plays a role in Francis's mystical vision–his encounter with the leper, the legend of his stigmata. These signs of abjection are celebrated as icons of self-dissolution. But it is notably absent from this *lauda*. The abject, as Julia Kristeva describes it, plays a crucial role in the annihilation of self that is so often used to describe the mystic. The writer of abjection, she claims, exists in a condition of "waste" or rejection. The writer of abjection *becomes* waste.[44] The abject takes us to the very border of our condition as living creatures–to the point where we might come into our closest encounters with death. "Mystical Christendom turned this abjection of self into the ultimate proof of humility before God," she writes.[45] Certainly the life of Francis–as it takes its shape from other texts–would give evidence of this sort of abjection. But this *lauda*, in its clean brightness, seems to give none.

The dampening of this sister mother's power, however, might give some indication of how Francis–with intent–seems to be

[44] Julia Kristeva, *Powers of Horror: An Essay on Abjection,* trans. Leon S. Roudiez (New York: Columbia University Press, 1982), 13.
[45] Kristeva, *Powers of Horror,* 5.

cleaning this mystical text of signs of abjection. If it was a song to be sung on the street, it was meant to pacify and give comfort. And the images of fecundity with the power to comfort are saccharine and tame: the sweet taste of fruit, the innocent promise of a bud, the tickle of new grass. They are the images of a birth that might, still, be permanently severed from death. The placenta, as Simone de Beauvoir points out, is not such an image. Instead, "That membranous mass by which the fetus grows is the sign of its dependency."[46] The fetus as icon of fertility, of fecundity, reveals not only the power of birth, but the fragility of dependence. "To have been conceived and born an infant is the curse that hangs over [man's] destiny, the impurity that contaminates his being."[47] The mother, argues Beauvoir, "dooms him to death. The quivering jelly which is elaborated in the womb (the womb, secret and sealed like the tomb) evokes too clearly the soft viscosity of carrion for him not to turn shuddering away."[48] Francis tempers the mother's power. She is not *truly* a mother. She is merely a "sister mother"– an incomprehensible hybrid of female biological functions. She is not given power because, perhaps, she would then be able to govern us enough to inflict us with *both* birth and death. Here, Francis seems only to give her the authority to nourish. The earth, too, is a creature to domesticate and civilize.

Laudato si, mi Signore, per quelli che perdonano per lo tuo amore a sostengo infirmitate e tribulazione. Beati quelli che 'l sosterrano in pace, ca da te, Altissimo, sirano incoronati.	*Praised be, my Lord, for those who for your love forgive, and every trouble, every illness bear. Blessed are those who meekly endure, for You, most High, will crown them finally.*

Commentators report that this was the original ending to the *lauda*, when it was first scribed in 1225. Francis again stresses the contingency and dependence of all creatures. But they are not

[46] Simone de Beauvoir, *The Second Sex*, trans. H.M. Parshley (New York: Alfred A. Knopf, 1953), 146.
[47] Beauvoir, *The Second Sex*, 147.
[48] Beauvoir, *The Second Sex*, 148.

contingent as an infant is contingent–so fragile that even the skull is soft. Rather, they are subject to, obedient to this Most High that works in and through them. They may be fragile, but not like the rotting fruits of that wild and abundant earth. His alien glory is a shield around them. For the sake of this Most High they are willing to forgive when it is most unappealing, to bear every possible illness, to suffer every possible form of trouble. The reward, for this obedience, is that they will wear–at the end of time–the crown. The meek will be the ones to inherit the earth. Francis holds out the carrot of justice. The great mother of this mortal earth is only a sister. She is not the one who made us, but is only a fellow mortal–suffering the fate of all contingent things. The stage that she has set, for us to live on, does not gives evidence of the justice he needs to see. Her justice, like everything else, rots.

But Francis will not want a justice that rots, nor will he suffer his creatures to wait for a justice that will only arrive at the end of time. We wait to *to be crowned*, but Francis makes the promise of this glory immanent, at hand. He wants to bring us justice–in some form–*now*. This also means we suffer its price. But this would not be the end. Francis would still make a late addition to the *lauda*, extending the scope of his concern.

Laudato si, mi Signore, per sora nostra Morte corporale,	*Praised be, my Lord, for our sister our bodily death,*
da la quale nullo omo viventi po' scampare.	*from which no living man can ever flee.*
Guai a quelli che morrano ne le peccata mortali!	*Woe to all those who die in mortal sin,*
Beati quelli che troverà ne le tue sanctissime voluntati,	*and blessed they who in your holy will are found,*
Beati quelli che troverà ne le tue sanctissime voluntati,	*for in no way will they by their second death be wronged.*
ca la morte seconda no li farrà male.	*So praise and bless and thank my Lord, and be*
Laudate e benedicite mi Signore, e rengraziate e serviteli cub grande umilitate.	*subject to him with great humility.*

Commentators report that this final stanza of the poem was added, by Francis, only days before his own death (what followers were to call his *transitus*) in 1226. Francis does not end the song, then, with

113

the promise of justice but with the promise of immortality. Those who follow the rules, who are obedient, who subject themselves to the "sweet tyranny" of the demand to praise, will be rewarded. They will be offered the view from on top: they will be shown that death is an illusion. The harmony that is promised–to live with the most blessed souls, in the eternal spheres–is also accompanied by what is, perhaps, the most intense subjection. Francis (on his own deathbed) finds death, herself, subject to mortality. He subjects her to the creaturely condition.

Death, like the sister mother earth, is a woman. Death will not be a *power* with which Francis must contend. She will be the submissive sex. Death is not the figure of fearsome intelligence and cunning who must be challenged to a chess match. Death is a woman. Feminist thinkers, like Beauvoir, have made much of the connection between woman and death. Death as a woman, says Beauvoir, becomes "a false infinite, an ideal without Truth, she stands exposed as finiteness and mediocrity and, on the same ground, as falsehood."[49] Rather than read death as an end, then, she becomes a means through which man can comprehend the immortality promised to him by the father. Woman, as the condition of possibility of birth, threatens always to remind him of this contingency. And yet, "she also enables him to exceed his own limits."[50] It is by passing through the false infinite that is death that the infinite becomes effective, real.

As Francis copes with the end of the body, the contingency of the body, it would appear that he seeks also to pass through this mortality–into the real infinite. No man can ever flee sister death. But to be given up to her, he suggests, is not the end. Francis, instead, mortalizes death. Does this characterization–the creation of death as a sister creature–typify what Dastur argues is the Christian pattern of negotiating with death? Does Francis simply turn her into a bad infinite, a false infinite, and subject her (like everything that is not divine) to the creature condition? Does he recognize her, only to reject her? Can it be said that he is, really, a friend to this creature? Does his mystical vision hinge on a gesture of coldness and cruelty towards death? Do the final lines of this *lauda* indicate that he has found a way to trump this female creature's power?

---

[49] Beauvoir, *The Second Sex,* 187.
[50] Beauvoir, *The Second Sex,* 148.

Dastur argues that our relation to death can be more than a simplistic anxiety that leads us to fear death as the enemy, that leads us to reject or deny it. She argues that anxiety (a Heideggerian sense of anxiety, properly understood), when embraced, can give rise to a kind of transfiguration. We can, "let ourselves be born by it in order thus to achieve that moment when it changes into joy."[51] She suggests that this sort of shift can change our very understanding of what death is. When we are able to see both joy and death resonate together at the same moment, she argues, we begin to see that death is not an enemy but, "the very condition of our being born." It is, "no longer an obstacle, but rather a springboard." Death is not the end of the human, but that which gives us the opportunity to be human in the first place. Death is not a "scandal" but, instead, the "very foundation of our existence."[52] It is death upon which we are ultimately dependent. Death makes creatures of us all.

It is true that Francis dissociates death and fecundity, in his *lauda*. He does not suggest that death is ripe, productive. It is true that his gendering of death, to some degree, renders her less powerful, less potent. He names death a "sister" and not a "mother." We are not *ultimately* dependent upon death. Rather, we and death are co-dependents. It is fair to say that Francis–who was not above utilizing the techniques of discipline and punishment at his disposal–maintains some illusory degree of control over death, by naming her a fellow creature.

Yet there is some gesture of camaraderie in this rhetorical device, as well. By making death a creature–one of the many creatures that he *praises*–Francis also seems to recognize a fellowship, a kinship, that would otherwise be incomprehensible. In this, he seems to pass beyond a "rejection" of death and into something else. It may not be death who stands as the condition of our existence. But Francis does seem to suggest that we (death, and the rest of us) are in this together. For this–for our entanglement, for our mutual dependence, for the attempts we each make to navigate the terrain of this earthly existence–he seems to think that death, as one of the creatures, is worthy of a kind of praise. Death, like the other creatures, has her "thisness," she too is illuminated with a particular kind of light.

---

[51] Dastur, *How Are We*, 42.
[52] Dastur, *How Are We*, 44.

Beatrice Marovich is a PhD candidate in Drew University's Graduate Division of Religion. She specializes in theories of divinity and is currently writing her dissertation, tentatively titled "Dream of the Creature."

UNCOUPLING THE HERMIT: RICHARD ROLLE'S HERMIT-*ING*

Christopher Roman

> . . . because *ontos* is always a question of *ethos* and *praxis.*
> In that sense, the tone of a thing tells us more than
> anything else what it *is,* for its tone is its ethic, its
> practice, its ontology, *its rapport.*
>
> – fragilekeys[1]

Be aware of deception. Rolle's *The Form of Living* wrestles with
deception; not to beware, but to be *aware.* How does one form
living in the face of such common deception? And, as Rolle is
concerned with deception, as such, living then must be something
taken from deception; it is something that must be formed, shaped
out of what is before us. Of course, there are those who cannot rise
to love God: "þay fallen in lustes and lykynge of þis world, and for
þey þynken ham swete" (7-8).[2] They "þynken" them sweet; their
taste for *faux* sweetness has left them fallen. They have no form–
those who are deceived. Rolle addresses *The Form* to one who
wants to fashion a solitary life, but this solitary life is shaped from
this miasma of deception. The *problem* of reality is paramount. On
the one hand, there are many things that lead the solitary astray:
the devil, sin, the flesh. On the other hand there is revelatory depth
beneath these obstacles–a way to live that is bound to these
obstacles that reveals truth. Rolle is not rejecting the act of rejecting
sin; as he repeats, it is sin that will lead the soul to everlasting
torment that is without comparison. However, that reality–the

---

Thank you to Andrew Albin (Fordham University) for his assitance with
relevant passages to *Melos Amoris.*
[1] http://fragilekeys.com/2012/04/26/common-ontology/.
[2] All citations from *The Form of Living* come from *Richard Rolle: Prose and
Verse*, ed. S. J. Ogilvie-Thomson, EETS (Oxford: Oxford UP, 1988).

reality of sin–is at the same time a real deception–it leads one to live a false life so that the solitary does not know who they are, does not allow themselves to be led by God or joined with Him. However, it is the *awareness* of deception that is necessary since it produces the furniture of the hermit's room.[3]

What am I to you? Initially, the solitary does not know itself. Rolle devises a chart of being with two axes. On one axis, Rolle explores the being of the contemplative in love: how do I recognize myself in you? On the other axis, Rolle sets out the being of Love itself. The question of how to love God is found on this second axis. Rolle needs to address the act that will lead to burning, the fire of love. Rolle emphasizes a kind of stability: "verray loue is to loue hym with al þi myght stalworthy, in al þi hert wisely, in al þi soule deuotely and sweetly" (705-707). Might stalworthy, hert wisely, soule deuowtly and sweetly–these three flow to constitute the gift of the contemplative to God. *I will give my will, my heart, my soul–these are the elements of my solitary body.* The solitary body is not anatomical, but a being like an exploded diagram. The will, the heart, the soul are the organs that matter; they float around each other in concentric orbits around the God-touch. This is the becoming that the mystic opens itself to. These three organs reach out to sense–this is the open space by which the contemplative touches a withdrawing God-object.

The form of living, this *progressive* verb–living–indicates that this form is found in the shifting, and it will not be fixed. "'*Ontology*' means doctrine of being."[4] So begins Martin Heidegger's 1923 lecture course where he lays out the philosophical investigation of ontology that finds full fruition in *Being and Time*. This early lecture course, however, provides us with Heidegger's definition of phenomenology as a mode of research, one that "needs to be understood *in accord with its possibility* as something which is not publicly and self-evidently given . . . Objects come to be defined just as they give themselves."[5] From this we can understand Rolle's need to develop an awareness of deception–it is not self-evident.

---

[3] Although *The Form of Living* was written for a very specific anchoress, in this commentary I am going to use anchorite/anchoress/hermit/solitary interchangeably. This may undermine historicism, but I am aiming for how this text speaks trans-historically.

[4] Martin Heidegger, *Ontology–the Hermeneutics of Facticity*, trans. John van Buren (Bloomington: Indiana UP, 2008), 1.

[5] Heidegger, 58.

As well, we notice that as sin presents itself it remains fixed. It is *always already* the devil, the sin, the fleshy world. In recognizing that there is evil, the index of the transcendent is evident . It is in shifting, in living, that the solitary recognizes their capability, their thing-hood. The solitary is a shape that must be made. As Graham Ward writes, "an orientation toward ontology–some model of the relationship between existence and existents, being and becoming– is necessary. The question also presupposes that an enquiry into the relationship is possible. The question demands that there is or can be an identification of a 'thing,' an understanding of thinghood."[6] For Ward, the debate surrounding the ontological nature of God is between God as beyond (such as found in Jean-Luc Marion or Heidegger) and God in the Augustinian sense, as source. For Ward, then, the debate is between a philosophical and theological line of questioning one in which the former is contained in the latter (for Augustine, and, thus, Ward). Ward's concern with "thinghood," however is important for Rolle's sense of the God-object and the solitary that I mentioned earlier. For Ward "its 'thinghood' and the varieties of 'thinghood' of which it is composed is never stable, never static. Its thinghood is in suspension, as the 'what' is what it is in the fullness of its becoming."[7] Ward echoes an object-oriented ontology here in that what Ward calls "suspension," OOO philosophers would call *withdrawal*. Ward further elucidates, "whether a thing is can never be fully defined. That there *is* can be affirmed, but the nature of that *is* is not a thing that can be grasped or even experienced as an *is,* as presence, as that which can be isolated as present to itself."[8] Ward writes that only in the line of questioning do we have a sense of God's presence, but we will never know God-in-himself; "the

---

[6] Graham Ward, "Questioning God" in *Questioning God,* ed. John D. Caputo, Mark Dooley, and Michael J. Scanlon (Blooming: Indiana UP, 2001), 279. Also see Joannes Scottus Eriugena, who, in the *Periphyseon writes,* "Divine essence, which in Its pure state surpasses all intellect, is rightly said to be created in the things made by, through, in, and directed toward Itself; so It is recognized in Its creations through the intellect (if the creations are solely intelligible) or the senses (of they are sensibles) of those who search for it with proper zeal" (*Periphyseon: On the Division of Nature,* ed. and trans. Myra L. Uhlfelder [Indianapolis: Bobbs-Merrill, 1976], 17).

[7] Ward, 280.

[8] Ward, 280.

questioning of God (both subjective and objective genitive) never ends; it just plumbs deeper into the mystery of the Godhead as the Godhead unfolds its own infinite nature."[9]

If the fundamental question of ontology is 'what is?' then *The Form of Living* investigates that question through the lens of the becoming continuity of the hermit-God relationship, and in that becoming the God-object floats. Therefore, Rolle is concerned with separating how what *is* relates to that which *negates*. And, what negates is what stands still. For Rolle, the problem of ontology is finding the ways in which the solitary can fulfill their capability. Grace Jantzen's commentary on a queer theology assists us in thinking through Rolle's attempt to "uncouple" the hermit from traditional frames of reference, to be aware of what is not self-evident. Jantzen is interested in a theology that "gets rid of the straight and narrow boundaries of traditional Christendom and is open to difference, fluidity, curvature."[10] This fluidity and curvature finds fulfillment in the aesthetics of the self:

> those of us who already take up queer positions have some extra practice in the creativity and the cost of an aesthetics of the self. We are learning how to dig deep into our best possibilities, and not to allow ourselves to become flat mirrors of our contexts, reflecting and reinforcing its self-perceptions . . . the mirror we hold up to our culture, religious and secular, is a mirror of curves and corners that reveals the multiple distortions of discursive and material reality.[11]

Rolle repeats in many of his works the formula "knowest thi self" (453-454). The need to know oneself is integral in understanding the life of solitude, as well as how that life opens towards God.[12]

---

[9] Ward, 282.

[10] Grace Jantzen, "Contours of a Queer Theology" in *Feminism and Theology*, ed. Janet Martin Soskice and Diana Lipton (Oxford: Oxford UP, 2003), 344.

[11] Jantzen, 351.

[12] Rolle's need for ontological prescription finds its counterpart in Heidegger's commentary on the relationship between object and hermeneutic: "the theme of this hermeneutical investigation is the Dasein which is in each case our own and indeed as hermeneutically interrogated with respect to and on the basis of the character of its being and with a

Rolle's hermitic ontology is based on fulfilling being; in a word, how the hermit is becoming-*hermit.*

At the heart of Rolle's ontology is the role of God in the hermitic life. But role is too static of a word: God is a catalyst in the relationships. It is the middle of the river. God is revealed through the connections between solitary and God. God is not present to itself because it is never fixed. The solitary's relationship with the *unknown* is where they find God. So, God is not a stable object, rather, something only definable in terms of movement, in terms of love. God is an unhittable moving target. God is negated when the relationship between God and solitary is disrupted by sin, deception, or falsity. Early in *The Form of Living*, Rolle warns that people are not what they seem. It is easy to see "worldisshe men and wommen that vsen glotony or lecherie and other oppyn synnes, bot þei ben also in sum men þat semen in penaunce and in good lif" (18-20). Rolle emphasizes the "semen" throughout this text. Worldly people wallow in gluttony and lechery, so it is easy to see what not to do in their case; they are actively and publicly sinning, but they are also standing still–they are gluttony, they are lechery, and it fixes them like so many pins inside so many bugs.

The lecherous, the greedy, they are, perhaps, easy to spot. Rolle poses the question about those we might identify as role models: the priests, the bishops, the enclosed, who, to all appearances, are living a holy life. What if they are also–on the inside–actually sinning and leading an unholy life? Rolle emphasizes that what happens in these situations is that the devil especially likes to pick apart the holy: "when he seth a man or a womman amonge a þousand turne ham holy to God . . . a thousand wiles he hath in what manere he may deceeyue ham" (21-25). Further, Rolle writes, if he cannot make them publicly sin so that others can see them for what they are, "he begileth many so priuely þat þai can nat oft tymes fele þe trape þat hath take ham (26-28). The devil then sets a trap that the holy person is not aware of–in other words they are living what they *think* is a holy life, but in truth they are ensnared in a devil's web because they are living in imagination, as opposed to what is. They are fixed. In order to live more harmoniously with God this trap must be avoided.

---

view to developing in it a radical wakefulness for itself," (*Ontology–the Hermeneutics of Facticity,* 12). The wakefulness is what Rolle is addressing against the problem of deception.

But, first Rolle insists we understand the very nature of the snares, so that the hermit can continue being. Again, Rolle wants us to know ourselves in order to live in God. Many of these initial traps have to do with pride: "sum men he taketh with errour þat he putteth ham in; sum with synguler witte, when he maketh ham wend þat þe thynge þat þei thynken or done is beste, and fortþi thei wol no conseil have of other þat ben better and connynge þan þei" (29-32). The nature of pride is that it cuts oneself off from relationships; we fix ourselves. The self is entirely centered on the *itself* and is not opened. Further, this stain of pride attacks what could be beneficial spiritual activities. For example, Rolle writes that one could "delite in ham self of þe penaunce þat þei suffren" (35-36). Penance, abstinence, good works: for Rolle these are easily bent to be sinful as the solitary fixes them onto oneself. The activity stops; it becomes *not* a process, but is embraced only for false outputs. Because the solitary places themselves in the middle of the act, cutting off the benefits that connect one with God.

Therefore, Jesus cannot be loved "bot in clennesse" (159-160). This cleanness has to do with righting the self outwards in understanding true Being. The original tempter came "in an angel of lighte" (who "hideth yuel vndre þe liknesse of good") (182-184). The solitary's work is in being able to separate the "liknesse of good" from Real good. So, the Real works beneath the level of appearance. And this "liknesse" can easily be faked while the Real beneath is hidden from uncritical eyes. Rolle places the solitary in a unique position: "the state þat þou art in, þat is solitude, þat is most able of al othre to reuelaciouns of þe Holy Goste" (138-139). The solitary, though, has a certain predilection for privation, the ability to push the body is a hallmark of hermitic living. However, Rolle emphasizes that the solitary should not be excessive in their habits since this leads to further deception. If the solitary eats, drinks and sleeps too well then it "makes vs slowe and cold in Goddis loue" (190). On the other hand, if there is too much penance the solitary risks "destrue" of the self (192). In both cases, extremes lead to misconception. In the first case, easy living leads to too much comfort and thus a contentment in earthly pleasures and a distancing from God. In the second case, bodily punishment leads to an erasure of the body, a body that is necessary to live a contemplative life. There also develops a sense of competition with excessive ascetic practices—the solitary begins to pride themselves on their extremes and, thus, prove that these practices are not for God, but, rather are done out of their own excessive sense of self.

What is the relationship between self and solitary, then? We can begin in thinking about the connection between body and soul. Rolle writes, "I know þat þi lif semeth yeuen to þe service of God. þan is hit sham to þe, bot if þou be as good, or bettre, within in þi soule, as þou art semynge at þe syght of men. Therfor turne þi þoȝt perfitly to God, as hit semeth þat þou hast þi body" (233-234). Even if the solitary is publicly identified–bodily–as someone whose spiritual practices are strong–*semeth*–it does not guarantee that they are actually living a good life devoted to God; there is a delineation being made here: one between the body and the activities devoted to it and the activities of the soul which must be connected to those bodily activities. The becoming-solitary cannot separate oneself into two modes of being; they must flow together. Therefore, the solitary must move both body and soul toward God, aligning the soul with the body. The body is already *acting like a hermit,* but the solitary's soul might not be. Note Rolle's mapping here, since usually it is the body that leads the soul astray. Here, it is the soul that must correct itself to the habitation of the body.

For Rolle, the concept of "perfit love" indicates this alignment of body and soul in space. In order to achieve this, the solitary must also contemplate time. The solitary must keep four things in mind:

> on is þe mesure of þi life here, þat is so short is þat vnnethe is oght; for we lyve bot in a point . . . Anoþer is vncerteyntee of oure endynge; for we wot neuer whan we shall dey . . . The þrid is þat we shal answare before þe righteous juge of al þe tyme þat we han had here: how we haue lyved, whate oure occupacioun hath bene and whi . . . The fourth is þat we þynke how mych ioy is þat þay shal haue, þe which lesteth in Go[ddis] love to har endynge. (280-288; 297-298)

Not only does the solitary need to think of their life as a point–to reveal themselves within the control of eternity, but the solitary is encouraged to see that life moved forward into eternity. As Eileen Joy writes, "every point of each of us coincides with every point of everyone else in a single point which is where we all are. There is nowhere else. The idea of distance, or separation, or estrangement, is a dream. Which is not to say we should not mind the gaps."[13] Rolle asks the solitary to consider this distilled point of time in which they exist and connect to everything else. In this way, Rolle sets up the contemplative life as a revelation: it will need to be revealed, accounted for at the time of judgment, but the contemplative, as a way to make sense of the point of time they currently occupy will also set themselves into an eternal future. As Heidegger remarks:

> Taking historical consciousness to be an exponent of being-interpreted in the today draws its motivation from the following criterion. The manner in which a time (the today which is in each case for a while at the particular time) sees and addresses the past (either its own past Dasein or some other past Dasein), holding on to it and preserving it or abandoning it, is a sign of how a present stands regarding itself, how it as being-there *is* in its there.[14]

The hermit regards itself. The "uncerteynte" of the ending of life is countered by the comfort of being "breþere and felewes with angels and holy men, louynge and hauynge, praising and seynge þe kynge of joy in þe fairheed and shynynge of his mageste" (299-301). The nature of time is both finite—life, narration of that life—and eternal—love of God, joys of heaven. But, the contemplative cannot have one without the other. It is in the taking account of time—seeing it for what it is; seeing it for how it projects forward—that the contemplative is the most successful in their living.

Rolle emphasizes a certain kind of life as the source of contemplative power, hence his emphasis on living *appropriately*. The ideal of living appropriately is made clear in his discussion of being "right disposed" (323). Being "right disposed" means to understand the character of the human being: "what thynge fileth a man . . . What maketh hym clene . . . what holdeth hym in clennesse . . . what þynge draweth hym for ordeyne his wille al to Goddis wille" (323-327). Again, we return to the concept of

---

[13] Eileen Joy, "You Are Here: A Manifesto" in *Animal, Vegetable, Mineral: Ethics and Objects*. ed. Jeffrey Jerome Cohen (Washington, DC: Oliphaunt Books, 2012), 154.
[14] Heidegger, 28.

knowing oneself, but also, as is indicated in the use of the third-person "hym," Rolle seems to be widening his reach and suggesting an anthropology that guides the contemplative: what is this "hym?"

It is in this "hym" that Rolle addresses the nature of hermitic being in the relation between the heart, the mouth, and the deed. These sites of the body are vulnerable to sin and must be carefully guarded and made right, but they also indicate the foundation of hermitic being. These three complement the orbiting will, heart, soul in which Rolle's ontology is based: the heart, mouth, and deed are points in the hermitic being that cause perturbations in the local–they uncouple the hermit from one environment (the world) into another (the hermitic space) or, if not properly aligned with God, they re-couple the hermit to the world. In other words, the heart, mouth, and deeds *are* hermitic being in that it is through them that being is constituted.

The heart is where the emotions and thought are situated. Rolle writes that the sins of the heart consist of "il thoghtis, il delite, assent to syn, desire of il, wikked wille . . ." (329-33). The heart is not only connected to emotional stuntedness, for example "il dreed, il loue, errour, fleishly affecioun to þi frendes or to others þat þou lovest" but also poor thinking, "vnstablenesse of thought, pyne of penaunce, ypocrisi, loue to plese men, dred to displese ham, sham of good deed" (3301-332, 340-342). Thoughts and emotions are situated in the heart and this catalogue of problems that Rolle reports indicates both the inability to align the heart with God, as in the "assent to sin," and also an unhealthy relationship with the community and the self. Being too concerned with pleasing or displeasing others leads one astray from the ability to love God, but, also, leads one to be ashamed of one's good deeds. Earlier in this litany of sins, Rolle writes of "perplexite (þat is dout what is to do, what nat, for euery man oweth to be sikyre what he shal do and what he shal leue)" (336-338). The idea of "perplexite," this inability to decide, speaks to the bent nature of the self–it is being upset by a lack of becoming, of distraction that clouds the contemplative being.

If the sins of the heart indicate the ways in which the emotions and thoughts can ground the hermit in the wrong path, the sins of mouth indicate the public nature of the contemplative being. The environment of the hermit is important in that Rolle's text is attempting to move, to cause vibrations in the solitary. Rolle recognizes that the solitary can never be completely severed from the world–as was indicated earlier, the body is in a relationship with the soul–however, he works to change the track of the solitary so that they are moving towards God. With his discussion of the mouth, Rolle connects the disjointedness that results from the relationship between God and community. Not only is it sinful to slander God or swear in his name, but to "gruch ayayns God for any anguys or noy or tribulacioun þat may befalle in erth" (352-353), indicates a lack in understanding of God's being on the part of the community. To "gruch" would imply that God does not know what it is doing, and, thus putting oneself at odds with a divine will. God is no longer part of becoming if it is out there acting *apart* from the community.

As mentioned earlier, *The Form of Living* is concerned with deception–the world that presents itself is a series of flows and stops that *produces* the hermit. The concern in Rolle's hermitic ontology is what kinds of objects need to exist in order for the contemplative to exist. One key to hermitic relations is the attitude toward neighbors. The contemplative must avoid discord with the neighbors: "manacynge, sowynge of discord, tresone, fals witnes, il consail . . . turne good deeds to il for to make ham be holden il þat don ham (we owen for to lap oure neghbors dedes in þe best and not in þe worst)" (355-358). Rolle's capacious attitude towards neighbors, to hold them to the best intentions is a way to "uncouple" from judgement. As Slavoj Žižek remarks, "the person who mistrusts his others is, paradoxically, in his very cynical disbelief, the victim of the most radical self-deception . . . the true believer . . . sees Goodness in the other where the other himself is not aware of it."[15] To place oneself in judgement of the neighbor's deeds or even to cause *negative* political (treason, false witness) problems with one's mouth proves that one is out of joint with being.

Finally, Rolle describes the problems of the sins of deeds. Rolle begins with a roll call of the various ways one can break the law of the Ten Commandments. These are direct acts against the Law, but, again, Rolle widens actions to describe community disharmony. Rolle is critical of hurting "any man in his body or in his goodes or in his fame . . . , withhold necessaries fro þe body or yeve hit outrage . . . , feynynge of moore good þan we haue for to

---

[15] Slavoj Žižek, *The Fragile Absolute*. London: Verso, 2000, 119.

seme holier or connynger or wiser þan we bene" (367-372). Again, Rolle speaks to the way that these elements–God, self, community–constitute the being of the contemplative. It is of interest to note not only the power that the contemplative has in his community, and the damage the solitary can cause through making themselves out to be better than they are, but the political nature that it can also hold. Rolle warns against treason and false witness, and also harming goods. There is a sense that Rolle has cast a wide net–these are the problems of every *body* and, thus, his anthropology is of human failing, what is wrong or out of joint with Being. On the other hand, however, Rolle is suggesting that human being is not a lost cause–the nature of the human simply needs to be remedied in a clear fashion:

> the thynges þat clenseth vs of þat filthede ben þre, ayeyns þay þre manere of synnes. Þe first is sorowe of hert ayeynes þe synnes of thought; and þat behoueth to be perfite, þat þou wolt neuer syn moor . . . The tother is shrift of mouth again þe syn of mouth; and þat shal be hasted withouten delayynge, naked withouten excusynge, and entier without departynge, as for to tel a syn to oon prest and anoþer to anothre; sey al þat þou wost to oon, or al is nat worth. The þrid is satisfaccioun, þat hath þre parties, fastynge, prier, and almsysdede . . . for to foryeve ham þat doth þe wronge and pray for ham, and enfourme ham how þay shal do þat ben in poynt to perisshe. (399-410)

The advice that Rolle provides here is in protracting the body into stability. Stability, though, is a kind of flow. The mouth should be given "shrift" but also made transparent. Rather than try to spread around one's sins to multiple priests so that no one has any clear idea of the depth of sin, one should tell them all to one so as to avoid shallowness. The depth of the solitary needs to be revealed.

This becoming toward God by the contemplative is based on Rolle's discussion of the nature of love. Rolle's discussion of love involves two dimensions. First, Rolle addresses degrees of love. These degrees of love are levels to which the contemplative must attain or "win" (525). The other dimension of love that Rolle discusses is Love itself–the being of Love. If *The Form of Living* is a guide for contemplative to turn their life to God, Rolle's ontology is in the nature of Love itself. In a Socratic-like dialogue, Rolle begins with three questions: what is love?, where is love?, and how do I love? As mentioned previously, one can think of Rolle' analysis as a diagram–on one axis is the being of the contemplative, on the other, is the love that God reveals. In the final *how* of the dialogue the two axes meet.

The three degrees of love are "insuperabile," "inseparabile," and "synguler." The contemplative achieves "insuperabile" love when the love is stable in the face of all obstacles. In marriage ceremony-like language, Rolle describes the love as stable whether "in ese or in anguys, in heel or in sekeness, so þat þe þynke þat þou will nat for al þe world, to haue hit withouten end, wreth God oo time" (529-531). This love conforms with Rolle's wish for stability of heart. This is the foundational love that the other forms of love rest upon. Rolle writes further that this is a good love to have, but it is even better for the contemplative if they can move into other types of love.

If "insuperabile" love is marked by the external, "inseparabile" love is marked by the internal. Insuperabile love is threatened by the external, so that for Rolle love is truly inseparabile if it is stable and will not bow to anything that happens to the contemplative. Inseparabile is characterized by a oneness with Jesus. The contemplative is fastened to the thought of Jesus so that "þi thought and þi myght is so hooly, so entierly and so perfitly fasted, set, and stablet in Ihesu Criste þat þi þoght cometh neuer of hym, neuer departeth fro hym" (538-540). The prepositions "of" and "fro" indicate the contemplative's flow–they are immersed in Jesus–being both a part of and emanating out from. The only time the contemplative's thoughts depart from Jesus is in sleeping, but immediately upon waking the contemplative returns to Jesus-thought. There is a singularity in this thinking as the contemplative is aligned with Jesus, however, Rolle leaves his longest discussion for the third kind of love: synguler.

Synguler love is the highest form of love that the contemplative can experience and it is marked by the feeling of fire that the contemplative experiences. As Rolles writes, this love "hath no pere" (550). The contemplative experiences solace and comfort from Jesus only and nothing else. For Rolle, Jesus is the sole occupier of the heart at this level. The fire that burns in the heart is "so delitable and wonderful þat I can not tel hit" (556). The fire defies descriptions though it is can be likened to the fire one feels if one sticks their finger in the candle's flame (555). At this level the soul is Jesus-bound: "þe sowl is Ihesu louynge, Ihesu thynkynge, Ihesu desyrynge, only in coueitys of hym" (556-557). The gap between Jesus and the heart is lessened here–if there is a gap at all. The heart begins to embody the present progressive verb-form that is Jesus; the heart makes itself Jesus-*ing*, as it burns, thinks, desires. The soul makes a final transformation when it becomes song.

The soul–in the midst of its desire for Jesus, thinking of Jesus– becomes a song of Jesus. It is at this point that Rolle points out the contemplative will be overwhelmed to see Jesus and that the feeling of "deth swetter þan hony" (562) is proof the soul is secured to Him. As the contemplative is absorbed into Jesus-thought, Rolle still feels in his contemplative ascension that the payoff is to see Jesus, to have him confirmed visually. But, despite this death-wish, Rolle indicates that along with the song, it is here that the contemplative no longer "languishes" rather, it is here that the contemplative experiences the profound change of their body sleeping and the heart awake.

As Rolle points out, in the first two levels the contemplative languishes, like a sickness (567). It is only in the third degree that the heart/soul is awakened like a "brennynge fyre, and as þe nyghtgalle, þat loueth songe and melody" (571-572). This soul is only comforted in song and so will sing for the rest of its days of Jesus. Like song, the soul moves, but it is not graspable.[16] It is a flow both as a point (think musical notes) and as a movement (the notes roll along the notation, touch the ear). Rolle further wants to separate this song from regular every day singing. This genre of song is only experienced *at this level* of love. And, further, this love is a gift from God, it comes from heaven; when the contemplative

---

[16] See *The Melos Amoris of Richard Rolle of Hampole*, ed. E.J.F Arnould (Oxford: Basil Blackwell, 1957), especially chapters 44-46 for Rolle's discussion of the ontology of song in his mystical work. For example, from the beginning of chapter 46, Rolle writes of the nourishing song before the Almighty that reveals the lover: "Novum nimirum cantant canticum, quia novata natura in nitore nutriuntur quousque conscendant castrum cupitum et clare conspiciant Cunctipotentem. Optime orantes elevantur in altum et ordinem habentes muniminis mirandi, modulando in melos organizantur. Ingenter iubilant ante Auctorem, Regique referunt almiphonum amoris ac canunt conformes concentui preclaro et odas ostendunt amantibus excelsis iperlirico in ympno" (137-138).

has this song all the songs of earth seem "bot sorowe and woo" (583-584).

These three levels of love act as a guide to what the contemplative is capable of experiencing. The ontology of love desires Jesus, and the need to not be separated from Him; there is a level or eroticism that Rolle will explore further in the lyrics and in his centering of worship on the name of Jesus. Here Rolle's ontology is of a love that is there for the contemplative to experience as long as they can become aware of the fixed and flowing worlds. The world of some kinds of matter are a distraction that limits what the contemplative can experience—either by keeping them still or keeping them at the lower levels of the love experience.

For Rolle, this ontology of love has another dimension, that of the Loved. The questions that Rolle poses at the end of *The Form of Living* create an ontology of God that suggests being, location, and intersubjectivity between contemplative and God. God contains Love and is contained by it: "love is a brennynge desire in God, with a wonderful delite and sikernesse. God is light and brennynge" (633-635). This love emanates through God (of and from) so that love shows itself as object: "love is a thynge þrogh which God loveth vs, and loveth God, and euery of vs other" (639-640). For Rolle, love is an object by which God and contemplative touch. We can think of it as the object that Rolle is attempting to unravel; one that changes shape, size, dimension depending on who is touching it. It is the object that is the nexus. Like the power of gravity it couples "togiddre þe louynge to þe loued" (636-637). Rolle separates Love from loving here—love is the object, something necessary in order to Love. Love is a surface of God and it is that surface that we touch and love God and through which God loves us.

Love is, then, the turning from earthly things. This object joins the contemplative with God. As Rolle writes, Love "clenseth þe soule, and delyuereth hit fro þe peyn of hel" (667). So, the nature of Love, the essence, is of a cleansing pseudobezoar, one that joins, saves, and centers loving. This Love is this centering object where love can be experienced; without it there is no focus, no clear direction for the contemplative to move. The heart, Rolle remarks as he closes the discussion of this first question, is central, as well; the contemplative's "hert shal so bren in love þat hit shal be turned in to fire of love, and be as hit were al fyre, and he shal be so shynynge in vertuȝ þat in no partie of hym [he] be durke in vices" (674-677). The contemplative's heart becomes fire. It is important to note, however, that the contemplative's being becomes the phenomenon of Love–God is fire; He is the burning– the true contemplative becomes like that God-object with light emanating from them, as well.

Love is found, then, within a heart unconcerned with anatomical function. Rolle locates love not in works–not in the "hand ne in his mouth" (679). Works lead to flattery and the contemplative can be misled by works down a different path, so that they rest in their works assured by others that they are doing good. Again, Rolle warns his audience about those who "seemeth holy" (682). The deception covers over the lack of stability in those who devote themselves to garnering praise from others. Rolle insists that good works are truly good if they are based in thinking about and through God. Rolle further points out that no one can tell if he loves God: "then can non tel me if I love God, for noght þat þay may see me do" (698-699). There is a division between those who do good and those who do good based in love. However, as Rolle indicates, human beings are unable to tell the difference. Love, however, will continually work since it occupies the will "verraili, nat in werke bot as signe of loue" (700). Love is not found in the outward good works that are visible except as sign: "loue will nat be ydel" (702). Love here is located, then, in the heart and it is noteworthy that it emanates out only in significance. Love is found through good works, but it is not in the works themselves. One who is "possessed" by love will act out in goodness always, but the one who does good work is not necessarily occupied by love, especially if they act in order to get praise. For them, though Rolle does not say so explicitly, acts and love are separate objects, only colliding in the true contemplative's environment. On the one hand, love is foundation for good works, on the other hand, good works can happen without love, though, the implication is that these works are not "best" practices. If love is the object, the mediator in relations that is found in the heart, the gift of good works passes through it, charging it with higher value. Without love, as found in the one who seeks praise, the good work is cheapened by the giver, though the receiver still benefits from the gift (i.e. giving someone a blanket to keep them warm, even if one is doing it to receive praise, cheapens the giver's act for the giver, but not the receiver's warmth).

In answering the question, how does one love God?, then, Rolle further explores the nature of the will. The will must first be made meek: "he is stalworth that is meke, for al gostly streynth cometh of mekenesse" (708-709). The strength from humility argument that Rolle employs delivers the contemplative into the might of will that the contemplative will have as a heavenly reward: "þat þay may haue hit plenerly in þe toþer" (729-730). A meek will overcomes even the devil; Rolle sees humility, not passivity, as stronger. No matter what a person does on earth–fasting or suffering–without the meekness of will that is stable, for it is "nat stirred for any word þat men may say" (722), they are unable to have love. It is interesting to note on these last items that Rolle is critiquing traditional ascetic acts–fasting, suffering–as not enough. This repeats his critiques of good works earlier in that acts need Love behind them. In this way, any act, for it to be worthy, must have love–and as an add-in here–meekness of will.

The heart must also wisely love God. Wisdom consists of moving oneself away from the world. Those who are foolish "spend in coueitise and bisynesse about þe world" (738-739). Wisdom for Rolle most has to with object choice. A person who is unable to identity true value is unable to love wisely. So, for Rolle, those who love an apple, rather than precious stones (in order to buy a castle), we would see as a fool (739-741). Rolle, oddly uses this extended metaphor to warn the contemplative not to be so concerned with the world. The contemplative's precious jewels, however are "pouerte and penaunce and gostly trauaille" (742-743). With these jewels the contemplative can buy the kingdom of heaven. For Rolle wisdom–using the heart wisely–has to do more with turning to heart to God than solving real world problems. The wise heart knows where true value is: in recognizing the way the world distracts from loving God, and, thus, correcting from that distraction.

Finally, Rolle writes that the soul will love sweetly and devotedly. Sweetness is connected to the chaste body and clean thoughts. Rolle likes this love to rest and peace: "as þou ware in silence and sleepe, and set in Noe shippe, þat no þynge may letþe of deuocion and brennynge of swet loue" (769-770). The ship-rested love will accompany the contemplative until death–Jesus "resteth in þe" (772). The sweetness of love, then, brings the contemplative peace as it is stable rest–a resting place for Jesus.

Rolle then moves on to thinking through how one would know one was in love. Rolle has focused thus far on the getting-to-love and the experience of love, he further wants to explain how one could self-identify that what one feels is truly love. Here is a great level of uncertainty here for Rolle in that there is no objective way to verify love. Rolle writes that if one found oneself at the "synguler" level of experiencing love that one could be assured that what the contemplative was feeling was indeed love. In "synguler" love, "he þat is so hegh, he wold nat hold hym selfe worþier þan þe synfullest man that gooth on þe erthe (788-790). So, finding oneself in love is like recognizing that one is no better than the lowliest sinner.

Finally, Rolle addresses the issue of the state of the contemplative: how must they *be* in order to love God? For Rolle, this has everything to do with the body: "in moste reste of body and soule and leste is occupied with any nedes or bisynesse of þis world" (820-821). Further, Rolle writes that "I have loued for to sit, for no penaunce ne for no fantasie 'þat' I would men spake of me, ne for no such þyng, bot only for I knewe þat I loued God more, and langer lested with me comfort of loue, than goynge or standynge or knelynge" (829-831). In sitting, Rolle is rested, able to focus, able to aim his "hert most vpward" (833). Sitting, too, is a kind of flow: forming the body's shape, setting the spine, the legs, the arms. So, Rolle ends *The Form of Living* with a discussion of opening the body–the experience of the body in contemplation is key to focus and stability.

Rolle is first concerned with the hermit's concern, or, to put it another way, the hermit's *being*. The nature of the hermitic being is one that must be "unplugged" from one assemblage to be re-coupled to another. As Kevin Hart writes "the Christian experience of God is that he has left his trace in the life and death of Jesus, that consequently it both is and is not an experience. One could say, loosely, that Christianity involves an experience of absolute interruption."[17] Rolle's concern in this work is showing how, ontologically speaking, the world is necessary for the hermit-*being* and that hermit-being is entwined with an absolute

---

[17] Kevin Hart, "Absolute Interruption: On Faith" in *Questioning God*, ed. John D. Caputo, Mark Dooley, and Michael J. Scanlon (Blooming: Indiana UP, 2001), 194.

interruption that can be opened to comprehension (albeit not *full* comprehension, since the God-object withdraws) through Love.

As Žižek comments, "in true love, 'I hate the beloved out of love'; I 'hate' the dimension of his inscription into the socio-symbolic structure on behalf of my very love for him as a unique person."[18] This inscription for Žižek places *limits* on love, reduces love, and, thus, deceives us into loving the wrong kinds of things. Rolle wants to open the hermit to love, to avoid this deception. It is in his hermitic ontology that this "socio-symbolic" realm is punctured and Žižek's "absolute" (absolute interruption?) can be seen. Žižek writes that the Absolute is "something that appears to us in fleeting experiences–say, through the gentle smile of a beautiful woman, or even through the warm, caring smile of a person who may otherwise seem ugly and rude: in such miraculous but extremely *fragile* moments, another dimension transpires through our reality."[19] Rolle's hermitic ontology frames the experience of the hermit so that these fragile moments can be recognized.

It is in Žižek's late discussion of "uncoupling" from *The Fragile Absolute* that we see Rolle's challenge: "as every Christian knows, love is the *work* of love–the hard and arduous work of repeated 'uncouplings' in which, again and again, we have to disengage ourselves from the inertia that constrains us to identify with the particular order we were born into."[20] With Rolle (and Žižek), then, we can ask, how do we continually uncouple and not fall into a rigidity that leaves the hermit unsatisfied and destroyed while avoiding the rigidity of fundamentalism in which the smile from the ugly goes unrecognized or the fixed becomes a resting place? We must keep hermit-*ing*.

---

[18] Žižek, 118.
[19] Žižek, 119.
[20] Žižek, 119-120.

Christopher Roman is Associate Professor of English at Kent State Tuscarawas. His publications include *Domestic Mysticism in Margery Kempe and Dame Julian of Norwich* (2005), as well as articles and reviews on mysticism and anchoritism in *Mystics Quarterly*, *Florilegium*, and *Speculum*. His recent work deals with digital humanities studies, critical animal theory, and speculative realism and their collision with concepts of the medieval. He also likes comic books.

THE AUTHORITY OF REASON: ON JOHN SCOTTUS ERIUGENA'S *PERIPHYSEON*, I.508C-513C

Cinzia Arruzza

INTRODUCTION[1]

Even reason herself teaches this. For authority proceeds from reason, but true reason certainly does not proceed from authority. For every authority which is not upheld by true reason is seen to be weak, whereas true reason is kept firm and immutable by her own powers and does not require to be confirmed by the assent of any authority. For it seems to me that true authority is nothing else but the truth that has been discovered by the power of reason and set down in writing by the Holy Fathers for the use of posterity.[2]

This astonishing passage comes at the end of a digression on the relationship between authority and reason following Eriugena's treatment of the ten Aristotelian categories in Book I of the *Periphyseon*.[3] The occasion for this digression is the problem of the

---

[1] I would like to express my gratitude to Eugene Thacker and Nicola Masciandaro for their insightful and helpful comments.

[2] Johannes Scotus Eriugena, *Periphyseon*, edited by E. Jeauneau, Corpus Christianorum Continuatio Medievalis [CCCM] 161-165 (Turnhout: Brepols, 1996-2003), I. 3052-3059; PL 122:513B-C. Translation: Eriugena, *Periphyseon (The Division of Nature)*, translated by I. P. Sheldon-Williams, revised by John J. O'Meara, (Montreal: Éditions Bellarmin, 1987), 110. Subsequent cross-references to the PL edition omit the volume number.

[3] On Eriugena's treatment of Aristotle's categories see: C. Erismann, "'Processio id est multiplicatio': L'influence latine de l'ontologie de Porphyre: le cas de Jean Scot Érigène," *Revue de Sciences philosophiques et théologiques* LXXXVIII (2004), 401-46; J. Marenbon, "John Scottus and the

applicability of the categories of acting and suffering to God. The Alumnus, the student of the dialogue, is puzzled: the reasoning up to that point would suggest that these categories, as well as the previous eight, cannot be applied to the Creator due to the Creator's transcendence to substance. Moreover, to attribute the categories of acting and suffering to God would imply that accidents can be predicated of God's nature. But, on the other hand, denying the possibility of the applicability of those categories to the Creator would have as a consequence that no active or passive verb could be used in the case of God. This would imply that the Scriptures are deceiving when they say that God is loved or that he loves, that he is moved or that he moves.[4] The Alumnus is stuck between the danger of impiety—into which he would fall by attributing falsehood to the Scriptures—and ridiculousness, for, as he admits: "if I say it is false [i.e., that God does not admit acting and suffering], *reason itself* might easily make a laughing-stock of me."[5]

In order to help the Alumnus out of his puzzlement, the Nutritor, the teacher of the dialogue, begins a digression which will lead him first to claim that the Scriptures cannot be in contradiction with true reason, and second, that reason has priority over authority. At the very beginning of this digression we find a long quotation from Dionysius's *De divinis nominibus* (I.1), whose authority the Nutritor paradoxically uses in order to undermine the supremacy of authority over reason.

The conclusion reached by the Nutritor in agreement with the Alumnus, i.e. that reason has priority over authority, will determine the correct order of the inquiry and of the exposition: "And that is why reason must be employed first in our present business, and authority afterwards."[6] This conclusion is not particularly surprising, when one considers both Eriugena's

---

Categoriae Decem," in *Eriugena : Studien zu seinen Quellen,* ed. W. Beierwaltes (Heidelberg: C. Winter, 1980), 116-34; G. d'Onofrio, "'Disputandi disciplina': Procédés dialectiques et 'logica vetus' dans le langage philosophique de Jean Scot," in *Jean Scot Ecrivain,* ed. G.-H. Allard (Paris: Vrin 1986), 229-263. On space and time in particular see M. Cristiani, "Lo spazio e il tempo nell'opera dell'Eriugena," *Studi Medievali,* 3rd series, 14 (1973): 39-136.
[4] *Periphyseon,* I. 2856-2868 (PL 508C-D).
[5] *Periphyseon,* I. 2856-7 (PL 508 C).
[6] *Periphyseon,* I. 3060-1 (PL 513 C); Sheldon-Williams, 110.

rationalistic attitude within the dispute on predestination between 850 and 851 and his peculiar solution to the problem of divine predestination and foreknowledge, which ended up causing him major trouble with the ecclesiastical authorities.[7] In the *De praedestinatione liber*, Eriugena coherently applied his own rationalistic interpretation of the Augustinian claim that true philosophy is true religion, and *vice versa*, by using the arts of the trivium in order to reconstruct the true meaning of the *auctoritates*. As he shows in I.1, to say that true philosophy is true religion is to say that dealing with philosophy is identical to clarifying the correct rules of the inquiry into God, where the boundaries between rational investigation into God and religious veneration of God are blurred.[8] Regarding the interpretive methodology to be applied, while the scriptural text or a given sentence of a Church Father is the starting point of the interpretive process, the end point is the outcome of rigorous reasoning, largely resorting to the resources offered by grammar, rhetoric and dialectics. The guiding principle here is that whenever the *auctoritas* appears to contradict logical reasoning, we must have fallen into an interpretive mistake, which can be corrected by an adequate use of the liberal arts. As an index of this complex relationship between reason and authority in Eriugena's commentarial activity, one might see the fact that in the thirteenth century large excerpts of the *Periphyseon* were used as glosses to the *Corpus Dionysiacum* and were organized together into a commentary on the Mystical theology.[9] In what follows, I will first address the question of the relationship between *ordo verborum* and *ordo rerum* in Eriugena's thought. Then I will analyze the arguments Eriugena provides in order to reach and

---

[7] On the political context and content of the debate on predestination and of Eriugena's intervention, see M. Cristiani, *Dall'unanimitas all'universitas: da Alcuino a Giovanni Eriugena: lineamenti ideologici e terminologia politica della cultura del secolo IX* (Rome: Istituto storico italiano per il medioevo, 1978) and the introduction by E. S. Mainoldi to Giovanni Scoto Eriugena, *De praedestinatione liber, Dialettica e teologia all'apogeo della rinascenza carolingia*, (Florence: SISMEL – Edizioni del Galluzzo, 2003).

[8] *Iohannis Scotti de divina praedestinatione*, ed. G. Madec, Corpus Christianorum Series Latina [CCSL] 50 (Turnhout: Brepols, 1978), I.1.

[9] See J. McEvoy, "John Scottus Eriugena and Thomas Gallus, Commentators on the *Mystical Theology*," in *History and Eschatology in John Scottus Eriugena and His Time*, eds. M. Dunne and J. McEvoy (Leuven: Leuven University Press, 2002), 183-202.

support the claim that reason has priority over authority, paying particular attention to his peculiar use of the *De divinis nominibus*'s passage and of Dionysius's authority.

ORDO VERBORUM AND ORDO RERUM

In the *Expositiones in ierarchiam coelestem* (II. 124), Eriugena translates and comments on a passage from Dionysius's *De coelesti hierarchia* (II.1; PG 3:137A) in which Dionysius explains why intelligible beings in the Scriptures are represented through corporeal images and symbols.[10] Dionysius argues that the Scriptures have resorted to symbols appropriate to our capacity of understanding and has employed them *atechnōs*, i.e. without *technē*, or artlessly. The adverb *atechnōs* refers to the simple and artless way in which the Scriptures make themselves understandable to the human mind, a simplicity that Dionysius opposes to the artificiality of rhetoric and of the liberal arts.[11] As is well known, Eriugena mistranslates the adverb *atechnōs* as "valde artificialiter," "highly artificial," and then comments upon this passage by drawing a similarity between theology and poetry. Here theology is presented as an exercise for the mind aimed at an anagogic development of reason, progressing from sensible images to the perfect knowledge of intelligible things.[12] Following Roques, this is much more than a simple mistranslation or an interpretative mistake: Eriugena is actually inverting the meaning of Dionysius's passage because he cannot accept the notion of an opposition of the Scriptures to the liberal arts. The rules of the liberal arts,

---

[10] For the critical editions of these works, see *Iohannis Scotti Eriugenae Expositiones in Ierarchiam Coelestem*, ed. J. Barbet, CCCM 31 (Turnhout: Brepols, 1975) and Dionysius Areopagita, *De coelesti hierarchia*, in *Corpus Dyonisiacum*, II, eds. G. Heil and A. M. Ritter (Berlin: Walter de Gruyter 1991).

[11] Roques stresses this opposition between divine revelation and the liberal arts in R. Roques, 'Connaissance de Dieu et théologie symbolique d'après l'*In ierarchiam coelestem Sancti Dionysii* de Hugues de Saint-Victor,' in *Structures théologiques de la gnose à Richard de Saint-Victor* (Paris: Presses Universitaires de France, 1962), 294-364.

[12] See on this W. Otten, "Religion as Exercitatio Mentis: Exegesis between Faith and Reason," in *Christian Humanism. Essays in Honor of Arjo Vanderjagt*, eds. A. A. MacDonald, Z. R. W. M. von Martels and J. R. Veenstra (Leiden: London, 2009), 65-66.

indeed, are the same as the rules of intelligence[13] and, Eriugena later argues, there would be no Scriptures at all without the rules of the liberal arts.[14] These exist eternally in God's Wisdom and are the most perfect and highest image (*significatio*) of Christ.

At the very beginning of the *De divina praedestinatione*, where Eriugena deals with the correct order of the argumentation, we have found not only a strong praise for philosophy, but also the equation of true philosophy to true religion.[15] Both philosophy and religion, when they are true (i.e. enlightened by the intellect), share the same rules, so that loving wisdom is equated to striving to know God. Eriugena describes the different parts that constitute the study of wisdom (dialectics, heuristics, apodictic, and analytic) and insists on the justification of the use of dialectics in the theological domain. The initial justification for the resort to dialectics is the usefulness of the knowledge of the rules that govern a correct discourse in the struggle against heretical false arguments. Theology, furthermore, needs dialectics both in order to defend itself and in order not to be helpless in front of the sophisms and false syllogisms of the heretics.[16] The presupposition of this use of philosophy is that philosophical discourse can grasp truth *because* reality and true philosophical knowledge have the same structure, and because things themselves are not different from their being known. This means that there exists the possibility of a correspondence between *ordo rerum* and *ordo verborum*.

The rules for a correctly articulated argument are not a pure invention of the mind with no connection to the order of the world. On the contrary, such rules organize universal reality as such. As stressed by Moran, the arts are conceived by Eriugena both as identical to the primordial causes, i.e. to the unchanging ideas in God's mind, and as the faculties or powers of the human mind.[17] This is why they both play a mediating role between God and human being, and grant the possibility of true knowledge. Through the knowledge of the arts, a human mind can have access at the same time to the primordial causes of the whole reality, to

---

[13] See R. Roques, "'Valde artificialiter' : Le sens d'un contresens," in *Libres sentiers vers l'érigenisme* (Roma: Edizioni dell'Ateneo, 1975), 45-98.

[14] *Expositiones*, I. 560-1; PL 140.

[15] *De praed.*, 1. 1, 16-18.

[16] *De praed.*, 1. 3, 45-47.

[17] D. Moran, *The Philosophy of John Scottus Eriugena. A Study of Idealism in the Middle Ages* (Cambridge: Cambridge University Press, 1989), 207.

reality as such, and to its own mind. The task of the philosopher, therefore, is to identify the laws of reality, the natural order of things, and to articulate his discourse in such a way that the order and structure of reality can be exposed as the order and structure of the discourse. This also explains why heretical claims can be unmasked and denounced as logical mistakes.

The notion of a correspondence between *ordo rerum* and *ordo verborum* is present in several passages of the *Periphyseon* (see for example *Periphyseon*, II.26; II.570-571), where it is often a matter of carefully choosing the order of arguments and how to proceed in the dialogue. Whereas sometimes it seems that the choice of the order of the arguments is dependent on the will of the Nutritor (*Periphyseon* I.3062, I.3240-3241, II.575) or related to the pedagogical relationship between the master and the student, in several passages the verbs used–*exigo, pono, expeto*–allude to a much more binding order (*Periphyseon*, I.3476-3478, II.40, II.2324-2325, III.2421).[18]

The fact that the recreation of the structure of the universe in thought requires the use of the liberal arts and a correct employment of logic indicates that a pure intellectual intuition of the universal substance escapes human beings. As noticed by d'Onofrio,[19] Adam, in his prelapsarian condition, does have access to the pure intellectual contemplation of divine truth without needing to resort to deductions. Since in the state of grace before the fall everything exists in its universal form, Adam *qua* genus, (i.e. *qua* universal human nature) contemplates the genera of things, and not the particulars. It is opportune to stress here that the prelapsarian condition of the creature is not to be understood as a

---

[18] These oscillations could be explained as the sign of the coexistence of different orders (logical, pedagogical, and epistemological), which are intertwined within the treatise. On this line, see G. H. Allard, "Quelques remarques sur la 'disputationis series' du 'De divisione naturae,'" in *Jean Scot Erigène et l'histoire de la philosophie*, ed. R. Roques (Paris: Editions du CNRS, 1977), 211-224. At the same time I find convincing Jeauneau's insistence on the strong structural unity of the treatise. Jeauneau suggests that Eriugena operates as an architect and adopts an helicoidal trajectory in order to recreate the universe, by following a descendant and ascendant dialectics and progressively remodeling and recreating all the conceptual material he touches upon: E. Jeauneau, "L'homme et l'œuvre," in *Études érigéniennes* (Paris: Etudes Augustinienne, 1987), 45-46.
[19] G. d'Onofrio, "'Disputanti Disciplina'," 246-251.

condition historically preceding sin, but rather as one *ideally* and *ontologically* preceding it: the prelapsarian man is the genus, i.e. human nature created as pure of sin and in full possession of its intellectual capabilities among the divine Causes. This idea is based on Gregory of Nyssa's distinction between the creation of man in the image of God, or ideal creation, and what God adds to this ideal creation, and to human nature, because he foresaw man's sin. While in temporal terms, Adam and Eve have been created with a sexed body from the very beginning, yet in ontological terms, the sexuation of the bodies is an accidental addition to the ideal human nature as originally conceived of by God.[20]

According to Eriugena, on an ontological level, the fall is the cause both of the determination of the genera *via* the rupture of the original unity and the process of particularization, and of a decadence of human intellectual capacities. This is why logical operations of reason, guided by the intellect, are needed in order to grasp the original truth of the universal substance. When they are correct, or, when reason is enlightened by the intellect and not deceived by the senses, then these operations are capable of recreating the order of the universe in thought.

It is now clear why, on the one hand, the question of the *ordo verborum*, of the correct articulation of arguments and of the form of exposition, is so relevant in Eriugena's work, and why, on the other hand, the liberal arts are indispensable.

RATIOCINATIONIS VIOLENTIA

The digression on the relationship between reason and the Scriptures begins with the Alumnus's reference to the "violence of the reasoning" which forces the Alumnus to make conclusions seemingly in contradiction to the Scriptures. This reference to the *ratiocinationis violentia* is relevant because it attributes binding necessity to the conclusions reached through the correct use of reason. This necessity is not disavowed, but rather, even more strongly asserted in the Nutritor's answer:

Do not be afraid. For now we must follow reason, which investigates the truth of things and is not overborne (*opprimitur*) by any authority, and is by no means

---

[20] See for example, *De hominis opificio*, 16, 184D-185A. On this topic see C. Arruzza, *Les mésaventures de la théodicée* (Turnhout: Brepols, 2011), 263-268.

prevented from revealing publicly and proclaiming the things which it [both] zealously searches out by circuitous reasoning and discovers with much toil.[21]

Responding to the Alumnus's puzzlement, the Nutritor insists that *ratio sequenda est*, that we need to follow reason. Having stated this, the task of the Nutritor is to show that following reason cannot be in contradiction to the Scriptures. The argument articulated by the Nutritor can be summarized as follows: we have two sources of authority, one is reason, whose correct use leads to conclusions which have binding necessity, while the other is the Scriptures, which hide truth in *secretis sedibus*, in secret places. Whenever there is an apparent contradiction between the correct use of reason and the text of the Scriptures, we need to keep in mind first, that God is superessential and because of his absolute transcendence he escapes any possible definition, and second, that true reason teaches us that whereas affirmations about God can be wrong, negations are never wrong.[22] This means that the symbols and names used within the Scriptures need interpretation and should be understood as always metaphorical and never as properly predicated.

Since reason's correct deductions play a fundamental role in demonstrating the necessity of negations, and therefore in granting a correct understanding of the truth hidden under the symbols used by the Scriptures, it is clear that the Scriptures and true reason are not incompatible but rather, complementary. To this claim Eriugena also adds a metaphysical argument stating the common origin of authority and reason:

> So do not let any authority frighten you away from the things which the rational deduction from right contemplation teaches you. For true authority does not conflict with right reason, nor right reason with true authority, since there is no doubt that both flow from the same source, the Wisdom of God.[23]

---

[21] *Periphyseon*, I. 2869-2873; PL 508D-509A. Sheldon-Williams, 105 (translation partially modified).
[22] *Periphyseon*, I. 2938-2939; PL 510C.
[23] *Periphyseon*, I. 2973-2977; PL 511A-C. Sheldon Williams, 108.

Authority and reason, then, are two different, but reciprocally consistent manifestations of the same divine wisdom that ontologically undergirds them both. The Nutritor reassures the Alumnus (*nulla itaque auctoritas te terreat*), or rather, invites him to stand firm against any attempt at undermining the conclusions of true reason through an appeal to authority. This is apparently still not sufficient for the Alumnus, for despite being convinced by the master's reasoning, he asks him to provide more supporting evidence by resorting to the authority of the Holy Fathers.[24] This time, however, the Nutritor refuses to comply with his student's request. The *ordo verborum* must correspond to the *ordo rerum*, and since reason is prior to authority in dignity and nature, "that is why reason must be employed first in our present business, and authority afterwards."[25]

The Nutritor's argument for the priority of reason is quite confusing. He begins by saying that what is prior by nature has greater dignity than what is prior in time.[26] Then, referring to Augustine's *De ordine*,[27] he states that we were taught that reason is prior by nature, whereas authority is prior in time. Augustine's passage refers to the correct path for those who want to apply themselves to the study of divine things. In this passage, Augustine argues that in the process of learning we are guided both by authority and by reason, but that whereas authority is prior in time, reason is ontologically prior (*re autem ratio prior est*). The temporal priority of authority refers to the fact that authority is the access door for those who want to learn. In other words, authority is the proper starting point: whereas simple-minded people content themselves with authority, those who want to learn apply reason to authority's teachings, developing their capacity of reasoning beyond authority's nursery in order to grasp the universal principles and what transcends those universal principles.

In Eriugena's passage, however, Augustine's reference is followed by a commentary which overturns Augustine's suggestion while pretending to be a simple explanation:

---

[24] *Periphyseon*, I. 3042-44; PL 513A.

[25] *Periphyseon*, I. 3060-1; PL 513 C. Sheldon-Williams, 110.

[26] *Periphyseon*, I. 3045-6; PL 513B.

[27] Augustinus, *De ordine*, II.9. 26, ed. W. M. Green, CCSL 29 (Turnhout: Brepols, 1970).

We have learned that reason is prior by nature, authority
in time. For although authority was created together with
time, authority did not come into being at the beginning
of nature and time, whereas reason arose with nature and
time out of the Principle of things.[28]

In spite of Eriugena's "*enim*"[29] and of my attempts at a charitable
reading of this text, I cannot see how Eriugena's statement follows
from Augustine's text. Indeed, in my view, Eriugena is rather
radically shifting the discourse from a consideration related to the
correct pedagogical method to one concerning the metaphysical
relationship between authority and reason. On a metaphysical
level, reason precedes authority also in time, in the sense that while
reason comes *together* with the beginning of time and nature,
authority follows only later. In this way Augustine's teaching about
authority's priority in time is overturned, for reason is shown to be
prior both by nature *and* in time. And indeed, the conclusion of
this reasoning is that the correct *ordo verborum* is the one which
resorts first to reason and afterwards to authority. In other words,
whereas the Alumnus's request to provide some evidence coming
from the authority of the Holy Fathers is consistent with
Augustine's pedagogical suggestion, the Nutritor's conclusion is
not.

THE FREEDOM OF THE COMMENTATOR
    After having shown the pattern of Eriugena's argument for the
priority of reason, it is time to deal with his peculiar use of
Dionysius's passage from the *De divinis nominibus*. At line 2891, the
Nutritor suggests they resort to the evidence provided by Dionysus
in order to solve the apparent contradiction between true reason
and the Scriptures, which is puzzling the Alumnus. Yet, a few lines
later he suggests the reorganization of Dionysius's *ordo verborum* in
order to make this difficult and somewhat obscure text more
understandable.[30] This apparently innocent clarification will prove
to be not innocent at all because the reorganization of Dionysius's
text corresponds to a precise argumentative strategy.

---

[28] *Periphyseon,* I. 3048-3051; PL 513 B. Sheldon-Williams, 110.
[29] "Quamvis enim natura simul cum tempore create sit . . ."
[30] *Periphyseon,* I. 2896-2900; PL 509 C.

First, Eriugena starts quoting Dionysius's text leaving out the beginning of the chapter.[31] What he leaves out, however, is not fortuitous, for in those lines Dionysius argues that the truth established about the divine things is not established through the persuasive discourses of human wisdom, but rather through the demonstration of the divine power inspired to the holy authors by the Holy Spirit. Indeed, it is the divine power, which moves those authors, that allows a supra-rational union with God, i.e. a union which transcends the limits of our narrow intellectual capacities. As in the case of the passage from the *De coelesti hierarchia* discussed above, Dionysius seems to want to oppose the power of divine wisdom, and therefore the truth revealed through the inspiration by divine power, to the limits of profane wisdom. Dionysius's passage is based on 1 Cor. 2:4: "This is what we speak, not in words taught us by human wisdom but in words taught by the Spirit, explaining spiritual realities with Spirit-taught words."

There is, however, no mention of this introductory passage in Eriugena's quotation and subsequent commentary–an omission which might reveal the same difficulty as accepting any opposition between the Scriptures and the liberal arts that we have already found in the passage from the *Expositiones* quoted above.

In the passages quoted by Eriugena, Dionysius is restating the basic principles of negative theology, namely, God's absolute transcendence with regard to being and intellect, and the impossibility of attributing any name to God in a proper way. God's absolute transcendence is the reason why the Scriptures have supreme authority and it is not allowed for human beings to say or think anything about God except what has been revealed to them by the Holy Scriptures. When he opens his commentary on this passage, Eriugena restates the necessity for following the authority of the Scriptures, arguing that this has been sufficiently proved by Dionysius's words.[32] Yet, he adds immediately after:

---

[31] The first passage quoted is *De divinis nominibus* I.1, 108, 6-109, 2, ed. B. R. Suchla, in *Corpus Dionysiacum*, I (Berlin: Walter de Gruyter, 1990); PG 3:588A2-10. The second is *De divinis nominibus* I.1, 109, 7-110, 6; PG 3:588B1-C8.

[32] *Periphyseon*, I.2931-2; PL 510B: "Haec de sequenda auctoritate solummodo sanctae scripturae in divinis maxime disputationibus sufficient"; translation slightly modified.

147

Indeed reason (*ratio vero*) is wholly concerned with suggesting, and proving by the most accurate investigations into the truth, that nothing can be said properly about God, since He surpasses every intellect and all sensible and intelligible meaning, Who is better known by not knowing, of Whom ignorance is true knowledge, Who is more truly and faithfully denied in all things that He is affirmed. For whatever negation you make about Him will be a true negation, but not every affirmation you make will be a true affirmation.[33]

Now, in Dionysius's passage there is no mention of the role played by reason or its logical operations in this process. On the contrary, the whole text, and what follows in the subsequent chapters, insists on the constitutive weakness that characterizes human reason, on the necessity of overcoming its narrow boundaries, as well as on the boundaries set by language, by honoring the obscurity of the divine Thearchy through silence. While Eriugena approves of Dionysius's negative theology, he grants a crucial role to human wisdom and its tools by insisting on the divine origin of the liberal arts and of the correct logical reasoning in general. In this way he uses Dionysius's text for a purpose that is significantly different from the purpose for which it was originally written. Indeed, the apophatic approach to God appears, in Eriugena's commentary, as the outcome of the rigorous application of reason and of the liberal arts, which lead us to the overcoming of representation: the mystical contemplation of God is, then, the necessary outcome of an eminently logical process. It is certainly true that Dionysius stresses the necessity of a correct, non-literal understanding of the symbols adopted by the Scriptures in order to name God. However, for Eriugena, the impossibility of naming God more strongly opens a decisive space for human reason and for its proper tools.

The insistence on God's absolute transcendence is the argumentative dispositive adopted by Eriugena in order to arrive at the conclusion that reason is prior to authority and that right reason and right authority cannot be in contradiction because they have the very same source. The impossibility of taking literally the names given to God, attributes, in Eriugena's commentary, the

---

[33] *Periphyseon*, I. 2931-2939; PL 510B-C. Sheldon-Williams, 107.

crucial role of negation to reason's operations. This opens a space of radical interpretive freedom in front of the text of the Scriptures, a space which is the proper domain of reason's accurate investigations, for these investigations alone are entitled to discover and expose the hidden truth in the Scriptures. Reason's freedom in this process lies in the fact that the correct conclusions of correct reasoning are binding (*violentia ratiocinationis*), so that in the last instance, reason, while honoring the Scriptures's authority, obeys its own necessity, i.e. the binding necessity of truth. This is the point of the passage at lines 3052-3059, quoted at the beginning of this short commentary. There, the Alumnus concludes that true reason does not require the assent of authority, or, that in the moment in which it grasps the truth, it is self-sufficient and does not require further proof. Authority, on the contrary, requires the assent of reason. Of course, here the Alumnus is talking about the authority of the Holy Fathers, and there is a difference between the authority of the Scriptures and that of the Holy Fathers, for only the former has been shown to be absolutely binding. Nevertheless, the fundamental idea remains that reason is bound by the revealed text of the Scriptures, because this text is *true*, as it has its origin in the very divine wisdom which is the origin of human reason and of the liberal arts. This means that the truth of the Scripture is its immanence to reason and that this truth can be discovered in its hiding places through reason's deductions.

CONCLUSION

By briefly commenting on this passage from the *Periphyseon*, I have tried to show Eriugena's own freedom in using his sources, in this case, the short quotation from Augustine's *De ordine* and the long passage from Book I of Dionysius's *De divinis nominibus*. While being in agreement with Dionysius's insistence on negative theology, Eriugena uses Dionyius's text in order to reassure the Alumnus that reason and the liberal arts, which reason uses to carry out its investigations, are indeed the prominent source of authority–a conclusion which does not belong to Dionysius' text. On the basis of this conclusion, Eriugena interprets the apophatic climax of negative theology not as an irrationalistic move, but rather as the necessary logical conclusion of correct and rigorous reasoning, in which reason exhausts itself and its representational capacities, and both authority and dialectics are suspended. Finally, by quoting and commenting on this passage from *De divinis nomibus,* Eriugena performatively grants to himself as a commentator the freedom he wants to grant to reason, which lies in the fidelity of reason to its own necessity, the necessity of truth.

Cinzia Arruzza is Assistant Professor of Philosophy at the New School for Social Research. She works on ancient metaphysics and ancient political thought. She published *Les mésaventures de la théodicée. Plotin, Origène, Grégroire de Nysse* (Brepols 2011). She is currently working on a translation, introduction and commentary of Plotinus, *Ennead II 5 [25]* (under contract with Parmenides Press) and on a book on philosophy and politics in Plato's *Republic* and in its contemporary interpretations.

SILVERING, OR THE ROLE OF MYSTICISM IN GERMAN IDEALISM

Daniel Whistler

1. THE MAKING OF MIRRORS

In Spring 1801, absolute idealism materialised in Jena as the shared project of F.W.J. Schelling and G.W.F. Hegel. Central to it were the critique of contemporary philosophy as "reflective" and the assertion of a new "speculative standpoint"–even if the very constitution of the *meanings* of "reflection," "speculation" and their relationship was a task that consumed the subsequent years. For what followed over the next fifty years was (in part) a series of experiments in speculative philosophy, attempts to model thinking as a "magical and symbolic mirror."

The concepts of both reflection and speculation gain their sense from the workings of the mirror: its ontology of original and image (which both is and is not the original) and its evaluative criteria of fidelity (seeing face-to-face) and inaccuracy (seeing darkly). The description of thought as mirror (while traditional) takes on a new urgency from 1801 onwards in the task of differentiating between two types of mirror: a narcissistic, reflective mirror which is to be avoided and a magical, speculative mirror which all philosophers must strive to silver. What distinguishes these types of mirror–that is, the conditions of silvering that account for the transition from reflection to speculation–are Schelling and Hegel's concerns.

What is more, it is important to bear in mind that what *concretely* constitute these mirrors are the philosopher and her text. It is for the philosopher to think and write in such a way that reality reflects itself in a speculative rather than merely reflective manner. It is for the philosopher to silver herself so as to become speculative. Behind Hegel and Schelling's appropriation of this optical imagery therefore lie the questions: how does one become a speculative philosopher? What practices and exercises are required to transform oneself and one's writing from a reflective state to a speculative one? In other words, in what do speculative forms of life consist?

In what follows, I consider two passages from Schelling's later work in which he attempts to model a speculative form of life. What is most revealing about these examples of "the formation of the speculative"[1] is that Schelling's chosen dialogue partners are not canonical philosophers, but heretical mystics: Böhme and Swedenborg. In order to theorise the becoming-speculative of the philosophical mirror, Schelling resorts to mystical texts; and yet he is always clear–although for very different reasons at different moments–mysticism is only a dialogue partner. The mystical text cannot be the answer, even if it does still point the philosopher on her way.

Consideration of a passage repeated in both the Lectures on Philosophy of Art and the Lectures on Method (*On University Studies*) will help bring out further the key issues at play in this recourse to mysticism. Schelling writes, "Art contemplates the intimate essence of the science of the absolute (philosophy) as in a magical and symbolic mirror."[2] The artistic medium reflects–and so mediates–philosophical ideas. And there is, of course, also an art to philosophising itself: the philosopher too must hold up a mirror to her thinking through the written or spoken word. Articulation is necessarily mediation. So, one of the stakes in philosophising is the nature of the philosopher's mirror–what it reflects and how it reflects it. That is, what is at stake is how the mirror is manufactured, the silvering process that goes into its creation. The art of the philosopher includes the art of making mirrors as well as looking into them–the production of "that dull surface without which no reflection and no specular and speculative activity would be possible."[3] The philosopher mediates

---

[1] F.W.J. Schelling, *Briefe und Dokumente* vol. 2, ed. Horst Fuhrmans (Bonn: Bouvier, 1962-75), 436.

[2] F.W.J. Schelling, *Philosophy of Art*, trans. Douglas W. Stott (Minneapolis: University of Minnesota Press, 1989), 8; *On University Studies*, trans. E.S. Morgan (Athens, OH: Ohio University Press, 1966), 150.

[3] Rodolphe Gasché, *The Tain of the Mirror: Derrida and the Philosophy of Reflection* (Cambridge, MA: Harvard University Press, 1986), 6. In many ways, what follows is an implicit commentary on the opening to Gasché's

reality through herself and her text—and it is not just the success of such mediation that distinguishes a good from a bad philosopher, it is also the type of mediation she forges in the first place.

However, as the above quotation implies, the philosopher still possesses a quite unique relation to her ideas: for while the artist can only reflect on such ideas from without, the philosopher reflects what she already thinks. The philosopher stands in both a mediated *and immediate* relation to philosophy. What Hyppolite writes of Hegelian thought applies to the above too: "The immediate itself reflects itself, and this identity of reflection and the immediate corresponds to philosophical knowledge as such."[4] In other words, the artist is forever attempting in vain to recover a lost immediacy; the philosopher negotiates *an immediacy always already present.* Schelling's acknowledgement of this presence is seemingly what forces him to begin with philosophy already presupposed— that is, to philosophise "like a shot from a pistol" or to "fall head over heels into the absolute."[5]

And yet, as this essay progresses, we will come to see Schelling criticise precisely this philosophical illusion of the givenness of thought. That is, the above proposes an idealist fiction: that thought is given first (and given first to the philosopher alone). And while he remains committed to this fiction, Schelling will never tire of putting it into question as well.[6] Throughout his works, he uncovers the pre-philosophical, pre-textual practices that give rise to thought. Ideas are mediated and reflected prior to philosophy. Hence, while *to the philosopher* thought appears immediate, such immediacy depends on the forgetting of the very process of becoming-philosophical (the *Bildung* of the philosopher or "the formation of the speculative").

---

work and his marginalisation of Schelling's role in "the formation of the speculative." See especially ibid., 23-4.

[4] Jean Hyppolite, *Logic and Existence,* trans. Leonard Lawlor and Amit Sen (Albany: SUNY Press, 1997), 84-5; this translation from Gasché, *The Tain of the Mirror,* 34.

[5] Respectively: G.W.F. Hegel, *Phenomenology of Spirit,* trans. A.V. Miller (Oxford: Oxford University Press, 1977), §27; Frederick C. Beiser, *German Idealism: The Struggle against Subjectivism 1781-1801* (Cambridge, MA: Harvard University Press, 2002), 588.

[6] Implicit here is a rejection of any simplistic distinction between the "early", idealist Schelling and the "late", critical Schelling.

Already a tangled dialectic is emerging–and this tangle will only increase as we weave our way through Schelling's engagements with mysticism. Philosophical ideas are immediate but need to be mediated to retain their immediacy. This is the necessity of silvering or the requisite indifference of mediacy and immediacy–the *speculative* ideal. At the same time, such immediacy is also dependent on *prior* practices of becoming-philosophical in the first place (breeding speculative forms of life). Immediacy is dependent on both prior and posterior mediation to be articulated as immediacy–and what is more it is also dependent on the philosophical *forgetting* of precisely these practices. What follows is (to some extent, at least) a survey of the ways in which Schelling encounters the mystical text *in order to remember*–to remember, that is, the vast panoply of mediations necessary for philosophical claims to immediacy. Together these recovered exercises in mediation form the art of immediacy.

I argue, however, that it is Schelling's recovery of the *pre*-philosophical practices of mediation in particular which constitute his most significant achievement in this regard. As the above analysis of Schelling's appeal to "the magical and symbolic mirror" of speculation has already made clear, it is these extra-textual exercises that are most prone to be forgotten. I contend that Schelling's relative neglect of them in his analysis of Böhme's mysticism gives rise to some of the instability in his attitude to theosophy during the 1830s and 40s, while his metaphilosophical reflections in *Clara* (with Swedenborg as exemplar) give rise to a more fruitful idea of the life the philosopher must live to become speculative.

2. BECOMING-SPECULATIVE: HEGEL AND SCHELLING'S COMMON PROJECT

When embarking on his *Naturphilosophie* in 1797, Schelling saw speculation as a sickness, a by-product of man's sentimental alienation from nature:

> *Mere* speculation, therefore, is a spiritual sickness in mankind, and moreover the most dangerous of all, which kills the germ of man's existence and uproots his being . . . Every weapon is justifiable against a philosophy which makes speculation not a *means* but an *end.* For it torments human reason with chimeras which,

because they lie beyond all reason, it is not even possible to combat. It makes that separation between man and the world *permanent.*[7]

One speculates only when cast adrift. The task of the philosopher is thus the annihilation of speculation, which is also the annihilation of philosophy itself (and ultimately consciousness). Very quickly, however, Schelling found himself dissatisfied with such terminology and by 1799 "speculation" gained a very different valence: it became the ideal towards which *Naturphilosophie* moved–the perfection of this branch of the philosophical enterprise is dubbed a "speculative physics."[8] At the same time, Schelling begins to formulate more determinately a form of philosophising opposed to speculation, one that embodies all that is wrong with how we usually think–"reflection." Reflection is the abject other of speculation, and it is the former rather than the latter that now designates a spiritual sickness in which the subject is alienated from the object, preventing secure knowledge. Hence, the 1803 edition of the *Ideas for a Philosophy of Nature* exactly inverts the 1797 passage:

> As soon as man sets himself in opposition to the external world. . . reflection first begins; he separates from now on what nature had always united, separates the object from the intuition, the concept from the image, finally himself from himself . . . *Mere* reflection, therefore, is a spiritual sickness in mankind, the more so when it imposes himself in dominion over the whole man, and kills at the root what in germ is his highest being, his spiritual life, which issues only from identity.[9]

---

[7] F.W.J. Schelling, *Ideas for a Philosophy of Nature*, trans. Errol E. Harris and Peter Heath (Cambridge: Cambridge University Press, 1988), 11. The 1797 variant is printed in a footnote.
[8] F.W.J. Schelling, *Introduction to the System of a Philosophy of Nature* in *First Outline of a System of the Philosophy of Nature*, trans. Keith R. Peterson (Albany: SUNY Press, 2004), 195.
[9] Schelling, *Ideas*, 10-11. For a detailed account of the above, see Klaus Düsing, "Spekulation und Reflexion: Zur Gesammenarbeit Schellings und Hegels in Jena," in *Hegel-Studien* 5 (1969).

At the turn of the century, the conceptual pairing reflection/speculation orientated Schelling's approach to philosophy. Nevertheless, the idea of speculation and its relation to reflection remains underdetermined in Schelling's writings[10]–until, that is, the Spring of 1801 and the arrival of Hegel in Jena as a collaborative partner. A more substantial conception of the reflection/speculation binary seems to have emerged in conversation; it is first hinted at in Schelling's *Presentation* published in May 1801;[11] then fully elaborated in Hegel's *Differenzschrift* released in September.

Initially at least, speculation and reflection are to be understood as opposed: "Since, for speculation, cognition has reality only within the absolute, what is cognised and known in the reflective mode of expression and therefore has a determinate form, becomes nothing in the presence of speculation."[12] Speculating is equated with doing philosophy well and getting at the truth; reflective thought plunges into error. It is a sickness to be cured with the medicine of the speculative standpoint. Moreover, first and foremost, this sickness takes the form of *narcissism*. In reflection, "I remain entirely self-obsessed . . . I never get away from myself," never "leave the circle of consciousness."[13] The mirror-image shows no more than what was present to begin with– and usually rather less. A reflective philosopher therefore becomes trapped in the continual repetition of the same–an "inevitable vicious circle"[14] of sterile limitation: "In its striving to enlarge itself

[10] See Düsing, "Spekulation und Reflexion," 116.
[11] In the Preface, Schelling employs "speculation" positively (F.W.J. Schelling, *Presentation of my System of Philosophy*, trans. Michael G. Vater in *Philosophical Forum* 32.4 [2001], 346) and denigrates "the standpoint of reflection," associating it with thinking from antitheses (ibid., 348) and Fichtean idealism (ibid., 345). In the main body of the work, he goes on to contrast what is "for reflection or in appearance" with "the standpoint of reason" (ibid., 351).
[12] G.W.F. Hegel, *The Difference between Fichte's and Schelling's System of Philosophy*, trans. H.S. Harris and Walter Cerf (Albany: SUNY Press, 1977), 99.
[13] F.W.J. Schelling, *Werke*, vol. 4, ed. K.F.A. Schelling (Stuttgart: Cotta, 1856-61), 81.
[14] Ibid.

into the absolute, the intellect only reproduces itself *ad infinitum* and so mocks itself."[15]

On the other hand, the speculative mirror breaks out of the vicious, nihilistic circle of reflection. It gains access to "the great outdoors" behind the looking-glass–and it is to this extent, of course, that the mirror is, as Schelling calls it, "magical." What is reflected in the speculative mirror is not just the philosopher gazing in, but the totality of reality. But this is already to implicitly question the possibility of such a speculative mirror: is such a mirror "magical" because it is in fact a phantasy of intellectual desire? Is there any way to silver a mirror such that it would do what Schelling and Hegel hope for? Put simply, how is speculation to be achieved? Schelling and Hegel's early answer runs as follows: the great outdoors is not to be accessed by smashing through the glass, but instead through radicalising the mirror's limitations, its ineluctable insistence on reflecting back the same.[16] There is no immediate path to speculation: it is to be captured by diversions, strategies and feints. Out of such concerns emerges the ideal of "mediated immediacy"–and, as this paper proceeds, a very Schellingian variant of such mediated immediacy will emerge: an *art* of speculation.

Reflection is defined by dichotomy. "Reflection works only from oppositions and rests on oppositions."[17] In particular, the reflective mirror is that which distinguishes original from image. In so doing, it establishes a hierarchy between the two: the original becomes conceived as ontologically prior to the image and so the cause of the latter. It is here that Hegel and Schelling pinpoint the genesis of cause and effect and the type of mechanical thinking that is based upon them–"an eternal and flowing source of error."[18] Speculation rejects all these dichotomies and hierarchies by asserting the ultimate identity of original and image. As Hegel categorically states it, "the principle of speculation is the identity of subject and

---

[15] Hegel, *Difference*, 89-90.

[16] Hence Meillassoux criticises Hegel and Schelling for not breaking out of the correlation, but absolutising it. The great outdoors becomes the "great" indoors in a theorisation of total immanence. See Quentin Meillassoux, *After Finitude*, trans. Ray Brassier (London: Continuum, 2009), 37-8.

[17] Schelling, *Presentation*, 348.

[18] Schelling, *Werke*, 4:343-4.

object."[19] No duality emerges; instead, there is a sort of participatory metaphysics in which each image is reality in a specific form–and the aggregate of such images presents the absolute, the totality of reality:

> Reason does not recall its appearance, which emanates from it as a duplicate, back into itself–for then, it would only nullify it. Rather, reason constructs itself in its emanation as an identity that is conditioned by this very duplicate; it opposes this relative identity to itself once more, and in this way the system advances until the objective totality is completed. Reason then unites this objective totality with the opposite subjective totality to form the infinite world intuition, whose expansion has at the same time contracted into the richest and simplest identity.[20]

Such a process of gathering together constitutes speculation itself, for all of reality now appears to the philosopher in her self-forged, magical mirror.

Three aspects of this programme for becoming-speculative require note. First, speculation is to be distinguished from reflection in terms of its achievement of totality. Speculation "carries totality within itself"[21] in contrast to the "arbitrary separation of the individual from the whole effected by reflection."[22] As a collection of all possible images of the absolute, the speculative text is nothing less than the absolute itself. Speculation is all-encompassing: nothing is left out–not even, as we shall see, ghost stories and angelic realms.[23]

Second, the identity of the original with its image is once again mediated, rather than immediate. This is "the identity of identity and non-identity" proclaimed by Hegel in the

---

[19] Hegel, *Difference*, 80.
[20] Ibid., 113.
[21] Ibid., 89.
[22] Schelling, *Presentation*, 357.
[23] C.f. Grant's conception of an "extensity test" for an absolute system. Iain Hamilton Grant, *Philosophies of Nature after Schelling* (London: Continuum, 2006), 19-21.

Differenzschrift and Schelling in *Bruno* and the *Further Presentations*.[24] On the one hand, reflective thinking fixates on one particular image, thereby implicitly affirming the non-identity of such an image with reality as a whole. Here, "nonidentity is raised to an absolute principle."[25] On the other hand, the speculative philosopher is able to raise herself to totality so as to incorporate the particular image into a system. Speculation is only achieved by means of progressive systematisation.[26]

Third, this emphasis on the multiplicity of images in speculation (as opposed to reflective thinking's fixation on one) is of a piece with siding with *life over death*. The reflective understanding kills, because it places all phenomena in "static, dead pigeonholes;"[27] speculative reason, however, gives rise to life, since it describes a process of becoming.[28] What is seemingly forgotten, though, in Hegel and Schelling's early assertions on the supremacy of life is the necessity of mediation. The affirmation of life needs to be mediated through its opposite, death, and in Part Four of this paper I will reconstruct Schelling's argument that death (or the philosophical simulation of suicide) is a precondition for speculative philosophising.

---

[24] Hegel, *Difference*, 156; F.W.J. Schelling, *Bruno, or On the Natural and Divine Principle in Things*, trans. Michael G. Vater (Albany: SUNY Press, 1984), 192; Schelling, *Werke*, 4:431.

[25] Hegel, *Difference*, 81. See Gasché, *The Tain of the Mirror*, 26.

[26] For Hegel, this achievement is *reflection's own doing* – it negates itself by pursuing its own end absolutely. Reflection "has thrown itself into the abyss of its own perfection" (*Difference*, 140), he writes, and thereby becomes "speculative reflection" (ibid., 174), so that "philosophy [is] a totality of knowledge produced by reflection" (ibid., 103). For Hegel, therefore, speculation and reflection are not ultimately as opposed as they first appear. This is one of the points at which Schelling and Hegel diverge: for Schelling, reflection has "only *negative* value" (Schelling, *Ideas*, 11).

[27] Hegel, *Difference*, 80.

[28] Ibid., 91. See also the language of life and death in G.W.F. Hegel and F.W.J. Schelling, "The Critical Journal of Philosophy: Introduction on the Essence of Philosophical Criticism Generally and its Relationship to the Present State of Philosophy in Particular," in George di Giovanni and H.S. Harris (eds.), *Between Kant and Hegel: Texts in the Development of Post-Kantian Idealism* (Albany: SUNY Press, 1985).

Such–broadly–are the features of speculation and reflection as they emerge in Schelling and Hegel's writings at the turn of the nineteenth century. However, so far I have said very little, for it is difficult to see at first blush how the above connects with concrete philosophical practice. What does it mean, for example, for the philosopher to posit the identity of original and image? What would this look like in a philosophical text? It is at this point that a plurality of interpretations accumulates. It is precisely here that the endeavour to silver a speculative mirror becomes a matter of experimentation. In what follows, I pursue two such experiments from later in Schelling's career in which he attempts to make clearer what speculative silvering might look like–and, in particular, what exactly the philosophical art of mediating to produce immediacy might consist in. At stake, therefore, are rules for the construction of good philosophy–and it is at this point that the role of the mystical text in German Idealism takes centre-stage.

3. THE ART OF IMMEDIACY: WHERE BÖHME WENT WRONG
    The mystic most often associated with Schelling's philosophy is Jakob Böhme–and and it is certainly true that Schelling's engagement with his work was long, intense and eventful. Schelling was introduced to Böhme by Tieck in 1799; he obtained a copy of his works in 1804 and became infatuated by him by 1809.[29] As Cyril O'Regan puts it of the period around 1809, "many of Schelling's texts read almost as if they are paraphrases of Böhme."[30] Böhme is the Muse of the middle period, even if between 1807 and 1820 Schelling never once mentions his name.[31] In what follows, however, I consider the return Schelling makes to

---

[29] On the context of Schelling's early reading of Böhme, see Paola Mayer, *Jena Romanticism and its Appropriation of Böhme* (Montreal: McGill University Press, 1999).
[30] Cyril O'Regan, *The Heterodox Hegel* (Albany: SUNY Press, 1994), 462.
[31] This makes the task of assessing the extent of Böhme's influence particularly difficult. In the Anglo-American literature, Robert Brown's *The Later Philosophy of Schelling: The Influence of Böhme on Schelling's Works of 1809-15* (Lewisburg: Bucknell University Press, 1977) affirms Böhme's influence enthusiastically. In Germany, however, the 1970s saw a reaction against the Böhmean Schelling: Harold Holz, *Spekulation und Faktizitat: Zum Freiheitsbegriff in des mittleren und späten Schelling* (Bonn: Bouvier, 1970); Werner Beierwaltes, *Platonismus und Idealismus* (Frankfurt am Main: Klostermann, 1972).

Böhme's work at a much later date in his career—the 1830s and
40s. Here, rather than talking *like* Böhme, Schelling talks *about* him,
and, what is more, he talks about Böhme's work in terms of the
very kind of mediated immediacy that had been set out as the goal
of speculative thought as far back as 1801.

The 1841/42 *Lectures on the Philosophy of Revelation* were to be
the crowning achievement of Schelling's career. In Summer 1841,
the King of Prussia summoned Schelling to Berlin to slay "the
legions sprung from the teeth of Hegel's pantheistic dragon" (as the
King's own letter put it)[32]–and the Lectures were the immediate
result. They opened with a who's-who of nineteenth-century
intellectuals in attendance (Bakunin, Burkhardt, Engels, Alexander
von Humboldt, Kierkegaard, Ranke, Savigny, Trendelenburg), but
ended heaped in derision. Indeed, H.E.G. Paulus published a
pirated edition of the lectures for the very purpose of ridiculing
them.[33] In supplementary footnotes, Paulus berates Schellingian
positive philosophy as succumbing to the worst excesses of
theosophy—implicitly linking Schelling's name to Böhme's once
more.[34]

Schelling had a twofold response to Paulus's piracy: first, to
sue him; second, to add a new section to the lectures determining
his relation to Böhmean theosophy more precisely. Hence, the
Lectures on the Philosophy of Revelation of 1842/43 include an
additional lecture which explicitly picks up on the accusations:
"Have I myself not provided the impetus to bring positive
philosophy into contact with theosophy?"[35]

---

[32] Quoted in Alan White, *Schelling: An Introduction to the System of Freedom*
(New Haven: Yale University Press, 1983), 146.
[33] Republished (without Paulus' editorial interjections) as F.W.J. Schelling,
Philosophie der Offenbarung 1841/42, ed. Manfred Frank (Frankfurt am
Main: Suhrkamp, 1977). For accounts of the Paulus-affair, see Frank,
"Einleitung" to ibid., 46-52; Xavier Tilliette, *Schelling: Biographie* (Paris:
Calmann-Lévy, 1999), 351, 354-7.
[34] Bakunin, Engels, Leroux and Ruge also commented on Schelling's
proximity to theosophy. See the extracts in Schelling, *Philosophie der
Offenbarung 1841/42*, 542, 546, 552. For Engels, see his "Anti-Schelling"
(http://www.marxists.org/archive/marx/works/1841/anti-
schelling/index.htm; last accessed: 09/12/12), passim.
[35] F.W.J. Schelling, *The Grounding of Positive Philosophy: The Berlin Lectures*,
trans. Bruce Matthews (Albany: SUNY Press, 2007), 174.

There is much in Schelling's reading of Böhme that reflects standard philosophical prejudices against mysticism. A glance at Schelling's treatment of Böhmean theosophy in his 1833 *Lectures on the History of Modern Philosophy* makes this "standard" attitude most clear. Here theosophers, like Böhme, are characterised as "philosophers of not-knowing"[36]: instead of argument, they employ "ecstatic intuition and immediate revelation."[37] In this state of immediate ecstasy, "language and knowledge cease" and "all communication of knowledge [becomes] impossible."[38] Such is *the problem of articulation* that plagues mystical thinking: the very immediacy of the experience of God which is the mystic's greatest asset becomes her downfall when it comes to communicating this experience—or even preserving it in clear concepts. Mystical experience is incapable of the mediation appropriate to articulation. As Schelling puts it, "all experience, feeling, vision is in itself mute and needs a mediating organ to be expressed."[39] For the theosopher, though, mediation is conceived as an external, destructive agent which pollutes the privileged experience with which she began. In consequence, Schelling concludes, "the true mark of mysticism is the *hatred* of clear knowledge."[40] Böhme and other theosophists fail to attain the speculative ideal of the indifference of mediacy and immediacy—and hence, it is no surprise that Schelling criticises them by returning to mirror imagery: they do not "place [experience] firmly before [them] . . . to look at it in the understanding as in a mirror (in reflection)."[41] The speculative philosopher, on the other hand, realises the following:

> Everything . . . must first be brought to real reflection, in order to achieve the highest representation. Here, then, lies the border between theosophy and philosophy which the lover of science will chastely seek to preserve,

---

[36] F.W.J. Schelling, *On the History of Modern Philosophy*, trans. Andrew Bowie (Cambridge: Cambridge University Press, 1994), 179.
[37] Ibid., 181.
[38] Ibid.
[39] Ibid., 185.
[40] Ibid.
[41] Ibid., 181.

without being led astray by the apparent wealth of the material in the theosophical systems.[42]

The philosopher must not run scared of mirrors as the theosopher does.

When Schelling returns to Böhme once more in the 1842/43 *Lectures on the Philosophy of Revelation*, such a critique still plays its part, but something very different is now going on as well. A sense of Schelling's new project of positive philosophy is required to discern this.

The task of the *Lectures on the Philosophy of Revelation* is to obtain knowledge of the divine as *actually existing* (i.e. as historically, rather than logically becoming). In other words, the requirement is to cultivate a state of rational ecstasy where God is encountered not as a concept of thought, but as a freely acting person. Positive philosophy leaves behind a philosophy of logic for a philosophy of existence, of freedom and of life. Thus on the one hand, Schelling mounts a critique of all previous philosophy as too rationalistic. Such philosophy has possessed no relation to concrete existence in the world: "Rational philosophy . . . is so independent of existence that it would be true even if nothing existed."[43] Hegel is of course the target of this attack. His system, Schelling claims, remains stuck within thought: it is "empty, logical" and "an unbridgeable chasm [separates] logical necessity and reality."[44] And so, on the other hand, Schelling attempts to set out the method for a non-logical philosophy, one that *does* access concrete being and so escapes the confines of thought. This philosophy does not begin in thought but *outside* it. Positive philosophy thus demands that reason be "set outside itself, absolutely ecstatic"[45]; it demands that reason "become motionless, paralysed . . . in order that through this subordination reason may reach its true and eternal content."[46] And this true content is "extralogical existence."[47]

---

[42] Ibid., 182.
[43] Schelling, *The Berlin Lectures*, 179-80.
[44] Ibid., 160.
[45] Ibid., 203.
[46] Ibid., 205-6.
[47] Ibid., 155.

It should be obvious how and why Böhmean theosophy could serve as a useful guide here. Böhme's visions of the divine make claim to the same kind of *ecstasis* as positive philosophy. They assume immediate access to the processes God actually undergoes, free of the dross of scholastic metaphysics. Böhmean mysticism accesses the divine through apparently immediate experience. Schelling's characterisation of Böhmean thought in the 1842/43 *Lectures* recognises this,

> In a third type of empiricism, the supersensible is made into an object of actual experience *through which* a possible ecstasy of the human essence in God is assumed, the consequence of which is a necessary, infallible vision not merely into the divine essence, but into the essence of creation and every phase of that process as well. This type of empiricism is theosophy, which is predominantly a speculative or theoretical mysticism.[48]

Böhme's writings exhibit "the inherently laudable aspiration to comprehend the emergence of things from God as an *actual* chain of events."[49]

And yet, while the aspiration may be there, Schelling contends that Böhme ultimately fails to fulfill it. Here the standard German Idealist critique of mysticism continues to play its part (Böhme lacks a rigorous method and so is plagued by the problem of articulation), but it is now obviously insufficient–for the aim of positive philosophy is precisely to throw off the burden of scientific rigour in the name of ecstasy. Schelling now seems to want to be a mystic. As such, his most substantial criticisms end up proceeding in a very different direction.

Namely, Böhme fails to encounter God as actual in ecstasy because he remains in thrall to logic and rationalism. Böhme is still too scientific, too philosophical. Despite its appearance to the contrary, Böhme's vision of God is *too mediated* to serve as a model for Schellingian positive philosophy:

---

[48] Ibid., 173.
[49] Ibid., 175.

We have advanced theosophy primarily as the antithesis of rational philosophy, and thus of rationalism in philosophy. Yet at bottom theosophy *strives* to move beyond rationalism without, however, being capable of actually wresting away rationalism's substantial knowledge. . . Theosophy wants of course to overcome such a knowledge, but it does not succeed, as is seen most clearly with Böhme. . . Although he calls it theosophy, thus making the claim to be the science of the divine, the content to which theosophy attains remains only a substantial movement, and he presents God only in a substantial movement.[50]

What separates theosophy from positive philosophy, Schelling now contends, is the remnant of abstract logical thought in theosophical speculation:

What in particular lies at the heart of Jakob Böhme's theosophy is the inherently laudable aspiration to comprehend the emergence of things from God as an *actual* chain of events. Jakob Böhme, however, does not know of any other way to bring this about than by invoking the deity itself in a type of natural process. The characteristic feature of the *positive* philosophy, however, consists precisely in that it rejects all processes taken in *this sense*, namely in which God would not only be the logical but also the actual result of a process. To this extent, the positive philosophy is more properly speaking in direct opposition with each and every theosophical aspiration.[51]

The question is therefore why Böhme fails to escape thought, logic and rationalism. And Schelling's answer is basically Kantian: Böhme wants an immediate experience of God, but *no* experience of the divine can ever be immediate. There is no "raw," naïve or immediate experience of an external entity and so Böhme's raid on immediacy must necessarily–even if surreptitiously–involve mediacy. It is Böhme's appeal to experience which is the problem,

---

[50] Ibid., 177.
[51] Ibid., 175.

because experience, Schelling insists, can never resist entirely the activity of reason. Experience is ineluctably logical, and so the mystic remains forever alienated from the actuality of the theogonic process, consigned to a merely conceptual vision of this genesis. Böhme's claim to "immediate experience" still smuggles in mediacy.

So, Schelling contends, a different method is required than that which mystics employ. *Ecstasis* must be cultivated in a different way, a way that avoids appeal to experience. Philosophy must therefore begin *from what exceeds or what is above experience*, with "a being that is absolutely external to thought . . . beyond all experience as it is before all thought."[52] However, of course, for a Kantian (like the late Schelling), what is outside the realm of possible experience is inaccessible to the human subject. In consequence, *indirection* is required to bring about human access to what exceeds experience. In other words, Schelling develops *an art of ecstasy*: in place of the mystic's blunt, direct appeal to immediacy, he develops a *strategic* approach to the transcendent. The immediate is not (*pace* Böhme) immediately available, rather it is only to be obtained as a result of the mediacy of feints and diversions.

In 1833, the speculative mirror was invoked as a means of making experience conceptual: only when immediate experience reflects itself in a mirror can it attain true rigour and be labelled knowledge. In 1842, Schelling appeals to this mirror once again; however, it is for precisely the opposite reason: mediation is no longer a way of transforming vision into thought, but of escaping thought into vision. The speculative mirror is invoked for the sake of the unthought. An immediate vision of God as he actually is is only available *via mediation.*

To return to the terms of my Introduction, the immediacy of the mystic vision is to be safeguarded by posterior exercises in mediation. But, of course, in the terms of my Introduction, this is still to uphold something like an idealist fiction in which the initial moment of vision is still given immediately. That is, in his writings on Böhme (both *On the History of Modern Philosophy* and *Lectures on the Philosophy of Revelation*), Schelling neglects the mediation necessary to obtain that moment of vision to begin with. He

---

[52] Ibid., 179.

neglects those crucial exercises that transform the mystic into a person able to have such visions. The genesis of the mystical form of life eludes him. A symptom of this can be located in Schelling's violent oscillations between conceiving Böhme as a fanatic (*On the History of Modern Philosophy*) and as a Hegelian (*Lectures on the Philosophy of Revelation*). To even attempt to position mysticism stably on the rational/irrational axis might itself seem misplaced[53]; granting its possibility, however, such positioning still assumes too much–namely, that the rationality of Böhme's mystical texts can be classified with respect to two components alone: (a) the immediacy of his visions and (b) the problem of articulation attendant upon subsequently describing them. What is missing here is any account of the processes by which the visions are themselves generated and the implications of that for positioning Böhme on the rational/irrational axis.

To see what such an account might in fact looks like, as well as its significance for both Schelling's encounter with mysticism and his own characterisation of speculation, one must turn to *Clara*.

4. SIMULATING SUICIDE WITH CLARA

Emanuel Swedenborg's *Heaven and Hell* opens as a project in scriptural exegesis. In the Preface, Swedenborg rails against those who understand the words of Scripture merely "according to their literal meaning."[54] The genuinely religious act of reading goes beyond literalism to plumb "the hidden depths that lie within the details of the Word."[55] There is a spiritual meaning as well–and the purpose of *Heaven and Hell*, according to Swedenborg in these first

---

[53] Indeed, this is a problem to which philosophy in general is often prone insofar as it attempts to circumscribe the nonphilosophical *by means of its own categories*. Mysticism is a particularly helpful example by which to disrupt philosophy's treatment of the nonphilosophical precisely because of the prevalence of mysticisms that either seem to call for multiple loci on the axis (e.g. medieval speculative mysticism, employing rigorous logic for an apophatic end) or resist the terms of the axis altogether (e.g. Islamic theoretical gnosis). On the latter example, see Seyyed Hossein Nasr, "Theoretical Gnosis, Doctrinal Sufism and their Significance Today" in *Transcendent Philosophy* 6 (2005).

[54] Emanuel Swedenborg, *Heaven and Hell: Drawn from Things Heard and Seen*, trans. George F. Dole (West Chester, PA: Swedenborg Foundation, 2000), 87.

[55] Ibid., 87.

few pages, is to reveal this spiritual significance and so make us better readers. Yet, there immediately arises a skeptical rejoinder to this project: why should we trust Swedenborg? What guarantees his dogmatic assertion of these "pure correspondences" hidden in the biblical text for which "every detail points to something spiritual"[56]? The answer is given casually, in passing almost: Swedenborg is so sure because he has been granted immediate experience of the spirit world of heaven and hell: "I have *also* been enabled to see what is in heaven and in hell, a process that has been going on for thirteen years. Now I am being allowed therefore to describe what I have heard and seen."[57] There is no doubting the correspondences in the Bible, for they are confirmed by what Swedenborg has seen with his own eyes. This passing remark reorients the whole project of *Heaven and Hell*: only minimally an exercise in scriptural hermeneutics, it is rather dominated by accounts of Swedenborg's discussions with angels and observations of heaven's geography. For example, he famously gives the following description of angelic town-planning:

> Whenever I have talked with angels face to face, I have been with them in their houses. Their houses were just like the houses on earth that we call homes, but more beautiful. They have chambers, suites, and bedrooms in abundance and courtyards with gardens, flowerbeds, and lawns around them. Where there is some concentration of people, the houses are adjoining, one near another, arranged in the form of a city with streets and lanes and public squares, just like the ones we see in cities on earth. I have been allowed to stroll along them and look around wherever I wished, at times entering people's homes. This has happened when I was fully awake, with my inner sight opened.[58]

What is most significant for present purposes is Swedenborg's attempt in the Preface to *Heaven and Hell* (and this is illustrative of his whole oeuvre) to present his project as both hermeneutically sophisticated and empirically naïve. The accounts he puts forward

---

[56] Ibid., 88.
[57] Ibid., 89; my emphasis.
[58] Ibid., 181-2.

arise from both a delicate process of textual archaeology and a simple act of sensing what is immediately accessible. Swedenborgian mysticism partakes in both immediacy and mediacy; indeed, I want to contend in what follows that at one moment in his philosophical trajectory Swedenborgian mysticism represents for Schelling an ideal, precisely owing to the indifference of immediacy and mediacy productive of the speculative standpoint. Swedenborg attains immediate access to the great outdoors of the spirit world without succumbing to the theosophical temptation to silence and the renunciation of language.

Schelling's unfinished novel, *Clara*, is haunted by Swedenborg's achievements. Indeed, it ends with an exposition of "the northern visionary's" doctrine of revelation–an exposition which leaves the characters with a warm glow of "the greatest joy."[59] What is more, the very climax of the third dialogue–the novel's heart and ground–makes reference to Swedenborg once again:

> Truly anyone who dared to speak authoritatively about this [spirit] world would have to have died and come back to this life from the other side, like Plato's Armenian, or must have had his inner being opened to him in some other way so that he could look into that world, as happened to that Swedish visionary.[60]

Swedenborg is here presented as an ideal figure, since he achieved the near-impossible: he experienced the spirit world without having to die (as is the case for most of us, even Plato's Armenian) without even (and this will become increasingly important) falling asleep or being hypnotised. Swedenborg saw the heavens "when I was fully awake, with my inner sight opened."[61]

For the Schelling of *Clara*, this is the very condition to which the philosopher aspires. The spirit world is that aspect of reality in

---

[59] F.W.J. Schelling, *Clara or, On Nature's Connection to the Spirit World*, trans. Fiona Steinkamp (Albany: SUNY Press, 2002), 77.
[60] Ibid., 55-6.
[61] For a more general exploration of Schelling's appropriation of Swedenborg, see Friedemann Horn, *Schelling and Swedenborg: Mysticism and German Idealism*, trans. George F. Dole (West Chester, PA: Swedenborg Foundation, 1997).

which the ideal potency (the potency of mind, the ethical and the religious) is at its most intense.[62] To fulfill the speculative aim of philosophically accounting for everything (thereby bringing the system to totality), the spirit world must be included as well. Philosophers need to provide accounts of the spirit world, like Swedenborg–and ideally philosophers would provide such accounts based on an immediate experience that can be clearly articulated without falsification, again like Swedenborg. The task for philosophers is, then, to become Swedenborg.

Hence, the whole of *Clara* is oriented around this problem: how can the living (and, in particular, living philosophers) come to know the spirit world? The model of death is one particularly powerful answer given throughout the novel, since dying is, of course, the most popular means of attaining access to this realm of reality.[63] What is at stake for an absolute philosophy that accounts for the spirit world is *the simulation of death* (achieving precisely what death does but while conscious). As Schelling puts it, "He who loves wisdom will work towards death even here."[64] So, each of the five dialogues in *Clara* sets out conditions for the accomplishment of the Swedenborgian ideal–that is, practical ways to die in life and so imitate the mystical text.

The first dialogue, for instance, interrogates the possibilities and dangers of organised religion for this end. *Clara* opens with a presentation of Catholic festivities on All Souls Day as a symbolic means of communing with the dead:

> We saw a crowd of people thronging toward a gentle incline . . . We joined them so that for once we, too, could watch the moving festival dedicated to the dead that is celebrated this day in Catholic towns. We found the whole area full of people already. It was peculiar to see life on the graves, forebodingly illuminated by the

---

[62] See Schelling, *Clara*, 79.

[63] One of the central arguments of *Clara* is that death is not a negative moment, but "an elevation into a higher potency, into a really different and higher world" (ibid., 46). See further ibid., 79. C.f. Deleuze, *Cinema II: The Time-Image*: "Philosophers are beings who have passed through a death, who are born from it . . . The philosopher has returned from the dead and goes back there" (trans. Hugh Tomlinson and Robert Galeta [London: Athlone, 1999], 208-9).

[64] Ibid., 44.

dully shining autumn sun. As we left the trodden path, we soon saw pretty groups gathered around individual graves: here girls in their bloom, holding hands with their younger brothers and sisters, crowned their mother's grave; there at the grave of her children lost so young a mother stood in silence with no need for consecrated water to represent her tears . . . Here all of life's severed relationships were revived for the spectators who were familiar with the people and the circumstances; brothers came again to brothers and children to parents; at this moment all were one family again.[65]

Schelling's interest in the philosophical potentialities of the religious community was long-standing: his lectures on the *Philosophy of Art* end with an invocation of religious festivity.[66] And here again we read Schelling posit from the very beginning of *Clara* communal celebration as a means of attaining access to the spirit world. In a proto-Bakhtinian (but also very non-Bakhtinian!) manner, the festival becomes a site for the revelation of truth.

But it is seemingly not for everyone: none of the characters in the dialogue feel able to immerse themselves in the festival. The priest and doctor merely watch, while Clara has shut herself away in a Benedictine monastery. Such behaviour exemplifies what is, for Schelling, the other, equally prevalent face of organised religion: *ascesis*. Religion often prescribes collective immersion in the name of truth, but often it prescribes solitary withdrawal–and Schelling is insistent that such ascetic withdrawal from the world (whether physical in Clara's case or intellectual in the case of the idealist philosopher) is precisely what *impedes* access to the spirit world. *Ascesis* is the danger which must be avoided. Such dangers are embodied in the "well-educated, young clergyman"[67] who

---

[65] Ibid., 9.

[66] "Music, song, dance, as well as all the various types of drama, live only in public life, and form an alliance in such life. Wherever public life disappears, instead of that real, external drama in which, in all its forms, an entire people participates as a political or moral totality, only an *inward*, ideal drama can unite the people. This ideal drama is the worship service, the only kind of *truly* public action that has remained for the contemporary age" (Schelling, *Philosophy of Art*, 280). See also Schelling, *Werke*, 6:573.

[67] Schelling, *Clara*, 10.

appears in this opening dialogue: his disconnection from the world and subsequent inability to recognise any positive connection between it and the next results in disparaging comments on the festival and ultimately in a sterile, pseudo-Kantian agnosticism. So, when the narrator comments, "We should support all festivals and customs in which we are reminded of a connection with the world beyond," the clergyman responds:

> Today's commemoration certainly has something moving about it; however, if its purpose is to support the thought that we can be connected to the inhabitants of that other world, then I would hold this commemoration to be one that is almost detrimental and I would submit that it be abolished in your church . . . We must honour these old divisions.[68]

It is to such comments that Clara responds with the voice of both speculation and mysticism: "What do cold words and merely negative concepts have to do with ardent longing? Are we satisfied in this life with a bleak existence?"[69]

An alternative is required, and this alternative must provide a means of accessing the spirit world without renouncing this one. It is with this aim in view that the discussion turns to philosophy as a form of worldly curiosity. Philosophising serves as an antidote to *ascesis*: "Merely exercising piety as a way of life, without combining it with lively and active scientific research, leads to emptiness."[70] Indeed, this is a theme which resurfaces again and again in Schelling's philosophy: knowledge of higher things (God, freedom, the mind) does not come at the expense of the lower. Schelling repeatedly berates those philosophical ascetics who indulge in ethereal but ultimately vacuous considerations of the spiritual. Hence, in the 1809 *Freiheitsschrift* he attacks "dreary and fanatic enthusiasm which breaks forth in self-mutilation or . . . in self-emasculation" and "which in philosophy is accomplished by the

---

[68] Ibid., 12. The clergyman closely mimics Kant's own assessment of speculative mysticism in the closing pages of *Dreams of a Spirit-Seer* (in *Theoretical Philosophy 1755-1770*, ed. and trans. David Walford [Cambridge: Cambridge University Press, 1992], 2:367-73). On Schelling's familiarity with *Dreams*, see Horn, *Schelling and Swedenborg*, 11.
[69] Ibid., 13.
[70] Ibid., 17.

renunciation of reason and science."[71] Similar sentiments are to be found in the Introduction to *Clara* as well: "Modern philosophy did away with its immediate reference to nature, or didn't think to keep it, and proudly scorned any connection to physics. Continuing with its claims to the higher world, it was no longer metaphysics but hyperphysics."[72]

This is also a theme emphasised in the second dialogue: becoming-Swedenborg (knowledge of the ideal in its highest potentiation) can only occur *by way of* the natural sciences. It is this point that the character of the doctor presses home to Clara, so as to counteract her flight to the monastery. *Naturphilosophie* is a necessary precondition for being a speculative philosopher. He begins in the first dialogue, "No one should devote themselves to this investigation [of the spirit world] until they have gained a firm and solid ground here, within nature, on which they can base their thoughts . . . Not 'top down' but 'bottom up' is my motto."[73] And he then continues in the second dialogue:

> They [the ascetics] start with what is most general and spiritual and are thereby never able to come down to reality or particulars. They are ashamed to start from the earth, to climb up from the creature as if from a rung on a ladder, to draw those thoughts that are beyond the senses first from earth, fire, water and air. And so they don't get anywhere, either: their webs of thought are plants without roots, they don't hang onto anything.[74]

Knowledge of what is higher must be mediated (reflected) by what is lower. This is our first clue to Schelling's philosophical reconstruction of the Swedenborgian mirror: it involves impurity– the mixing of realms and sciences. As we shall see, this impurity informs the Schellingian definition of dialectic.

Let me temporarily skip the third dialogue and turn to the final two. Here the problem of articulation that so worried Schelling

---

[71] F.W.J. Schelling, *Philosophical Inquiries into the Nature of Human Freedom*, trans. James Gutmann (La Salle: Open Court, 1936), 31.
[72] Schelling, *Clara*, 3. See further ibid., 4-5. Whether this introductory piece was actually intended as an introduction to *Clara* or not is a matter of debate (see Steinkamp's notes to these passages).
[73] Ibid., 15.
[74] Ibid., 28.

with respect to Böhme takes centre-stage once again–that is, if the philosopher is able to attain experience of the spirit world by following the rules set out in the earlier dialogues, there remains the problem of transforming such immediate experience into knowledge and subsequently into a textual artefact. This is again to insist on indifferentiating between immediacy and mediacy to achieve the speculative standpoint: the philosopher attains the great outdoors only through mirroring it. Further practices and exercises must be prescribed for the philosopher to turn experience into cognition and text.

The fourth dialogue thus gives rules on the manufacture of a speculative text. This is of course somewhat of a performative exercise, since the rules Schelling sets out for the amelioration of philosophical writing are precisely those meant to be embodied in *Clara* itself. So, the fourth dialogue begins:

> At about the same time, a few days or weeks or so later, a philosophy book arrived in which some of the excellent things it contained were written in a completely incomprehensible language and abounded, so to speak, with barbarism. Clara found it on my table and after she'd read it for a while, she said: Why do today's philosophers find it so impossible to write at least a little in the same way that they speak? Are these terribly artificial words absolutely necessary, can't the same thing be said in a more natural way, and does a book have to be quite unenjoyable for it to be philosophical?[75]

In place of this arid and alienating jargon, Clara and the priest agree that philosophical works should tend to "the language of the people" and even the language of the lover; they should be dialogues, dramatizing a debate to "make it live before our very eyes"; and they should respect the Aristotelian unity of action (something that *Clara*–as a novel–does not do).[76]

These rules are further grounded in a discussion of the nature of language in the fifth dialogue. Language itself possesses the potential for bearing witness to both the natural world and the spirit world, for it "contains a spiritual essence and a corporeal

---

[75] Ibid., 63.
[76] Ibid., 63-5.

element."[77] Language is both a physical entity (sound/graphic mark) and an ideal one (meaning): it oscillates between nature and spirit. Indeed, Schelling mentions examples where language has become the medium through which to attain occult experience of the spirit world:

> Certain strange cases that cannot be gainsaid are told of people in conditions of rapture coming to understand languages of which they had no prior knowledge, even of their coming to speak in other tongues, as the apostles once did. It would follow from this that in all languages, particularly in the original ones, something of the initial element's purity is still to be found.[78]

Such sentiments are repeated in the 1811 *Report on Schmid's Attempt at Pasigraphy* where once again the depths of language are foregrounded as *the* key tool for an occult heightening of the self:

> We know of a quantity of cases where people in a somnambulant condition have produced poetry which they were never again able to produce in a wakeful state . . . In the *Actis Naturae Curiosum* there is the story of a woman who in the condition of pregnancy fell into an ecstasy in which she sang unknown songs and talked in foreign tongues . . . All this is surely sufficient to prove that the source of language lies in man and, like so much else which hides in him, emerges more freely under certain circumstances and is developed into a higher, more universal sense of language.[79]

Hence, language performs the very ideal of Schellingian speculation in *Clara*: it approaches the spirit world without renouncing the real and the natural. To speak is to deny the power of the ascetic ideal (and here emerges the germ of a critique of

---

[77] Ibid., 72.

[78] Ibid., 72-3.

[79] Schelling, *Werke*, 8:450-1. When we turn to the discussion of the occult in the third dialogue, this linguistic backdrop needs to be borne in mind. Language forms the basis of occult experience and the oscillation of the dialectic merely mirrors the oscillation of the word.

apophaticism). What is more, this account of the ontology of language also throws light on Schelling's attack on artificial jargon in the fourth dialogue. The resources for good philosophy are already present in language *as it is*; there is no need to remould it in the scientific image. The linguistic barbarians attacked in the fourth dialogue are similar to the ascetics Schelling likewise condemns: both renounce the everyday and the real, thereby concealing, rather than revealing, the truth. The invention of a philosophical language is a redundant gesture; the language of the people already possesses speculative potential.[80] Therefore, Schelling's linguistic concerns are pragmatic: setting rules for the concrete situations in which language can best be employed and its potential mined. Specifically, the speculative ideal is effectuated in a language of sympathy, "a heavenly appearance even here"[81] in which the materiality of the sign is not renounced but perfected.[82] And this incorporation of sympathy into the speculative should not surprise us, for speculation is the overcoming of opposition for identity–the very same dynamic exhibited by a sympathetic understanding. Sympathy–and in particular a sympathetic use of language–is the speculative affect *par excellence*.[83]

It is in the third dialogue that the characters tackle the project of becoming-Swedenborg most explicitly. While the first two dialogues set out some general philosophical prerequisites for this end and the last two (posterior) practices for manufacturing a text that manages to capture experience of the spirit world in linguistic form, it is the third dialogue which directly takes on the challenge of specifying those *pre*-philosophical exercises by which a full

[80] In the contemporaneous *Stuttgart Seminars,* Schelling affirms the maxim, *vox populi vox Dei.* F.W.J. Schelling, *Stuttgart Seminars* in *Idealism and the Endgame of Theory: Three Essays,* ed. and trans. Thomas Pfau (Albany: SUNY Press, 1994), 237.
[81] Schelling, *Clara,* 72.
[82] So, Schelling speaks of "communication without signs via an invisible, but perhaps nevertheless physical, influence" (ibid., 73). And once again the amorous relation becomes a philosophical model.
[83] For more on the affect of sympathy in Schelling's philosophy and its relation to his rhetorical practice, see Joshua Ramey and Daniel Whistler, "The Physics of Sense: Bruno, Schelling, Deleuze" in *Gilles Deleuze and Metaphysics,* eds. Alain Beaulieu, Edward Kazarian and Julia Sushytska (Lexington, MA: Lexington, 2013), 95-6.

experience of the spirit world is made possible. Moreover, as I have already intimated, the characters realise that such exercises must be modelled on death, for it is through dying that this spirit world is typically reached. Speculative philosophers must simulate suicide to know all of reality–and the third dialogue sets about identifying how. Such a concern with suicide should not be read as a "mystic aberration" in Schelling's trajectory. An insistence on killing the self in order to philosophise is a recurrent one in his oeuvre. For example, it is crucial to the methodology of *Naturphilosophie*: the process of abstraction by which philosophy begins consists in an artificial annihilation of the conscious self: "I had to extract the I from its own intuition . . . to posit the I as unconscious; but the I, to the extent it is unconscious, is not = the I."[84] The philosopher must suppress the I to know nature, and it is only a short step from asserting that unconsciousness is a necessary prerequisite for philosophising to an interest in employing occult practices for such an end.

There is a moment each of us experiences on the verge of sleep, the characters speculate, that gives rise to an unconscious lucidity:

> At the moment of falling into one's final slumber, an indescribable joy flows from one's entire being, and here the soul is in its finest moral and spiritual activity at the same time . . . This mid-condition between waking and sleeping . . . is so infinitely different from anything that we call a dream that its clarity surpasses even the most

---

[84] Schelling, *Werke*, 4:88. For an analysis of similar claims made in the early *Critical Letters*, see Alberto Toscano, "Fanaticism and Production: On Schelling's Philosophy of Indifference," *Pli* 8 (1999). To make explicit the contemporary stakes of this discussion, c.f. Brassier's insistence on the question, "How does thought think the death of thought?"–namely for genuinely nihilistic thought of the outside to occur, "the subject of philosophy must [somehow] recognise that he or she is already dead." Ray Brassier, *Nihil Unbound: Enlightenment and Extinction* (Basingstoke: Palgrave Macmillan, 2007), 223, 239. As I have argued, the Schellingian suicidal exercises that form a speculative life are preparatory to the description of a realm outside of human life. What they make possible, to quote the final words of Thacker's *After Life*, is "to think a concept of life that is itself, in some basic way, unhuman, a life *without us*" (Eugene Thacker, *After Life* [Chicago: University of Chicago Press, 2010], 268).

vivid waking thoughts, and any normal mode of existing seems to be only a dream . . . Everything is differentiated in detail and is completely without confusion. This condition, however, usually lasts only a second; it disappears in a sudden, shuddering movement.[85]

Such a moment of "waking sleep"[86] is death-like to the extent that death is itself the "last sleep" in which "those who have escaped sleep from within sleep . . . have thereby penetrated through to a waking state."[87] Yet it is available to the living. This leads the priest to affirm the maxim: "Only he who could do while awake what he has to do while asleep would be the perfect philosopher."[88] The third dialogue revolves around the ideal of conscious unconsciousness, death-in-life.

However, as Clara makes clear, if such a moment of dreaming lucidity is experienced at all, it "lasts a second" and then "disappears in a sudden, shuddering moment." The task for a speculative philosopher, therefore, is to *artificially* produce, reproduce and prolong this moment *at will*. It is here that she must appeal to occult practices and other "mysterious phenomena,"[89] such as hypnosis, since this moment of conscious unconsciousness is to be identified with the state of clairvoyance cultivated by the occult. Hypnosis is a strategy to effectuate "the highest clairvoyance."[90] Thus, Schelling describes the workings of hypnosis as follows:

> Through the influence of other people, human beings, acting *as if dead* toward everything apart from the influencer, and with their external senses completely *deadened,* can pass over into an internal clarity of the highest kind . . . If this is true, then I believe that here we would have the experience of a condition that we could justifiably call a higher one and that we could consider to be a wakeful sleep or a sleeping wakefulness. And I

---

[85] Schelling, *Clara*, 47.
[86] Ibid., 73.
[87] Ibid., 47.
[88] Ibid.
[89] Ibid., 48.
[90] Ibid., 49. See further Horn, *Schelling and Swedenborg,* 6-8.

would thereby compare it not to death, but to *the condition that follows death,* and one which I believe will be the highest and which will be a clairvoyance uninterrupted by a waking up.[91]

And yet the problem of articulation remains unsolved. In hypnosis, as in sleep and death, one ultimately loses consciousness and the experiences gained in a clairvoyant state are rarely preserved in memory. In other words, the above still does not amount to becoming-Swedenborg, for Swedenborg experienced the spirit world *"fully awake, with my inner sight opened."* He remembered every detail and was able to communicate it soberly in text after text. Hypnosis remains an approximation to this ideal: it fails to satisfactorily indifferentiate immediate experience and art.[92]

For the Schelling of *Clara,* this is the problem that *dialectic* answers. Dialectic is the philosophical tool for becoming-Swedenborg; however, it achieves this parity with the mystical text precisely by *abandoning* the Swedenborgian ideal *in its purity.* Mysticism is only part of the story; instead, the philosopher must diversify and embrace impurity–an impurity in which the philosopher oscillates or (in the language of *Clara*) "rotates" between mystic experience and concept-construction.[93] The rhythm of this rotation defines philosophical dialectic. Whereas the mystic is lucky enough to wholeheartedly pursue her end, the philosopher must compromise and become composite. It is with this in mind that the priest insists on Clara pursuing conceptual clarity *alongside* spiritual *ecstasis*:

---

[91] Ibid., 47-8; my emphases. And crucially the characters add that "approaching that higher sleep is very similar to approaching death." Ibid., 48.

[92] And so the doctor still insists in the third dialogue: "And yet . . . this condition [of clairvoyance] is still merely an approximation to the highest one" (ibid.).

[93] Ibid., 35. As is stated in the third dialogue, "What is delicate or spiritual receives its highest worth only by asserting its nature *through mixing* with a conflicting, even barbaric, element" (ibid., 77; my emphasis). Mixing is *the* formal criterion for Schellingian philosophy as a whole, see further Daniel Whistler, *Schelling's Theory of Symbolic Language: Forming the System of Identity* (Oxford: Oxford University Press, 2013), 238-9; and, in reference to the novelistic style of *Clara* in particular, see Philippe Lacoue-Labarthe and Jean-Luc Nancy, "Le dialogue des genres" in *Poétique* 21 (1975), 168-72.

What [Clara] lacked was the ability to unpack her thoughts and thereby clarify them. I know what an agreeable effect ordering one's own thoughts into a precise framework has; the soul is happy when it can have what it felt inwardly, as if by inspiration or through some divine thought, expressly worked out in the understanding, too, as if looking in a mirror.[94]

The speculative mirror reappears at the climax of *Clara*, once more as the culmination of philosophical activity. One must cultivate and ameliorate one's experience until it is "as if looking in a mirror." Speculation is only attained once the immediacy of experience has passed through the rigours of an art of immediacy. Such a process does not destroy immediacy; it makes the philosophical presentation of it possible. Ultimately, the speculative mirror potentiates, not annihilates, the mystic vision of the spirit world.

5. DEATH AND/OR THE DIALECTIC

Schelling is a philosopher of mediated immediacy; Schelling is a philosopher of the dialectic; Schelling is a philosopher who conceives death-like negation as a necessary moment in philosophising. *And yet* Schelling is not a Hegelian philosopher. The common search for the speculative standpoint connects Hegelian and Schellingian thinking, but once on their quest each embarks on a series of idiosyncratic experiments in the silvering of mirrors. German Idealism does not consist in a linear narrative; it does not posit one definitive orthodoxy and various alternatives to it. German Idealism is entirely constituted by non-standard speculations–the manufacture of weird and wonderful looking-glasses. For Schelling, mystical traditions form much of the material out of which such mirrors are silvered. Böhmean theosophy is such a crucial dialogue partner precisely because of what it lacks–a mirror adequate to its visions of God. Swedenborg, however, forges his own mirror–"a magical and symbolic mirror" that perfectly produces the indifference of mediacy and immediacy

---

[94] Ibid., 31. Schelling makes a similar point in the Introduction to the *Weltalter* fragments. See F.W.J. Schelling, *The Ages of the World*, trans. Jason M. Wirth (Albany: SUNY Press, 2000), xxxviii.

characteristic of the speculative standpoint. The philosopher strives in vain to replicate this Swedenborgian miracle. Ultimately and belatedly, she must choose between two inferior substitutes–*death or the dialectic.*

In the Introduction, I suggested that at issue in the language of speculation and reflection pulsing through Hegel and Schelling's work is the type of mirroring activity to which thoughts, feelings and visions are to be subjected. Such mediation must manage to keep the philosopher face to face with her material, free from falsification. Moreover, implicitly for Hegel and very explicitly (as I have argued) for Schelling, this question of the kind of mirror to be silvered leads directly to an interrogation of the very personality of the philosopher herself. The art of immediacy emerges out of a speculative form of life–those pre-philosophical, pre-textual practices that make one a speculative, rather than a reflective philosopher. What is more, the preceding has shown the significance of *mystical forms of life* for Schelling's depiction of the speculative philosopher.

The question is, therefore, not merely: who dares to face experience in a mirror–the philosopher or the mystic (as Schelling asks of Böhme)? Nor is it merely: which of them silvers a mirror capable of bearing the glare of experience? But more critically still: *who* are these philosophers and mystics–what breed of silverer are they? Schelling confronts the mystic with the challenge: who are you to do what you do?–just as we must challenge Schelling. And as a result of this challenge, he goes on to appropriate much from the mystic, even if (as is always the case in Schelling's post-1809 output) such appropriation is channelled through indirections and feints. Schelling learns from the mystic's failure, from the mystic's inimitable success, as well as from what can still be imitated. He plunders the mystical text, as he plundered vocabularies, styles and concepts throughout his career. Schelling's systematic eclecticism devours everything in the formation of the absolute system. He leaves nothing out–the mystical text included.[95] The impure

---

[95] This would give further significance to the remark attributed to Schelling from the 1820s, "If this Tafel [a Swedenborg scholar] could get Swedenborg into a system, that would be something!" See further Horn, *Schelling and Swedenborg*, 2. On systematic eclecticism, see Whistler, *Schelling's Theory of Symbolic Language*, Chapter Eleven.

mixture of the Schellingian dialectic is emblematic of this, cobbling together mystic intuition, conceptual analysis and scientific experimentation.

And yet in *Clara* the dialectic is only invoked under a veil of melancholy as an inferior surrogate for those neither inspired by mystic vision nor brave enough to die. In the wake of Caroline's death, Schelling surveys the prospects for those unlucky enough to have no sustained connection to the departed (whether in life, like Swedenborg, or though death)[96] and what remains is the dialectic. So, for the sake of the absolute system (and so the rational reconstruction of the spirit world), the philosopher must mournfully and regretfully carry on salvaging the scattered shards of mysticism.

ACKNOWLEDGEMENTS

Substantive comments from Nicola Masciandaro and Eugene Thacker improved this piece considerably (note 53, in particular, was born directly from their comments); Oliver Smith helped me hone in on what was of most interest in Schelling's critique of Böhme.

WORKS CITED

Beierwaltes, Werner. *Platonismus und Idealismus*. Frankfurt am Main: Klostermann, 1972.
Beiser, Frederick C. *German Idealism: The Struggle against Subjectivism 1781-1801*. Cambridge, MA: Harvard University Press, 2002.
Brassier, Ray. *Nihil Unbound: Enlightenment and Extinction*. Basingstoke: Palgrave Macmillan, 2007.

---

[96] As Schelling writes to Louise Gotter on Caroline's death: "I am left with the constant pain that will be allayed by nothing but my own death... God gave her to me, and death cannot steal her from me. *She will be mine again*, or rather, she is still mine during this brief separation." Quoted and translated in Horn, *Schelling and Swedenborg*, 22.

Brown, Robert. *The Later Philosophy of Schelling: The Influence of Böhme on Schelling's Works of 1809-15.* Lewisburg: Bucknell University Press, 1977.

Deleuze, Gilles. *Cinema II: The Time-Image.* Translated by Hugh Tomlinson and Robert Galeta. London: Athlone, 1999.

Düsing, Klaus. "Spekulation und Reflexion: Zur Gesammenarbeit Schellings und Hegels in Jena." *Hegel-Studien* 5 (1969): 95-128.

Engels, Friedrich. "Anti-Schelling." http://www.marxists.org/archive/marx/works/1841/anti-schelling/index.htm. Last accessed: 09/12/12.

Gasché, Rodolphe. *The Tain of the Mirror: Derrida and the Philosophy of Reflection.* Cambridge, MA: Harvard University Press, 1986.

Grant, Iain Hamilton. *Philosophies of Nature after Schelling.* London: Continuum, 2006.

Hegel, G.W.F. *The Difference between Fichte's and Schelling's System of Philosophy.* Translated by H.S. Harris and Walter Cerf. Albany: SUNY Press, 1977.

Hegel, G.W.F. *Phenomenology of Spirit.* Translated by A.V. Miller. Oxford: Oxford University Press, 1977.

Hegel, G.W.F. and F.W.J. Schelling. "The Critical Journal of Philosophy: Introduction on the Essence of Philosophical Criticism Generally and its Relationship to the Present State of Philosophy in Particular." In George di Giovanni and H.S. Harris (eds.), *Between Kant and Hegel: Texts in the Development of Post-Kantian Idealism.* Albany: SUNY Press, 1985. 272-91.

Holz, Harold. *Spekulation und Faktizitat: Zum Freiheitsbegriff in des mittleren und späten Schelling.* Bonn: Bouvier, 1970.

Horn, Friedemann. *Schelling and Swedenborg: Mysticism and German Idealism.* Translated by George F. Dole. West Chester, PA: Swedenborg Foundation, 1997.

Hyppolite, Jean. *Logic and Existence.* Translated by Leonard Lawlor and Amit Sen. Albany: SUNY Press, 1997.

Kant, Immanuel. *Dreams of a Spirit-Seer.* In *Theoretical Philosophy 1755-1770,* edited and translated by David Walford. Cambridge: Cambridge University Press, 1992. 301-60.

Lacoue-Labarthe Philippe and Jean-Luc Nancy. "Le dialogue des genres." *Poétique* 21 (1975): 148-75.

Mayer, Paola. *Jena Romanticism and its Appropriation of Böhme.* Montreal: McGill University Press, 1999.

Meillassoux, Quentin. *After Finitude.* Translated by Ray Brassier. London: Continuum, 2009.

Nasr, Seyyed Hossein. "Theoretical Gnosis, Doctrinal Sufism and
their Significance Today." *Transcendent Philosophy* 6 (2005): 1-
35.
O'Regan, Cyril. *The Heterodox Hegel.* Albany: SUNY Press, 1994.
Ramey, Joshua and Daniel Whistler. "The Physics of Sense: Bruno,
Schelling, Deleuze." In Alain Beaulieu, Edward Kazarian and
Julia Sushytska (eds.), *Gilles Deleuze and Metaphysics.* Lexington,
MA: Lexington, 2013. 87-109.
Schelling, F.W.J. *Werke.* 14 volumes. Edited by K.F.A. Schelling.
Stuttgart: Cotta, 1856-61.
Schelling, F.W.J. *Philosophical Inquiries into the Nature of Human
Freedom.* Translated by James Gutmann. La Salle: Open
Court, 1936.
Schelling, F.W.J. *Briefe und Dokumente.* 3 volumes. Edited by Horst
Fuhrmans. Bonn: Bouvier, 1962-75.
Schelling, F.W.J. *On University Studies.* Translated by E.S. Morgan.
Athens, OH: University of Ohio Press, 1966.
Schelling, F.W.J. *Philosophie der Offenbarung 1841/42.* Edited by
Manfred Frank. Frankfurt am Main: Suhrkamp, 1977.
Schelling, F.W.J. *Bruno, or On the Natural and Divine Principle in
Things.* Translated by Michael G. Vater. Albany: SUNY Press,
1984.
Schelling, F.W.J. *Ideas for a Philosophy of Nature.* Trans. Errol E.
Harris and Peter Heath. Cambridge: Cambridge University
Press, 1988.
Schelling, F.W.J. *Philosophy of Art.* Translated by Douglas W. Stott.
Minneapolis: University of Minnesota Press, 1989.
Schelling, F.W.J. *On the History of Modern Philosophy.* Translated by
Andrew Bowie. Cambridge: Cambridge University Press,
1994.
Schelling, F.W.J. *Stuttgart Seminars.* In *Idealism and the Endgame of
Theory: Three Essays,* edited and translated by Thomas Pfau.
Albany: SUNY Press, 1994. 195-243.
Schelling, F.W.J. *The Ages of the World.* Translated by Jason M.
Wirth. Albany: SUNY Press, 2000.
Schelling, F.W.J. *Presentation of my System of Philosophy.* Translated
by Michael G. Vater. *Philosophical Forum* 32.4 (2001): 339-71.
Schelling, F.W.J. *Clara or, On Nature's Connection to the Spirit World.*
Translated by Fiona Steinkamp. Albany: SUNY Press, 2002.
Schelling, F.W.J. *Introduction to the System of a Philosophy of Nature.*
In F.W.J. Schelling, *First Outline of a System of the Philosophy of*

Nature. Translated by Keith R. Peterson. Albany: SUNY Press, 2004. 193-232.

Schelling, F.W.J. *The Grounding of Positive Philosophy: The Berlin Lectures.* Translated by Bruce Matthews. Albany: SUNY Press, 2007.

Swedenborg, Emanuel. *Heaven and Hell: Drawn from Things Heard and Seen.* Translated by George F. Dole. West Chester, PA: Swedenborg Foundation, 2000.

Thacker, Eugene. *After Life.* Chicago: University of Chicago Press, 2010.

Tilliette, Xavier. *Schelling: Biographie.* Paris: Calmann-Lévy, 1999.

Toscano, Alberto. "Fanaticism and Production: On Schelling's Philosophy of Indifference." *Pli* 8 (1999): 46-70.

Whistler, Daniel. *Schelling's Theory of Symbolic Language: Forming the System of Identity.* Oxford: Oxford University Press, 2013.

White, Alan. *Schelling: An Introduction to the System of Freedom.* New Haven: Yale University Press, 1983.

Daniel Whistler is Lecturer in Philosophy at the University of Liverpool. He is author of *Schelling's Theory of Symbolic Language: Forming the System of Identity* (OUP, 2013), as well as co-editor of *After the Postsecular and the Postmodern: New Essays in Continental Philosophy of Religion* (CSP, 2010) and *Moral Powers, Fragile Beliefs: Essays in Moral and Religious Philosophy* (Continuum, 2011).

SOPHIA WITHIN, WITHOUT SOPHIA, WHITHER SOPHIA: THE LONGING OF PHILIP K. DICK

Aron Dunlap & Joshua Ramey[1]

"Tired of lazy tastebuds?" Runciter said in his familiar gravelly voice. "Has boiled cabbage taken over your world no matter how many dimes you put into your stove? Ubik changes all that; Ubik wakes up food flavor, puts hearty taste back where it belongs, and restores fine food smell . . . One invisible puff-puff whisk of economically priced Ubik banishes compulsive obsessive fears that the entire world is turning into clotted milk, worn-out tape recorders and obsolete iron-cage elevators, plus other, further, as-yet-unglimpsed manifestations of decay. You see, world deterioration of this regressive type is a normal experience of many half-lifers, especially in the early stages when ties to the real reality are still very strong. A sort of lingering universe is retained as a residual charge, experienced as a pseudo environment but highly unstable and unsupported by any ergic substructure. This is particularly true when several memory systems are fused, as in the case of you people. But with today's new, more-powerful-than-ever Ubik, all this is changed!"[2i]

---

[1] In the following text, Arabic numerals refer to our commentarial footnotes and Roman numerals refer to the bibliographic endnotes.

[2] Where are we? Whither Sophia? Characters do not find themselves, in the novels of Philip K. Dick, at the level of a reality that can be accepted as real, but are constantly attempting to attain to that real, to follow an Ariadne's thread back to something that could be counted on not to lie. Dick's great characters are under the influence—of a drug, a demiurge, or a web of illusions—and salvation is an effort to unravel this web or wait out the drug trip—even if it means becoming a stone for three million years (as in *The Three Stigmata of Palmer Eldritch*) or killing the demiurge. All to get back to the (really) real. But as debased as this second power reality may be, the key to getting back to the real is only found

187

from within the artificial world, the realm of lies–the realm, as *Valis* has it, of the "black prison." We might say that the story of salvation for Philip K. Dick is never a story but always a conundrum, in that one is forced to find the key to the real in the realm of the lie.

But how could anything found in the black prison lead to the truth? Every time the key is found, it is not the real key, but simply another step towards an ever-receding real key and the real, good world. Dick's novels always show us prisons that can be escaped from, but only into other prisons, like the escape, through Ubik, from tasteless real food into artificially satisfying false nutrition.

But when the real is reached within the illusion, death is near. When Sophia, the fifth and final savior to appear in *Valis*, is finally found she must immediately die, and send her seekers on yet another endless quest. What Dick's conundrums reveal is that all worlds–real worlds, fantasy worlds, illusory worlds, ephemeral worlds–are equally cracked, equally marked by a kind of wobble in their being, a smudge in their smooth reflective surface. Should you wish to depart from a given world, or should you find yourself forced out of it, your conduit must be that crack; follow it and you find yourself in a different world, but one that, inasmuch as it is defined by the element that sets it askew, is depressingly identical to the one you just left.

This second power of reality, the power of the black prison, is archetypically understood as a man, separated or divorced from a beautiful woman and perhaps some beautiful children, living out his days in some kind of exile, surrounded by a barren landscape where plants do not thrive and, where, in the words of the Sumerian *Descent of Inanna,* "ass does not lie with ass, nor man with maiden." This man is driven to find the key to return to a world in which a woman awaits and desires him and the earth flourishes.

While the protagonist must often follow the trace that is the wobble in his world, Dick's literary offerings, taken in and of themselves, have their own kind of wobble, which is the trace that Dick left for himself. It is often apparent as a kind of sophomoric philosophizing that Dick eventually made a monument to in his recently re-published *Exegesis.* The following passage is taken from *The Three Stigmata of Palmer Eldritch.* We've de-italicized the wobble.

"Its very simple Mayerson; I'll give you a translation world in which you're a rotting corpse of a run-over dog in some ditch—think of it: whatta goddam relief it'll be. You're going to be me; you are me, and Leo Bulero is going to kill you. That's that dead dog, Mayerson; that's the corpse in the ditch." And I'll live on, he said to himself. That's my gift to you, and remember: in German Gift *means poison. I'll let you die in my place a few months from now and that monument on Sigma 14-B will be erected but I'll go on, in your living body."*[3ii]

Within time, hyperuniverse II remains alive: "The Empire never ended." But in eternity, where the hyperuniverses exist, she has been killed—of necessity—by the healthy twin of hyperuniverse I, who is our champion. The One grieves for this death, since the One loved both twins; therefore the information of the Mind consists of a tragic tale of the death of a woman, the undertones of which generate anguish into all the creatures of the hologramatic universe without their knowing why. This grief will depart when the healthy twin undergoes mitosis and the "Kingdom of God" arrives. The machinery for this transformation—the procession within time from the Age of Iron to the Age of Gold—is at work now; in eternity it is already accomplished.[4iii]

---

[3] This bit of amateur etymology doesn't seem to add anything to the wonderfully disorienting plot that centers the novel, but the eruption of this jarring voice always leads us back to Dick himself and to his insuperable conundrum. This voice is for our disturbed author a trail of breadcrumbs so he can find himself again. The monstrous *Exegesis* is precisely Dick's concentrated effort to find himself apart from the literary artifacts he left us. This attempt to philosophize himself out of this world, hot on the trail of meaning, mirrors the attempts of his characters to set their world aright, or return (or find) their real reality. While this hurts the purely literary character of Dick's works—even his best books are cracked in this way—Dick is always true to his voracious lust for truth.

The defining truth of his work is that there is no world that is not cracked, and the voice which utters this truth is itself breaking.

[4] Even though it appears from this quotation as if "all things are well" for the One that dwells in eternity, the crack is apparent in even this world, the very sphere of God, inasmuch as it was of necessity that the woman died. Even if she should be reborn again via mitosis what would stop her from of necessity dying again?

Which is of course exactly the plot-line followed by *Valis*: the savior is born again, but must die again, and there is no end for this cycle. Dick's *Exegesis* is perhaps the purest rendering of obsessive machinations we have: new, uncracked worlds are generated at a phenomenal speed and are just as quickly shown to be faulty–"puzzled" as Dick would say–and to thus necessitate the creation of a new world, this time the right one . . .

That Sophia and her avatars must die is a theme that takes different forms in *Valis*, in which quite a few women die for not very good reasons. Horselover Fat's friend Gloria, with whose suicide the book begins, and Fat's ex-wife Beth (who doesn't die, but who, if we can sympathize with Fat, perhaps should have) are versions of the Sophianic "woman" who must die for the Kingdom of God to achieve touch-down. In *Valis* the character of Fat is helplessly attracted to helping such women, noting that the only things standing in the way of him and psychological health are dope and trying to help people. Since he actually gives up dope after his (second) suicide attempt we can assume that it is precisely women like Gloria, Beth and Sherri (Fat's friend who dies of cancer) who are his only and perpetual obstacle. We are shown little evidence that they will be overcome as easily as the dope was.

These women are variations on Sophia, who herself was, for Dick, psychologically rooted in his twin sister, Jane, who died days after birth and for whose death Dick blamed himself for much of his life. From an analytic perspective, the girl Sophia (in *Valis*) who gets killed by "Mini"–as Dick was when his sister was alive–has its predictable obverse in the devouring females (Gloria *et al*) who are blamed with all such violent appropriations: if someone gets eaten up, it's the girl that's to blame. We might call this a psychological symptom that poisons the universe of the text. Dick was no doubt aware of this, and the importance of *Valis* lies in his depiction of the losing battle he wages to delimit it in both his character and his writing. *Valis* is Dick saying: "I know I am crazy. I am trying not to be. I am losing."

Admittedly, psycho-biography is a dangerous method. In Dick's case, though, his own psychic history is woven into his texts in a way that one simply can't ignore. In *Valis*, his most personal novel, Dick himself is a character, the narrator and Fat's shadow, and Horselover Fat is of course just a multi-lingual pun on his own name. Thus, we are forced to analyze him as we interpret his text, because of the unhealthy lack of separation between the person Dick and his own literary offsprings. This is perhaps a way for Dick to score some free therapy, he being often quite as poor as *Ubik's* Joe Chip, who cannot even pay his front door to open (does there exist a better, more sad and more hilarious, image of the paranoid genius?). Dick, both author and narrator, is an exemplar of the over-analyzed obsessive, of whom we cannot say, as Lacan said of (the psychotic) Joyce, that he healed himself through writing. In fact, Dick may have done just the opposite.

The characters in *Valis* are, more than in any other of Dick's major works, walking archetypes. We have the polarization between belief and doubt (cynicism rather) embodied in David and Kevin, respectively. Then there is the aforementioned devouring female that takes form in the three women: Sherri, Gloria, and Beth, (and projected in an inverted fashion onto the child Sophia). It is Dick's anxiety concerning his habit of projecting his own guilt about the death of his sister onto his Sophianic characters that causes him to repeat this infantile devouring by having Mini destroy Sophia before she can lose her innocence, before she can become the devouring one. We must, of course, set aside the fact that this episode makes very little sense in the context of the story– how could this all-powerful creature, this fifth savior come to earth, be killed by a stupid accident?

What is truest in the world of Dick–and he always claimed to be only writing about Truth–is that the quest for personal salvation, as we see it undertaken by Fat, is precisely psychotic. The fact that Dick/Fat is helplessly motivated by this quest and that he *loses*, is his testament to our age, and to our need to finally understand that Christianity as a religion of love *cannot* also be a religion of personal salvation. And yet to turn to some kind of theory of corporate salvation (mankind is a person, *à la* Dick's beloved Meister Eckhart) is also a false path–in fact it is the path of the school of Idealism that perhaps had its birth in Eckhart's thought, and no doubt its apotheosis in the victory of Hegel's World Spirit). Christianity as personal salvation is psychosis. Christianity as corporate salvation is fascism. The "black prison" that defines Dick's *oeuvre* is a topographical object, like a Klein bottle or a cross cap, where the interior is a schizophrenic mind (absolute duality), but whose exterior is an alternate universe in which Hitler was victorious and all the world has only gained its

191

"One of these days," Joe said wrathfully, "people like me will rise up and overthrow you, and the end of tyranny by the homeostatic machine will have arrived. The day of human values and compassion and simple warmth will return, and when that happens someone like myself who has gone through an ordeal and who genuinely needs hot coffee to pick him up and keep him functioning when he has to function will get the hot coffee whether he happens to have a poscred readily available or not." He lifted the miniature pitcher of cream, then set it down. "And furthermore, your cream or milk or whatever it is, is sour." [iv]

The big economic forces had managed to remain free, although virtually everything else had been absorbed by the Government. Laws that had been eased away from the private person still protected property and industry. The SP could pick up any given person, but they could not enter and seize a company, a business. That had been clearly established in the middle of the twentieth century . . . If he could get back to the Company, get inside its doors, he would be safe. Jennings smiled grimly. The modern church, sanctuary. It was the Government against the corporation, rather than the State against the Church. The new Notre Dame of the world. Where the law could not follow. [v]

"Don't look so unhappy," Jennings said. He folded his arms. "The paper's safe—and the Company's safe. When the time comes it'll be there, strong and very glad to help out the revolution. We'll see to that. All of us, you, me, and your daughter."

He glanced at Kelly, his eyes twinkling. "All three of us. And maybe by that time there'll be even more members to the family!" [5vi]

---

health (unity) at the expense of nazification. The inhabitants of this prison wander from one realm into the other, fleeing one evil only to run into the other.

[5] Thin as it may be there is always a trace that the Dickian hero must follow, a trace both impossible to ignore (one gives up everything to heed its call) and flatly treacherous, inasmuch we never see the trace pay off. The short story *Paycheck* is almost an anomaly in this regard, though, in that the promise of a life free and good is emphasized so strongly at the end of the story—in fact, a little too strongly; we suspect that Dick is being ironic and wicked. This is a story of a man who gives up his paycheck for seven trinkets, like a hell-bent Israelite deciding not only to escape

192

Tim said, "The anokhi is the pure consciousness of God. It is, therefore, Hagia Sophia, God's Wisdom. Only that wisdom, which is absolute, can read the Book of the Spinners. It can't change what is written, but it can discern a way to outwit the Book. The writing is fixed; it will never

---

but to despoil the Egyptians while he's at it. He has hired himself out to do top-secret work for the Rethrick construction, at the cost of them removing his memories of that time. The action, then, happens quite literally in the unconscious, in a two year span that has been removed from his brain, though a little scar remains. He has left the clues for himself in the seven trinkets: charms, instead of money. Here we see perhaps the only Dickian moral: no matter how hopeless the search for the real may be, how paltry the traces that link us to it, no matter how certain it is that our effort will end in failure, such a failure is to be desired absolutely against the falseness of the prison, the worse lure of the paycheck, the false sovereignty of money (i.e. a naïve belief in the surface effects of this world). This is both the only way our hero, Jennings, can survive and the only way the revolution can come off. When Jennings first took the contract he was merely motivated by the paycheck, but at the bottom of that selfishness he sees a way for the whole system to be derailed. The Egyptians must have trusted their neighbors to lend them their valuables. Jennings has absolute faith because he knows that he has already laid the successful plan for himself. This is the Sophianic aspect, God's wisdom of the end of things, of the end of the rule of money, and the rebirth of love and family and freedom. That's a very hard thing to say with a straight face. Dick is able to give his protagonist a ridiculous level of confidence because of what he has accomplished in his unconscious before he was even aware of the traces, and of his impending adventure. But in order to enact the courage of his unconscious decision, he must penetrate into the heart of the corporation that imprisons him, going all the way in, as Lacan says. This is the arch-feminine act, something a man could only undertake under the influence, of drugs, the unconscious, what have you. It is he himself, in the caring arms of his own unconscious, that is the new Notre Dame of the world.

One should be astounded at the end of *Paycheck*, not that Dick finishes with a wicked flourish, but that, like the worship of money, the true religion is also one in which the truth lies at the surface.

change." He seemed defeated, now; he had begun to give up. "I need that wisdom, Angel. Nothing less will do." [6vii]

---

[6] In *The Transmigration of Timothy Archer*, just as in *Valis*, the wisdom of God, Sophia, must take on a tangible form for the obsessing subject, in this case the one-time Episcopal bishop of the diocese of California, Timothy Archer, who gives up his bishopric to chase down the truth behind Jesus Christ. He is led to cryptic fragments left by the Zadokites, fragments which contain sayings of Christ—but hundreds of years before Jesus walked the earth. These documents supposedly point to a psychedelic mushroom, *anokhi*, behind the experience of being born again. *Anokhi*, Hebrew for "I Am," the name of God, but for Timothy Archer this utterance of spirit has been transformed into a fungus that can be found should one only look hard enough. His pursuit leads to an untimely death in the desert surrounding the Dead Sea where he was sure that the truth of the *anokhi* could be found.

In books like this (Dick's last) we see that Dick takes his profession quite literally, for he reveals therein *science as fiction*. Unlike the tenets of orthodox Christianity which demand that a spirit (God) became a human being (Jesus of Nazareth), with no leftover, no mystery "behind" the incarnation, Timothy Archer is neither a theologian—one who knows that the truth lies at the surface—nor a scientist—who knows that the phenomena are always concealing a truth that is makeshift and transient. Timothy Archer attempts to play the theologian *as* a scientist. Thus he loses his faith but cannot stop himself from his addiction to the meaning generated by that now dead faith. He goes in search of a Christ that he has already disproved to himself. Thus, in the end he gets neither meaning nor knowledge, neither religion nor science, both of which for him are fictions. There is nothing redemptive here. For all of Dick's spiritualizing there is no "hope of the other side"; there is, in fact, no truly other side. There is only the organic cravings of a biological organism and its interface with an endless stream of meaningless information that stands in for God. Dick's work is proof that we can doubt our doubt and cast an ineradicable suspicion not only on our gods, but also on the foundation of our knowledge. The fantasy worlds of PKD are exquisitely broken in a way that is determined by the mode of entrance to that world. The way in will make you rue your decision to come. As noted before, we believe these defects can be found on a continuum between the

"The instinct for survival loses in the end. With every living creature, mole, bat, human, frog. Even frogs who smoke cigars and play chess. You can never accomplish what your survival instinct sets out to do, so

---

psychosis of a debased Christianity-as-religion-of-personal-salvation, and a mystical Eckhartian notion of the progressive enlightenment of a corporate humankind (which immediately turns into a kind of fascism; hence, the recurrent theme of Hitler in so many of the novels, *The Man in the High Castle* being only the most developed version of this theme). The thread that connects the dual worlds in all of Dick's work, and what gives the best of those works their inimitable vertigiousness, is desire. Ironically enough, the most religious of the sci-fi giants had no conception of spirit. Dick never had a feel for the first tenet of Judeo-Christianity, namely, the difference between creator and creation (which perhaps explains the consistent motif of the pot and the potter in his late works, a motif which never seems to fit or make sense with a given narrative, but which has a powerful pull to it–Dick using this ancient Hebrew metaphor for the creator to fill in a gap that he felt, if only unconsciously). Aside from naked desire (for drugs, for release, for health, for just fading out . . .) the only faculty of the mind which is something other than stunted is the imagination–and it is bloated and rotten from the inside out. In a Cartesian universe where doubt is the pillar of all knowledge, once this doubt can be shown as doubtable (essentially Dick's *modus operandi)* the imagination can have no relief from the other mental faculties, from judgment or will, which depend for their functioning on the real presence of other people and cannot be verified in mental thought experiments. This is why Dick's worlds are always built on the model of a double prison that folds in on itself, perhaps best represented in *Ubik,* where the two worlds seem to be equally in danger of being attacked by a devouring presence, Jory, as well as the decomposition which the "half life" is meant to fend off. The substance Ubik, a god-like restorer of youth and vitality, is clearly on the defensive here, and what is truly ubiquitous is neither the evil of decay nor the good of rejuvenation but the eternal war between them. On the other hand, the Sophianic character in *Ubik* is uniquely positioned to challenge that eternal war. We will return to her later.

ultimately your striving ends in failure and you succumb to death, and that ends it. But if you can fade out and watch—"
"I'm not ready to fade out," Jason said.
"—you can fade out and watch with happiness, and with cool, mellow, alpha contentment, the highest form of contentment, the living on of one of those you love." viii

Final scene of the film version of Total Recall *(1990): Quaid: "I just has a terrible thought. . . What if this is all a dream?" Melina: "Then kiss me quick . . . before you wake up."*

And who doubts that, if we dreamt in company, and the dreams chanced to agree, which is common enough, and if we were always alone when awake, we should believe that matters were reversed? In short, as we often dream that we dream, heaping dream upon dream, may it not be that this half of our life, wherein we think ourselves awake, is itself only a dream on which the others are grafted, from which we wake at death, during which we have as few principles of truth and good as during natural sleep, these different thoughts which disturb us being perhaps only illusions like the flight of time and the vain fancies of our dreams? [7] ix

What a chimera then is man! What a novelty! What a monster, what a chaos, what a contradiction, what a prodigy! Judge of all things, imbecile worm of the earth; depositary of truth, a sink of uncertainty and error; the pride and refuse of the universe. [8] x

---

[7] Earth is Mars dreaming. It is our green planet which has been forgotten, and even though Mars is dusty and red, it harbors a life giving gift. Sophia is hidden in the dream within the dream for Dick. We are still smack dab in the middle of the Cartesian hallucination, redoubled now. Thus, Sophia can never be real for us. She must always hover at the edge, tempting incarnation. *We* are the feared demiurge and trickster god. *We* are the creators of this earth and the dream we're now suffering. Descartes wondered whether the world that God had created was real; we took the doubt for a surety and built a "rational" world instead, one that we now desperately need to be wakened from.

[8] Philosophically, one might say that Dick is reviving a crucial critique of Descartes that was articulated first by Pascal: It is possible to doubt our doubting, and this leaves us no stable foot to

I studied philosophy during my brief career at the University of California at Berkeley. I'm what they call an "acosmic pan-enthiest," which means that I don't believe that the universe exists. I believe that the only thing that exists is God and he is more than the universe. The universe is an extension of God into space and time. That's the premise I start from in my work, that so-called "reality" is a mass delusion that we've all been required to believe for reasons totally obscure.[9][xi]

We are served by organic ghosts, he thought, who, speaking and writing, pass through this our new environment. Watching, wise, physical ghosts from the full-life world, elements of which have become for us invading but agreeable splinters of a substance that pulsates like a former heart.[xii]

She laughed a rich warm laugh. "You're the other one," Joe said. "Jory destroying us, you trying to help us. Behind you there's no one, just as there's no one behind Jory. I've reached the last entities involved." Ella said

---

stand on–Dick's universe, in which there is no escape from Descartes' demonic trickster god.

[9] This quotation, taken from an interview, also concerns the black prison, which Dick was able to construct extemporaneously. On the one hand God is all that exists, and, according to Dick's acosmic pan-entheism the universe should be completely transparent to us, reflecting God's goodness with no need for theophanies. On the other hand this universe is a delusion, all the more imprisoning for its non-existence. The fact that it is a lie makes it impossible to brush aside, and out of this prison universe only the most insanely dedicated, the most drug addled or sick, are able to glimpse the truth before the truth eats away their mind. But which is it? Is the universe a (benign) extension of a loving God, or is it a prison that violently obscures from us the truth? Is there a God behind god? Without Sophia we perceive the universe to flicker between the two in a schizophrenia-inducing display. This is the same conundrum delineated earlier, that if this world is unreal there can exist no key within it that would illuminate the real one– and yet we are driven to believe that there must be. The thread that Dick follows, and that he gets us to follow in his books, is thinner than a spider's line, evaporating in the morning sun, crumbs eaten by unministering birds . . .

caustically, "I don't think of myself as an 'entity'; I usually think of myself as Ella Runciter. [10][xiii]

"Oh hell, yes. Christ, I just now bought it downstairs at the tobacco counter. We're a long way into this. Well past the stage of clotted milk and stale cigarettes." He grinned starkly, his eyes determined and bleak, reflecting no light. "In it," he said, "not out of it." [xiv]

& I accept my own aging now. & I have my two fine cats. I guess now I don't need my psychotic fantasy-system so much—but I treasure parts of it, esp[.] the love & the beauty—& her. My psychosis put me in touch with "das ewige weibliche" *[the eternal feminine] in me, & for that I will always be grateful; it means I will never really be alone again: whenever I really need her, I will sense her presence & hear her voice (i.e. St. Sophia.)*

---

[10] Dick's purest Sophianic vision is embodied in *Ubik*'s Ella Runciter. Mysteriously dead at the age of 20 and the wife of the powerful Glenn Runciter, she guides her husband's company whilst in the limbo of half-life. There, we find out at the end of the book, she has devoted herself to battling the eater of life, Jory, a perverted adolescent half-lifer who attacks other souls and incorporates them for no clear purpose beyond shits and giggles—a formidable and grotesque trickster. The most compelling part of Dick's Sophianic vision in this novel is Ella's creation of Ubik, a rejuvenating substance in a spray can which is the only possible protection against Jory's malevolence. Dick does not spell out the manner in which Ella was able to create this balm, but from a Sophianic standpoint we have to assume that it is because she herself was "there in the beginning" (Proverbs 8:22) with the creator of life and half-life as well. She is not an entity but Woman in all her forms. She is the opposite of the devourer and as she fades into (real) death she makes way for her successor, Joe Chip, to carry on the battle against, not death, but the forces of an accelerated and perverted dying. When Joe Chip's face shows up on the coins in Glenn Runciter's pocket in the "real" world we understand this as a suggestion that Ella's loyal fight in the nether regions of half-life are perhaps more real than the daily ups and downs in the realm of what we call reality. Dick found in Ella, perhaps, an end to his perpetual cycling, and his ever-reaching-further schizophrenia.

At the center of psychosis I encountered her: beautiful & kind & most of all, wise, & through that wisdom, accompanying & leading me through the underworld, through the bardo thödol *journey to rebirth–she, the embodiment of intelligence: Pallas Athena herself. So at the core of a shattered mind and life lies this epicenter–omphalos–of harmony and calm. I love her, she is my guide: the second comforter & advocate promised by Jesus . . . as Luther said, "For the very desperate," here in this world secretly, for their–our–sake.*[xv]

Halting his work he turned his attention on her, faced her levelly. Her expression was cool and intelligent, with a faintly mocking quality which was particularly rewarding and annoying. "Hello," Jack said.

"I saw your 'copter on the roof," the girl said.

"Let him work," Arnie said peevishly. "Gimme your coat." He stood behind her, helping her out of her coat. The girl wore a dark wool suit, obviously an import from Earth and therefore expensive to an appalling degree. I'll bet that set the Union pension fund back plenty, Jack decided.

Observing the girl, he saw in her a vindication of a piece of old wisdom. Nice eyes, hair, and skin produced a pretty woman. This girl had such a nose: strong, straight, dominating her features, forming a basis for her other features. Mediterranean women reach the level of beauty much more easily than, say, Irish or English women, he realized, because genetically speaking the Mediterranean nose, whether Spanish or Hebrew or Turkish or Italian, played a naturally greater part in physiognomic organization. His own wife Silvia had a gay, turned up Irish nose; she was pretty enough by any standard. But–there was a difference.

He guessed that Doreen was in her early thirties. And yet she possessed a freshness that gave her a stable quality. He had seen such clear coloration in high-school girls approaching nobility, and once in a long while one saw it in fifty-year-old women who had perfect gray hair and wide, lovely eyes. This girl would still be attractive twenty years from now, and probably had always been so; he could not imagine her any other way. Arnie, by investing in her, had perhaps done well with the funds entrusted to him; she would not wear out. Even now he saw maturity in her face, and that among women was rare.[11][xvi]

---

[11] In *Martian Time-Slip* (1964), Sophia is still in the symbolic. She has not yet slipped into the real. She wears the wool suit, she submits herself to the disgusting flesh of the capitalist, she drinks the cocktail, drapes herself over the proper arm. She is in and of the world. This is Lacan's feminine act, "all the way in" the

"The existential psychiatrists often say to let them go ahead and take their lives; it's the only way for some of them . . . the vision becomes too awful to bear."
> *Jack said nothing.*
> *"Is it awful?" Doreen asked.*
> *"No. Just—disconcerting." He struggled to explain. "There's no way you can work it in with what you're supposed to see and know; it makes it impossible to go on, in the accustomed way."*
> *"Don't you very often try to pretend, and sort of—go along with it, by acting? Like an actor?" When he did not answer, she said, "You tried to do it in there, just now."*
> *"I'd love to fool everybody," he conceded. "I'd give anything if I could go on acting it out, playing a role. But that's a real split—there's no split up until then; they're wrong they say it's a split in the mind. If I wanted to keep going entire, without a split, I'd have to lean over and say to Dr. Glaub—" He broke off.*
> *"Tell me," the girl said.*
> *"Well," he said, taking a deep breath, "I'd say, Doc, I can see you under the aspect of eternity and you're dead. That's the substance of the sick, morbid vision. I don't want it. I didn't ask for it."*
> *The girl put her arm within his.*[xvii]

"But," he said, "that's the whole point; it's designed to make you flee—the vision's for that purpose, to nullify your relations with other people, to isolate you. If it's successful, your life with human beings is over. That's what they mean when they say the term schizophrenia isn't a diagnosis; it's a prognosis—it doesn't say anything about what you have, only about how you'll wind up." And I'm not going to wind up like that, he said to himself. Like Manfred Steiner, mute and in an institution; I intend to keep my job, my wife and son, my friendships—he glanced at the girl holding on to his arm. Yes, and even love affairs, if such there be.
> *I intend to keep trying.*[xviii]

---

symbolic, an action so far from within, it is subversive precisely because it is without break in the seam of the symbolic.

But of course, Jack doesn't end up with Doreen. Doreen enables the passage to the action, enables Jack to kill Arnie. And Jack must return to his unhappy, or at least imperfect marriage.

Well, thinking about this, about how Zoroastrianism teaches that we are met by the spirit of our religion when we die, & if we are a son of light, she is "Jung und Schön" [Young and beautiful]. But if we are a servant of the lie she is a wrinkled old hag... I dream I heard the magic bell, and & see her in bird feathers—like Papagena*... I am even more 1) uneasy as to whether I am in the "live" world (lower realm) or the "next world" (upper realms); but 2) pleased at how ma'at has judged me. There has been, admittedly, a lot of pain (over [past women in his life]) but the reward element predominates; I feel better & better, &, what is equally important, seem to understand more & more, exponentially. I am no longer chronically depressed & apprehensive (terror stricken). I've written (I feel) my best book so far** My mind is alive & active. I feel I am growing & developing. I finally got Laura & Isa*** down here. I'm economically secure. I'm no longer abusing drugs, legal or illegal—i.e., drug dependent. I am very happy. I even went to France. I had a lot of fun with Joan.**** My career is gosh wow (due in good measure to my own—and Thomas'—efforts). So I may be dead, as of 3-74. My cosmological concepts are so terrific, so advanced as to be off the scale. I create whole religions and philosophical systems. The very fact that I honestly ponder if I may be dead & in heaven is prima facie evidence of how happy & fulfilled I am. How many people seriously wonder this? (Maybe everyone, when they die.) If I am not dead, how do I explain 2-3-74? No one has ever reported such obviously post mortem experiences.

Well, I explain it in terms of a two part oscillation comprising my total existence: (1) the part where I am alive and in this world & my sister is dead & an idea in my brain; & the other part where I am dead & she is alive & an idea in my brain; & 2) the other part where I am dead & she is alive & I am a thought in her living brain—& I construe this matter as a riddle posed to me by the designer of the computer: Holy Wisdom, who is playful. But how do I explain why all of this was revealed to me & to no one else? I have no explanation; I know what I know but not why. Unless, of course, when you die it's all revealed to you routinely—

Or—having a deceased twin sister makes me unusual: in symbiosis to a dead (sic) person, & in telepathic contact with her. Or maybe I'm just a genius. No, I'm not. But I am curious. I love epistemological riddles. & so now I've got one, a superb one. It's ultimate. Just theoretically, its formulation couldn't be beaten. I love it. I'll solve it.

I regard the two-proposition formulation about "am I alive or . . ." etc. as a brilliant application of the "UBIK" puzzle to my own self. But I can't take credit for formulating it; it was presented to me. Whoever the funning player is, she is a delight. Sophia, I think it is you.

One thing I must posit as absolutely veridical: the power of Karma over me was broken completely in 3-74. So at the very least, I am 1) dead to the way-of-being in the world I had known; & 2) alive to a new free way of being, & progressively more so. (1978)

*Character in Mozart opera THE MAGIC FLUTE
**The reference here is to VALIS, written in 1978.
***PKD's two daughters, by his third and fourth marriages, respectively. PDK had arranged for each of them to visit him at his Santa Ana condominium during this period.
****Joan Simpson [with whom PKD had a romantic relationship in 1977] [12xix]

---

[12] More and more, the writing becomes autistic, self-enclosed. Hermetic. The characters start to lose their draw, their pull, as they are all pulled into the man. We lose PKD, or we start to lose PKD the moment he needs to live in his own dream. The moment he needs full resolution, full inclusion of himself within the godhead. Full communion with his dead sister, by identifying himself fully with her. But the cost of full and ideal identification with the sister is the full and complete split of PKD into two parts, into two halves. The becoming-gnostic of PKD. Not that he is suddenly converted to Zoroastrianism or Neoplatonism or Gnosticism. But rather that he becomes these things, he becomes the "binary computer" that sees itself as macrocosmic. And of course he wonders if it is real, if it really happened. Well of course it is real, of course it really happens. And yes, effectively, he dies. He loses his desire. His life gets cleaned up, he cleans up his act. His desire gets internalized, like Carl Jung retiring to build his tower. The self trying to include everything within itself. The self demanding satisfaction, and finally finding it.

"*Post mortem* experiences," indeed. "Two part oscillation": the one internalizing the other. What happened here? Was death internalized? Does the mystic take in the whole world, and lose his soul, or lose at least the ability to communicate—to shop for groceries, pay the bills, show up on time? Passing over into a self-with-self oscillation? To whom is Dick, at the end, speaking? To whom is he appealing? To whom are any of us speaking? "Admired in France." France, land of endless talk, land of *parler*. Where they dream of having the capability for such madness, such passion, such life.

But if we put PKD in the clinic, Lacan's or anyone else's, that is because it is where we have ended up–we, whoever we are, in the line of Burroughs, Kerouac, Henry Miller, D.H. Lawrence, maybe back as far as Donne, Petrarch, Augustine himself. A line of broken Western men, broken knights, wounded savants. The search for the lost Sophia, the search for the Self, the Soul. For She who is everywhere, everything. Elusive, untraceable. Driving crazy a line from knights errant to dead young rock stars, all longing and desperation and pale skin.

***

A legend: three men are sitting in a café, talking. They are discussing, with great seriousness, passion, and sincerity, some of the fundamental problems of the world. They converse with transparency, intimacy, and forthrightness. They hold back no secrets, they harbor no hidden agendas. Their desire is for truth alone, for truth to be shared, understood, and hopefully, against all hope, for truth to become action, to become life and time. They bring years of experience and dedication and sacrifice to the table. Years of solitude and grief and wandering in deserts, but also years of earnest expectation, joy, and moments of beauty that have promised infinite fulfillment beyond the charade of the world. You can see this in their eyes as they converse. This is no secret cabal, no private club. This is a conversation that should be, that wants to be, and that even is in principle open to any interlocutor, any listener, anyone in earnest.

Just beyond the three men, at the next table, is a beautiful dark-skinned woman. She is dressed in the most contemporary fashions, more glamorous, and yet more attentive to her surroundings than anyone else, man or woman, in the café. She seems to know nearly everyone by name. She even knows one of the men engaged in the serious conversation about the deepest, darkest problems of the world. She keeps staring at the man she knows. The man acknowledges her smile, looks her in the eyes several times. But she will not stop staring, stop smiling. Her gaze becomes rigid, fixed. There is something wrong. The man gets up, leaves the important conversation, and engages the beautiful dark-skinned woman in conversation. She remembers everything he ever told her, though it was years ago that they last spoke. She asks after his career, his son, his troubled marriage. The man does not remember anything about the woman, but asks anyway, trying to offer something resembling her intensity and enthusiasm.

Sensing he is trying to return to his conversation, his work, she desperately searches for more news to relate, something that would be relevant to the man steeped in such a serious conversation with his colleagues, his friends. She knows the man is a philosopher. She tells him she took a class once on the Italian philosopher, Vattimo. It was in 1990. The man suddenly realizes the woman must be much older than she seems, than her beauty and glowing skin betray. Finally the man tears himself away, makes it back to the table, the earnest, important exchange of ideas and communion of souls. The man can see that the woman has begun to talk to herself, to laugh to herself, or at her own thoughts. Or is she overhearing the important conversation, the big ideas, the ambitious theorems, the audacious hypotheses. Is she laughing at us? he wonders. Her laughter seems filled with pain. She was not like this, two years ago, when we met, he thinks to himself. I wonder what happened. I wonder if she is alone. I wonder if she was on meds and stopped taking them. I wonder if the others here in the café like her, tolerate her, know her, protect her, care for her, or if some other more sinister modality of human relation obtains between them. She seems to know everyone. But then she tries to stop another man who is just leaving, and he says he is just leaving.

Finally, mercifully, she goes outside to smoke a cigarette, leaving the three earnest men, our modest trinity, to their holy conversation, their intimate communion, their eternal peace of earnest talk. The men finally leave, one his way and two on theirs. Of the two, the man who knew her is guilt-stricken. Should he have brought her to the table? At one point she had nearly shouted to the man, "your son is French and American, isn't he?" "Yes, he is," the man smiles. What would have happened if she were brought to the table? Instead she waited outside smoking. When the man left, with his friend, he passed her on the opposite corner, pretending not to see her.

Filled with shame and horror and wonder, the trinity moves on to its next occasion of grace. Meanwhile the neglected woman, sick with grief, sick with drugs or loneliness or longing, sick with the problems of the world, waits to be taken home. What would have happened if the men had talked to her instead of talking to

God manifested himself to me as the infinite void; but it was not the abyss; it was the vault of heaven, with blue sky and wisps of white clouds. He was not some foreign God but the God of my fathers. He was loving and kind and he had personality. He said, "You suffer now in life; it is little compared with the great joys, the bliss that awaits you. Do you think I in my theodicy would allow you to suffer greatly in proportion to your reward?" He made me aware, then, of the bliss that would come; it was infinite and sweet. He said, "I am the infinite, I will show you. Where I am, infinity is, there I am. Construct lines of reasoning by which to understand your experience in 1974. I will enter the field against their shifting nature. You think they are logical but they are not; they are infinitely creative."

I thought a thought and then an infinite regression of theses and countertheses came into being. God said, "Here I am, here is infinity." I thought another explanation; again an infinite series of thoughts split off in dialectical antithetical interaction. God said, "Here is infinity; here I am." I thought, then an infinite number of explanations, in succession, that

---

themselves, about themselves? Would she have been too crazy to contribute? Would she have known the magic word? Would her inclusion have been the action the conversation was apparently about? Or is this only the form Sophia takes if she lets herself apparently be seen? Is Sophia only radiant, whole, wise, as long as she remains invisible, subtle, the substance of the conversation itself, the evidence of things unseen? Can Sophia only show up in the flesh as perverse, or as schizoid, as a drunk or a whore or just as unmanageable? Or can she never appear? Or is She somehow both the unhealable wound and the healing words, the force driving both men and women on, ever on, to whatever well of healing there may be–the next pill or nightclub or Philip K. Dick novel? Or is She the longing with which they long to but cannot hope to heal each other, at least not in time, never in time?

Amphilotropic. We coin this concept. This is the name of that which can be shared. Am, as in amphibian. Phil, as in love, or PKD. O, as in the null set, the emptiness. Or as in O Brother, Where Art Thou? Tropic, as in tending to create places or dimensions. This is a seal that cannot be broken, unless it is in the name of love, but then if it is broken in the name of love, it continues. Continues to respond, break, respond, break, respond, break, respond, break . . . have we lost count yet?

explained 2-3-74; each single one of them yielded up an infinite progression of flipflops, of theses and antithesis, forever. Each time, God said, "Here is infinity. Here, then, I am." I tried for an infinite number of times; each time an infinite regress was set off and each time God said, "Infinity. Hence I am here." Then he said, "Every thought leads to infinity, does it not? Find one that doesn't." I tried forever. All led to an infinitude of regress, of the dialectic, of thesis, antithesis, and new synthesis. Each time, God said, "Here is infinity; here am I. Try again."

. . .

"You cannot be YHWH Who You say You are," I said. Because YHWH says, 'I am that which I am,'" or, 'I shall be that which I shall be.' And you—"

"Do I change?" God said. "Or do your theories change?"

"You do not change," I said. My theories change. You, and 2-3-74, remain constant."

"Then you are Krishna playing with me," God said.

"Or I could be Dionysus," I said, "pretending to be Krishna. And I wouldn't know it; part of the game is that I, myself, do not know. So I am God, without realizing it. There's a new theory!" And at once an infinite regress was set off; perhaps I was God and the "God" who spoke to me was not.

"Infinity," God said. "Play again. Another move."

"We are both Gods," I said, and another infinite regress was set off.

"Infinity," God said.

"I am you and you are you," I said. "You have divided ourself into two to play against yourself. I, who am one half, do not remember, but you do. As it says in the GITA, as Krishna say to Arjuna, 'we have both lived many lives, Arjuna; I remember them but you do not.'" And an infinite regress was set off; I could well be Krishna's charioteer, his friend Arjuna, who does not remember his past lives.

"Infinity," God said.

"I cannot play to infinity," I said. "I will die before that point comes."

"Then you are not God," God said. "But I can play throughout infinity; I am God. Play."

"Perhaps I will be reincarnated," I said. "Perhaps we have done this before, in another life." And an infinite regress was set off.

"Infinity," God said. "Play again."

"I am too tired," I said.

"Then the game is over."

"After I have rested—"

"You rest!" God said. "George Herbert" wrote of me:

Yet let him keep the rest,
But keep them with repining restlessnesse.
Let him be rich and wearie, that at least,
If goodness leade him not, yet wearinesse
May tosse him to my breast.

"Herbert wrote that in 1633," God said. "Rest and the game ends."
"I will play on," I said, "after I rest. I will play until I die of it."
"And then you will come to me," God said. "Play."
"This is my punishment," I said, "that I play, that I try to discern if
it was you in March of 1974." And the thought came instantly, My
punishment or my reward; which? And an infinite series of thesis and
antithesis was set off.
"Infinity," God said. "Play again."
"What was my crime?" I said, "that I am compelled to do this?"
"Or your deed of merit," God said.
"I don't know," I said.
God said, "Because you are not God."
"But you know," I said. "Or maybe you don't know and you're trying
to find out." And an infinite regress was set off.
"Infinity," God said. "Play again. I am waiting." [xx]

Aron Dunlap is an assistant professor of liberal arts at Shimer College in Chicago. He works in the fields of Christian theology, psychoanalysis and literature and is currently finishing a book entitled *Lacan and Religion.* He also writes songs and performs with Good Dust.

Joshua Ramey is the author of *The Hermetic Deleuze: Philosophy and Spiritual Ordeal* (Duke University Press, 2012). His work on figures from Laruelle, Badiou, and Zizek to Warhol, Hitchcock, and Cronenberg has appeared in journals such as *Angelaki, SubStance, Political Theology, Discourse,* and *Journal for Religious and Cultural Theory.* He is currently co-translating François Laruelle's *Mystique Non-philosophique à l'usage des contemporains* for Palgrave-Macmillan Press, and is writing a monograph, *On Divination: Contingency, Metaphysics, and the Future of Speculation.* He teaches philosophy and writing at Haverford College.

[i] Philip K. Dick, *Ubik* (New York: Vintage Books, 1991), 127.

[ii] Philip K. Dick, *The Three Stigmata of Palmer Eldritch* (New York: Vintage Books, 1991), 205.

[iii] *Ubik*, 81-82.

[iv] Philip K. Dick, "Paycheck" (*Selected Stories of Philip K. Dick*, New York: Pantheon Books), 18-54.

[v] "Paycheck," 26.

[vi] "Paycheck," 54.

[vii] Philip K. Dick, *The Transmigration of Timothy Archer* (New York: Vintage Books, 1991), 208.

[viii] Philip K. Dick, *Flow My Tears, the Policeman Said* (New York: Vintage Books, 1993), 110.

[ix] Blaise Pascal, *Thoughts* (*Thoughts and Minor Works*, New York: P.F. Collier & Son, 1910), 145-146.

[x] Pascal, *Thoughts*, 147.

[xi] Philip K. Dick, "An Interview With America's Most Brilliant Science Fiction Writer," (http://www.philipkdick.com/media_aquarian.html, last accessed 2/21/13).

[xii] Philip K. Dick, *Ubik*, 213-214.

[xiii] Philip K. Dick, *Ubik*, 206.

[xiv] Philip K. Dick, *Ubik*, 182.

[xv] Philip K. Dick, *In Pursuit of Valis: Selections From the Exegesis of Philip K. Dick*, ed. Lawrence Sutin, (Lancaster, PA: Underwood-Miller, 1991), 37.

[xvi] Philip K. Dick, *Martian Time-Slip* (*Five Novels of the 1960's and 1970's*, ed. Johnathan Lethem (New York: Library of America, 2008), 90.

[xvii] Philip K. Dick, *Martian Time-Slip*, 98.

[xviii] Philip K. Dick, *Martian Time-Slip*, p. 100.

[xix] Philip K. Dick, *In Pursuit of Valis*, 39-41.

[xx] *In Pursuit of Valis*, 51.

THE VOICE OF THE MIRROR: STRANGE ADDRESS IN HILDEGARD OF BINGEN

Karmen MacKendrick

"YOU!" said the Caterpillar contemptuously. "Who are YOU?"
– Lewis Carroll, *Through the Looking Glass and What Alice Found There*

One might argue about whether the texts of Hildegard of Bingen (newly canonized, as of this May 10, as St. Hildegard) are properly mystical–at least insofar as the mystical text does not evade propriety altogether. Certainly Hildegard is a visionary, which is at least a nearby category. Many of her works, including perhaps the two best-known of her nine books (the *Scivias* and the *Book of Divine Works*), detail sets of visions she experienced (and, in some cases, beautifully illustrated as well). These visions come to Hildegard integrated with what she regards as divinely-inspired interpretation, however, and so the texts go on to provide such extensive exegesis that we might wonder whether any mystery at all can remain. I think that it can; occasionally in these texts, and still more in some of the songs on which so much of her current fame rests, we do find ideas and language turning about on themselves in those unexpected ways that reveal mystery, not by stripping it of its concealment, but precisely by showing us that not all is showable, or that the best ways of showing are sometimes indirect and elliptical. This may be as good a working definition of a mystical text as we are likely to find. I would like to focus here on one particular song, an antiphon to the Father from Hildegard's *Symphonia armonie celestium revelationum* (the Symphony of the Harmony of Celestial Revelation). I shall focus especially on the strangeness of address and indication that emerges within it. Hildegard's sense of divine address, of the way that "we" use "you" in relation to God, is unusual even among mystics, and in it her

209

musicality extends even more deeply and surprisingly than we would have thought.

The majority of Hildegard's songs are antiphons, meant to be sung before and after psalms, both hailing and responding (another third are responsoria, and it is probably not irrelevant that her songs so often enter into relation) (Newman in Hildegard, 1998, 13; Butcher, 2007, 24-25). This particular antiphon, addressed in its first line to the Father, is the first piece in the incomplete Dendermonde version of the *Symphonia*, the sixth in the larger Riesenkodex version. It is short enough to present here entirely:

> O magne Pater, / in magna necessitate sumus. / Nunc igitur obsecramus, / obsecramus te / per Verbum tuum, / per quod nos constituisti plenos / quibus indigemus. / Nunc placeat tibi, Pater, / quia te decet, / ut aspicias in nos / per adiutorium tuum, / ut non deficiamus, / et ne nomen tuum in nobis obscuretur, / et per ipsum nomen tuum / dignare nos adiuvare. (Hildegard, 1998, 104)

Barbara Newman offers us both poetic and literal translations of the song. Her sense of poetry is elegant, but to work as closely as we can with Hildegard, we might best turn to the more literal version:

> Great Father, / we are in great need! / Now then we beseech / we beseech you by your Word, / through which you created us full/ of the things we lack. / Now, Father, may it please you, / for it befits you, / to look upon us / and help us, / that we may not perish, / that your name be not darkened within us: / and by your own name, / graciously help us. (Hildegard, 1998, 105)

If we hadn't read Hildegard before, or if we weren't already inclined to be reading for mystery, we might be tempted to read this straightforwardly: we, a group of humans, ask another fairly anthropomorphic being (who can look, be pleased, assist, be addressed in parental terms, and so on) for assistance. But the more we look at this song, the stranger its request for assistance becomes, and the less tidy its divisions. Address and petition first become curiously blurred, the name fails to *be* named, and addressee and petitioner seem to turn about in a manner that renders the usual directionality of the *you* (and, accordingly, of the *we*) impossible to identify–without, however, identifying the two terms with each other.

I have argued elsewhere that prayer amplifies the element of address that we find throughout language, making it central even when the language may appear to be more descriptive or imperative. Divine names, particularly in prayer, are unusually vocative; that is, they call or draw more strongly than they point or describe (MacKendrick, 2008, 2011). This in itself is enough to make the language of prayer, including that of hymns and prayerful songs, a little strange. The strangeness of address here, however, runs more deeply and a little differently, in ways I hope to clarify.

The song opens with two modes of greatness that mirror each other as both image and opposite–the greatness of the father, the great need of the petitioner. Hildegard is fond both of mirroring (that is, of the use of these sorts of structures in which one phrase or image reflects another) and of the metaphor of the mirror as a description of the way in which we are the image of the divine– "All celestial harmony," she declares in her *Causes and Cures,* "is a mirror of divinity" (as epigraph, Hildegard 1998).[1] The symphonies of celestial harmony, then, are symphonies of the mirror of divinity. If the symphony provides something like an image, however indirectly, the songs must mirror the divine harmonies in their own. The symphony is not itself celestial harmony, but is rather the effort to come as near as we can to giving that harmony voice. Each song is a voice of the mirror. As this suggests, the reflection of the Father's greatness in the petitioners' need is neither singular nor simple; Hildegard's language evokes less a single figure gazing at its reflection than the dizzying recursion of an image in facing mirrors. The poetic structure itself repeats and redoubles in the words that open lines: *magne* and *magna,* then repetitions of *obsecramus, per, ut,* and *et.*

For Hildegard, this multiple gaze peers out from the very moment of creation, as she shows in her exegesis of the prologue to the fourth gospel in her visionary *Book of Divine Works.* She writes of the opening phrase "In the beginning was the Word," "I am the One by whom every reasonable being [i.e., every being that has

---

[1] The *Causes and Cures* is available in English translation by Priscilla Throop (Charlotte, VT: MedievalMS, 2008).

reason] draws breath." As the close affiliation here of reason and breath makes clear, Hildegard is typically medieval in her sense of the closeness of spirit and flesh–a point not irrelevant, as we shall see, to her use of language in song. "The body is the garment of the soul," she writes, "and it is the soul which gives life to the voice." The two together sing praise (Hildegard, in 1987, letter to the Prelates of Mainz, 358). From this breath of reason comes a stranger fusion still: "And so to gaze at my countenance I have created mirrors in which I consider all the wonders of my originality, which will never cease. I have prepared for myself these mirror forms so that they may resonate in a song of praise" (Hildegard, 1987, Vision 4, 128). The mirrors in which God delights in gazing, the mirrors that are creation itself, also, in a curious synaesthesia, delight resonantly in songs of praise–and the divine gaze upon a creation made in order to reflect strangely mirrors the delighted song of creation reflecting upon the maker who gazes. Even recursion, then, is not complex enough for a mirror so deeply synaesthetic and so causally complicated.

In this divine gaze at the wonder of mirrors that sing, delight is not neatly distinguished from desire–nor are the two, as I shall argue in more detail below, sharply distinguished in the Antiphon. We are reminded in Hildegard's exegesis–"I have prepared for myself these mirror forms so that they may resonate in a song of praise"–of the famous opening of Augustine's *Confessions,* in which he declares to a God for whom he is still searching that "to praise you is the desire of man, a little piece of your creation. You stir man to take pleasure in praising you, because you have made us for yourself" (Augustine, 1991, 1.1.1). This opening is full of desire, too, and of bafflement, as Augustine prays to find God without being sure how to look–and so, necessarily, without quite knowing where to address his prayer (see Mackey, 1997, especially 19). For neither Augustine nor Hildegard, however, is this praising function somehow a matter of reassuring an insecure God or stroking a divinely inflated ego. It is, rather, a resonant mirroring of a desire and a delight that amplify in complex ways: the desire and the delight of humanity amplify those of God and vice versa; desire amplifies delight, and vice versa again. As an invitation, resonance also demands silence: if I invite what resonates, I must give it the aural space, a perhaps contemplative place, in which to do so. The words of the song are those of desire requesting–*we beseech you*–but Word itself is given by and as the aim of the desire, by and as the

God sought (the exegeted prologue continues, "And the Word was with God, and the Word was God"). All words are called through the Word. Hildegard's Father has made humanity through words, through the means of beseeching God: "I spoke within myself my small deed, which is humanity," God declares in this same exegetical passage (Hildegard, 1987, Vision 4, 129). And God has made humanity so that they may make words: "Human beings were to announce all God's wondrous works by means of their tongues that were endowed with reason" (Hildegard, 1987, Vision 4, 122). But, as we shall see, for Hildegard there is an important qualification both to the divine creative voice and to the praising human one—they do not simply speak, but sing, and that will matter.

Making through the means, if not of desire itself, then at least of desire's expression, becomes stranger still as the song continues. Through the Word, we are *created . . . full of the things we lack.* And through words, we, in Hildegard's company, create anew the fullness implicit in this lack, create the expression of the desire and beseeching, an expression that is the creation of beseeching and the sustaining of desire. Language desires, and, at least sometimes, desire languages, is pulled into words (not always, to be sure: it may be precisely what stops our speaking, too, creating both the rushing flow of words and the stuttering gap).[2] Full of the things we lack, we are not only full of lacking, or empty of fullness, but also possess that fullness of which, and by which, we are dispossessed, the fullness of delighted desire. The words by which we beseech are our words, too. We give back not simply *what* we were given (words in desirous song), but that *by which* we *are* given—words, through Word itself. We give our own givenness, because we are given in desire (the divine desire to delight in the song of its own countenance), full of the things that we lack, given by the fullness of the words by which that lack takes on a fullness of its own. Here too Augustine echoes in Hildegard's thought. For him we may be given over, in memory or in the commitment of desire, to a God we nonetheless cannot fully find or grasp.

Even without its synaesthetic element, this is an entanglement too deep for simple reciprocity. That is, we cannot simply say,

---

[2] For a much longer and more involved meditation on this curious duality, see the chapter "Fold" in my *Word Made Skin: Figuring Language at the Surface of Flesh* (New York: Fordham, 2004).

"God makes us by verbal means, and we sing God a song back." We do not reciprocate in the sense of an economic exchange but rather, like those singing mirrors, resonate, reverberate. There is a great deal of mutual implication already in these opening lines, especially when they are set in the greater context of Hildegard's work: delight and desire, word and Word, praise and gaze, praise and petition, mirror and song, sight and audition.

Other puzzles remain in this strange little song. What, especially, are we asking (for)? Aside from repeated but interestingly open requests for help or aid, two requests are specified, though it is not clear how distinct they may be from one another: that we may continue to be, and that we may read internally the divine name: *that we may not perish, that your name be not darkened within us.* The name to which we call in prayerful song is the name within us, then—and as the metaphor of darkness (or obscurity) suggests, it is a name not just sounded, but written: read aloud, perhaps, since we need light (not-darkness) to call it. In its sounding and its inscription, we are both made and sustained, created and kept from perishing. If we are full of the things that we lack, and are so by virtue of the Word, so too we find with *in* us the very word,[3] the name, *out* to which we call, as if to draw ourselves to it even as we draw and desire what we do not have. Synaesthetically, the name is visible to the ear, is read aloud (and read musically: this is not just a poem, but a song) in the resonating chamber of our empty fullness. It is by that name that we are helped—helped, in part, to call it. We participate in our own sustaining.

We must be cautious, however, not to read these resonances and intersections as if they were identifications, even of a complex sort. It is here that Hildegard's distinction from at least some lines of mystical thought, particularly the more Neoplatonic, becomes evident. Hildegard is no pantheist, not even an emanationist. For her, emphatically, God is not every thing, not even in the curious manner of someone like Meister Eckhart (for whom God is distinct from all things by being alone indistinct from all things), but is unique and singular—and forgetfulness of that fact is grounds for

---

[3] As Nicola Masciandaro reminds me, Hildegard's *aspicias in nos* may also be rendered *gaze into us*, by which the Word is invited to see into the heart. We might add that when the Word sees word within, the mirroring and echoing effect is further multiplied.

the strongest condemnation. In the same passage of analysis in which the creator God delights in the mirrors' song of praise, Hildegard writes in the voice of this unique God: "By my Word, which was and is without beginning in myself, I caused a mighty light to emerge." Here, again, we see the synaesthesis of the aural and visual. "And in this light are countless sparks, which are the angels. But when the angels came to awareness within their light, they forgot me and wanted to be as I am. Therefore, the vengeance of my punitive zeal rejected in thunderclaps those beings who had presumed to contradict me. For there is only one God, and no other can be God" (Hildegard, 1987, Vision 4, 128-29). The angels' rejection of divine uniqueness, their desire not for God but to be (as) God, stands as a warning to human arrogance (but also to a common mystical desire for theosis): no other can be God.

But to be unique and singular is not to be isolated or disconnected, and Hildegard's is a cosmology not only of image and repetition, but of dense interconnection. These are not altogether different claims: image and repetition are often for her the language of that connection, as they would have been for many of her contemporaries. "God, who created everything, has formed humanity according to the divine image and likeness, and marked in human beings both the higher and the lower creatures" (Hildegard, 1987, Vision 1, 11). These "marks" are signatures and similarities: body parts are paralleled with the creation account, the humors (black and yellow bile, phlegm, and blood) with the elements (earth, air, water and fire), the planetary bodies with the health of the human body, the forms of plants with their medicinal uses. Humans are no more disconnectable from other organisms than from God, from other heavenly bodies than from the earth.[4] To pluck one string of the cosmos–the human body, the natural world, the art of music, the planets, the elements, the humors, the angels–is to set all of it vibrating.

Vibrating, it sings–and in this antiphonal song, the human soul sight reads that helping name. Not obscured, the name is nonetheless a mystery. The addressee goes unnamed in the song, unless we count such terms as "Word" or "Father" as naming. The name read is unnamed; the demand of the call is only to keep

---

[4] Evidence for this sense of entanglement in Hildegard is too widespread in various works to be given a precise source; however, for her comments on cosmology in *Divine Works,* see especially Vision 2, Sections 32-46.

reading–that is, to keep calling out. As a mystery, the obscured undarkened name is a paradox. At its root, a mystery demands closed eyes (it is not to be seen by the uninitiated) or closed lips (it is not to be told to them, either)[5]–but for Hildegard the mysterious name is undarkened and sung out. This it can be, perhaps, only because it is and is not a mystery (it is both concealed and revealed), is and is not a name. It is *you*, addressed by *we*. So who are *you*?

The directionality here has become deeply odd, and that oddness is in some measure a deictic one. Among the many strange things that can happen to deixis in mysticism, including a dissolutional fusion of the *you* and *I*, Hildegard's is perhaps one of the most intriguing, grounded as it is in the connective point of language to music, and of both to the origin, the sustaining, and the celebration of creation.

At least outside of mystical texts and contexts, there is such a thing as fairly straightforward deixis. Deictic terms are those given some measure of their meaning by context; they point, but to know at what, we must know something of the context of the pointing. Because it functions in a particular setting, deixis is not quite ostension. A deictic term such "I" or "this" will pick out different objects when voiced by different users or within different contexts. Ostension is a different mode of pointing, which will, at least presumably, always find the same object or set of objects; it means only to define by pointing to, often by pointing not to a whole set but to an exemplar. Ostension is a common intuitive theory of language; to know what a word means, we find examples of those things named by that word, and we point to them (or to at least to one of them)–perhaps quite literally–and, having formed the proper association, we may be said to *know* what the word means. No doubt one reason that this seems at first pass so reasonable a linguistic theory is that it is in fact the way many of us first acquire nouns, with the aid of parental pointing and terms such as "doggie!" uttered in tones meant to encourage mimicry.

---

[5] The *Online Etymology Dictionary* is typically helpful here, writing of "mystery": "from Anglo-Fr. *misterie (O.Fr. mistere), from L. mysterium, from Gk. mysterion (usually in pl. mysteria) 'secret rite or doctrine,' from mystes 'one who has been initiated,' from myein 'to close, shut,' perhaps referring to the lips (in secrecy) or to the eyes (only initiates were allowed to see the sacred rites)" (http://www.etymonline.com/index.php?term=mystery&allowed_in_frame=0).

Of course, such pointing is pretty limited, which is why this intuitive theory nonetheless is not a widely held theory of the way that languages work. It runs into particular drawbacks in the language of theology. In *The Teacher*, Augustine's son Adeodatus, as he tries to work out how words mean, suggests an ostensive theory of language, which Augustine fairly gently but thoroughly dismantles. The first problem comes in relation to verbs—how do I point at "running" without making the viewer think that "running" is the word for feet, or perhaps indicates the motion of striking the ground? But unsurprisingly, Augustine's deeper concern is more abstract. The poles of being itself—that is, nothing and the fullness of being that is God—cannot be pointed to (and this despite the fact that, engagingly enough, a little-used sense of "ostension" is the display of the sacramental host for adoration) (Augustine, 1995, 98, 102).

While it is alarmingly easy to have conversations with minimal meaning, it is hard to talk about nothing—our desire to reify is strong. Perhaps the primary effect of this fact is the amusement of logicians ("I'm sure nobody walks much faster than I do," says the insulted messenger in Lewis Carroll's *Through the Looking Glass,* to which the king replies, "He can't do that, or else he'd have been here first" (Carroll, 1999, 225)). Clearly, however, we cannot point at nothing and point at all. Rather more detrimental effects come from our desire to point to God— particularly the effects of theological certainty and unyielding dogmatism, the sense that we *know* just what we mean by the term and just what the term means for us. Though, as we've duly noted, ostension is not deixis, such pointing doesn't work in a context, either. There is, at least for Augustine or for Hildegard, no place from which we can legitimately say of God, "that's him," "that's me," ore "here it is, this one." Our pointing can be neither exemplary, the way it is ostensively, nor, it seems contextual. How, then, can we say of a mystic's God, or more properly *to* such a God, "you?"

Neither the prayerful *you* nor the divine *I* performs quite a normal deixis. With Hildegard, I shall dwell primarily on the *you,* but it is useful to see how strange the *I* is here as well. Of itself, famously, God in the Hebrew tradition taken up by Augustine and Hildegard's Christianity, asked for its name, declares instead, "*'ehyeh 'ašer 'ehyeh,"* generally rendered "I am that I am," though more literally "I will be what I will be" (Exod. 3:14). The "I am" as it begins could almost be a straightforward statement of presence, but then it explicitly turns back upon itself. In thus circling, it renders strange, as if it were so purely pointing (its name is nothing but its self) that we who are not it have no idea where to point if we want to speak of it. The "I" here seems to negate the very possibility of properly naming. A curious negation, as Nicola Masciandaro points out, is inherent to deixis—"What makes deixis work . . . is that it says by not saying, and more precisely, that it negates its own inability to signify by speaking language, that is, by referring to the actual event of our being in language, in the same manner that 'I' means 'the one who is saying 'I'" (Masciandaro, 2012, 4-5). This negation is not Aristotelian; it does not resolve into the elimination of one contrary—rather, it circles back. "The negativity of deixis," Masciandaro writes, "thus resolves to a deeper auto-deixis, its pointing to itself" (2012, 5).

The name "I am" says only I, pointing to itself as if purely indicating, but the *I* says a mystery by circling back upon itself, names a mystery by offering only this circle instead of a name. The deictic indicative requires a certain immediacy, even a presence, but we see now that it is odd enough that even simple repetition can trouble the sense of the present: it is all very well for "I" to point at itself, but where do the rest of us point? Nor are matters much simplified if we turn to the future "I will be," which not only mystifies us as to the whereabouts of the I, but even as to the when.[6] There is nowhere to point, but we do not point at nothing. Hildegard's *we* calls out to a divine *you*, not to nothing, and it calls out urgently: we are in great need. We ask help through the name that says only in a looping *I*, while we call to *you*.

The calling function is, again, sometimes a fairly clear one, but in prayerful language a bit more complicated.[7] Unlike the "I" or the "he" or the "this," the use of "you" makes it hard for any listener or reader to pull back, to feel him or herself to be wholly outside the deictic context. Perhaps this is why its use in writing is relatively restricted; beyond prayer or the deliberately addressed

---

[6] cf. T.S. Eliot, "Burnt Norton": "I can only say, *there* we have been: but I cannot say where./ And I cannot say, how long, for that is to place it in time." In Eliot, 1943, II.68-69.
[7] For more detail on these complications, see the chapter "Prayer" in my *Divine Enticement,* much inspired by Jean-Louis Chrétien's *The Call and the Response,* 2004.

epistle, the second person appears infrequently in essay or literature, but often in poetry, which may well seek to connect with its readers rather more directly than narrative or drama might; and in pornography, which in its own rather different mode certainly seeks such a connection. The basic, doubly deictic question, "Is that you?" is so common that we tend not to hear its strangeness— the strangeness, in this instance, of the fact that an honest negative answer is impossible. "You" is simply the second person, the one (or, in English, more than one) beyond the first person, the condition of the possibility of conversation. If *I* ask, *you* can only answer in the affirmative.[8]

The effect of a *you* that somehow fails to call is thus both odd and poignant. A few examples may make this clearer. David Markson's 1988 novel *Wittgenstein's Mistress* gives us one such instance: the narrator, who is either the last animal on earth or quite mad, hears a voice calling with a double deixis–"*You? Can that be you? . . .* And here, of all places!" (Markson, 1988, 47)–but she finds no caller, only, in a moment that at once echoes and alters Hildegard's, her own reflection in a window, or in a highly glossed canvas (Markson, 1988, 48). In a sense, of course, the *you* is present here, as the narrator herself, but she cannot occupy the second person position after all–there is only one person, and the addressor is absent, or only imagined. The auto-deictic *you* is far sadder than the auto-deictic *I.* Rainer-Maria Rilke offers us a different, more directly religious, failure in his poetic account of the Christic passion in "The Olive Garden": "And why is it your will that I must say/ You are, when I myself no longer find You . . . I am alone with all of human grief, which through You I undertook to lighten, / You who are not" (1990, 39).[9] Rilke comes close, in this *you*, to drawing together Augustine's impossible ostensive

---

[8] Of course we may answer in the negative, but when we do so, we are generally assuming that the question is actually mis-directed. That is, if someone asks me, "Is that you?" and I answer "No," what I mean is approximately, "I think that you are looking for someone else," even though the correct answer to "Is that you?" would have to be "Yes." "You" picks out any addressee, but when it is used in a question, we may reasonably assume that a *particular* addressee is implicitly intended–the deixis is standing in for ostension.

[9] "und warum willst Du, daß ich sagen muß/ Du seist, wenn ich Dich selber nicht mehr finde . . . Ich bin allein mit aller Menschen Gram,/ den ich durch Dich zu linern unternahm,/ der Du nicht bist" (Rilke, 1990, 40).

poles, nothing (no one) and God–but both only by addressing them in their failure. The addressor is narratively present here, but alone, or at least without the addressee: the poetic voice bitterly addresses a void, addresses the fact that address is impossible now. In a more complex failure, T.S. Eliot's grim rejoicing in "Little Gidding" includes the description of a self split in order to address: "I met one walking, loitering and hurried . . . Both intimate and unidentifiable. / So I assumed a double part, and cried / And heard another's voice cry: 'What! are *you* here?' / Although we were not. I was still the same, / Knowing myself yet being someone other / And he a face still forming" (Eliot, 1943, II.86-102). One doubles to address what is nonetheless not oneself, calling out to the reflected face, but hearing it call out, too: *Could that be you?* This *you* does not address falsely (from or to one who is-not), as in both Markson and Rilke; nor does it perfectly point back on itself, though it comes closer to this latter. Rather, in the double part assumed by the *I* is the double cry of a mutual *you,* a cry that forms those addressing and addressed by it, neither quite the same nor fully formed yet in their distinction. It is this lingering indistinction that keeps this final *you* from being quite successful. This will come closer to Hildegard's strange address, in which the voice is redoubled, but she will insist nonetheless upon a clear priority and distinction between creator and creation–a priority and a distinction that do not preclude mutuality.

There *is* a second person in Hildegard's antiphon: the speaker is not the Father, nor the Word. And there is a speaker, or there are speakers (though the numbers become, as so often in mystical discourse, strangely shifting and paradoxical) a choral many *we* who address; there is an addressee of the *you,* a Father in whose existence the speaker (or singer) seems confident. But her–or, rather, given the *we,* our–spoken or sung words do seem to give back to the Father what the Father through the Word gave to us: the fullness of lacking; that is, desire. That curious creative combination of fullness of lack (desire is never only lacking) flows multidirectionally through the W/word–and not least through the strange word *you.* The address here lacks a name, but not desire: it is entirely beseeching, asking only to address, to call upon. But the address is also directed through the Word by which the one calling was created–called into being as desiring, and by the divine desire to see and to hear. The antiphon vibrates, *resonates,* at the frequency of *you.* It echoes a divine eagerness to resonate, for which creation is made, and a human eagerness to resonate, as that for which we are made.

I have repeatedly used the idea of *resonance* here as a term particularly appropriate to the very musical cosmology and world-view of the writer of this small song. We don't often think about the resonance of language, but Jean-Luc Nancy, struggling to make sense of sense itself, writes, "Perhaps it is necessary that sense not be content to make sense . . . but that it want also to resound" (Nancy, 2008, 6). *Resonance*, re-sounding or sounding again, emphasizes the sense–the sensuality, even–of sound. Nancy writes of the act of listening to music, in which we attend to resonance explicitly (and to language, if at all, with as much attention to sensuousness as to meaning):

> It returns to itself, it reminds itself of itself, and it feels itself as resonance itself: a relationship to self deprived, stripped of all egoism and all ipseity. Not "itself," or the other, or identity, or difference, but alteration and variation, the modulation of the present that changes it in expectation of its own eternity, always imminent and always deferred, since it is not in any time. Music is the art of making the outside of time return to every time, making return to every moment the beginning that listens to itself beginning and beginning again. In resonance the inexhaustible return of eternity is played– and listened to. (Nancy, 2007, 67)

With these thoughts we can really begin to see how central it is that Hildegard is a musician. Hildegard claimed that her songs were received in her visions, though it is not clear if by this she included their melodies or only their lyrics (Pfau, in Hildegard, 1998, 75). What is a little more clear is that this distinction is imperfect. We find in the antiphons an example of the "medieval conception of melody as a movement of the voice, as *cantus* declaiming language through melodic inflections" (Pfau, in Hildegard, 1998f, 75, citing Treitler, 145-46). Marianne Richert Pfau notes that "the words in music in Hildegard's compositions are mutually influential. The text determines many musical choices; the music may clarify textual syntax and large-scale form that in turn contribute to the meaning" (in Hildegard, 1998, 94). I have noted that for Hildegard the world is brought into being by divine voice, and that creation is interconnected by resemblances that vibrate in a deeply musical interconnection. Her metaphors of the human-divine connection are often explicitly musical, as when she writes of the resonance of songs of praise.

Humanity is for her the image of God, a claim that oversimplifies the complex of images that Hildegard sees at every level of the cosmos. In a sense, the human voice is the image of the creative divine voice–but it is not a weakened copy. If anything, it is a weaker version of its own original perfection; for Hildegard, original sin is the loss of harmonious voice. In this notion, she both takes up and quite intriguingly nuances the Augustinian reading of original sin, through which the notion comes to be dogmatic or doctrinal for Christianity. For Augustine, the original disobedience is one that resonates, or multiplies in images of itself: Adam's[10] disobedience of God echoes in the continued dissonance not only of human and divine will, but of human will with itself and with human flesh (see Augustine, 2003, especially 14.24). Hildegard, however, makes explicit, and makes more than metaphorical, the musicality of this image. In a letter to the prelates of Mainz, she uses this reading to make a subtle argument in favor of song–and against the injunction that forbade her house from musical celebration (her argument was evidently effective, as the injunction was subsequently lifted).

"Adam lost [the voice of the living Spirit] through his disobedience. Because he lost his innocence, his voice in no way harmonized with the voices of the angels who sing God's praise . . . a harmony he had possessed in Paradise." The loss of Paradise is the loss of song. Conversely, when the prophets composed songs and accompanied them on musical instruments, they acted "[s]o that human beings would not live from the memory of exile, but with thoughts of heavenly bliss . . . and furthermore so that human beings would be enticed to praise God" (Hildegard, in 1987, 356). Music is the best form of praise because it acts as its own enticement, thereby enhancing itself, and because it echoes the

---

[10] The emphasis on Adam, rather than Eve, in the reading of the Genesis story is not simple sexism, though it is not unreasonable to suspect that sexism is active as well. Among more theoretical grounds, however, is the fact that Augustine, in keeping with the medical knowledge of his time, understood human heritage to be entirely seminal (with the sperm as homunculus). If original sin is to be inherited, as he believed it was, it would have to come through the father.

perfect praise of the voice that harmonizes with the very angels. Indeed, Hildegard insists, "before the Fall [Adam's] voice carried in itself, in full, harmonious sound the loveliness of every musical art" (Hildegard, in 1987, 357). Our music is imperfect, but it is as close to perfection as the praising voice can come—when we only speak, or are inharmonious, our praise is lessened. The Devil, Hildegard argues, so hates songs of praise that he sows discord—from that between humans and God in Eden all the way to that between Hildegard and the prelates—in order to silence them (Hildegard, in 1987, 358).

In this antiphon, we see a musical deixis, or a deixis that gives way to musicality. The *you* does not point, but resonates. We find neither identity nor difference, but "alteration and variation . . . modulation." *You* resonates with the *we* as the plural of "a self deprived . . . of all egoism and all ipseity" (Nancy, 2007, 67), a self full of the things that it lacks, made a resonating chamber for the divine that does more than simply reflect. That singing, praying self resonates with its addressee; God reverberates with the creation that the resonant divine voice has called into being, and eternity returns to the measured time of the song. Reason breathes from the diaphragm, and the body gives voice to the soul.[11]

It is creation that allows God to see God, creation that acts as a mirror—a mirror that shows (wonder) by singing (praise)—but in singing it does not simply show, but necessarily shares. Creation mirrors God in this synaesthetic image, an outpouring of divine joyful desire echoed back, as such desire so often is, in song. The knowledge or seeing thus given back to the creator is not an epistemological necessity (it does not seem that Hildegard's God requires creation for self-knowing), but rather a gift that returns joy by holding that mirror up to it. Resonance is responsive, but it is not simply response, nor even a circle of response and call; in it, the singing vibration is shared. God says, and the world is—both because God's speaking is creative power, and, less evidently, because all speaking does implicitly address: to speak, God speaks to, and the face formed in the mirror sings back in praise.

---

[11] Brendan Doyle notes the deep physicality of Hildegard's music, and remarks, "this makes wonderful sense if we realize that she was a physical scientist as well as a musician." Introduction to the Songs, in Hildegard, 1987, 364.

Hildegard's *we* call out from creation to the resonant joy and desire found only in the great need and the *you*.

Hildegard's musical deixis, then, functions quite unusually. It does not simply point, not even in a given context—and this though Hildegard, unlike many mystical theologians, does seem to have a clear sense of a God as distinct and singular, capable of firmly declaring its own singularity. Neither does the pair *we-you* simply collapse, as if to conflate the *we* and the *you*—not only would this be for her a sin worthy of severe condemnation, but it would silence the music itself, the rapid back and forth of vibration. Despite Hildegard's frequent use of mirror imagery in descriptions of creation, the song is no simple mirror either; the singing *we* are not a poor imitation of the divine voice that sang creation into being, but the closest that postlapsarian creation can approach to the perfect harmonies of Paradise. The antiphon does not quite serve as a responsory, even in the complexly looped manner of much prayerful call-and-response, in which an originary voice is hard to pinpoint, and every call seems already to be and to have been an answer. Nor does it, quite, loop in the manner of autodeixis, in which the context refracts the pointing back to the source of the term. Rather, altogether musically, deixis becomes reverberation, in which one vibration—the call of created desire, the creative divine voice—sets up another on the same frequency, so that we have the "same" sound, but more so, louder by addition, enriched by another voice, closer to Paradisical perfection. Humanity's very need, put into song, perfects divine delight. Hildegard's musicality informs her cosmology both intellectually and sensuously. Taking seriously the notion of a world called into being by voice, she likewise takes seriously the fullness of desire that calls back, the soul as a resonating chamber for the voice that reads aloud the unnamed name of the *you*, in an address and a reply that can only call to both gratifying completeness and endless need.

WORKS CITED

Augustine of Hippo. 2003. *City of God*. Translated by Henry Bettenson. London: Penguin.

_____. 1991. *Confessions*. Translated by Henry Chadwick. Oxford: Oxford University Press.

_____. 1995. *The Teacher.* In *Against Academicians and The Teacher.* Translated by Peter King. Indianapolis: Hackett Publishing.
Butcher, Carmen Acevedo. 2007. *Hildegard of Bingen: A Spiritual Reader.* Brewster, Mass: Paraclete Press.
Carroll, Lewis. 1999. *Through the Looking Glass.* In Lewis Carroll, *The Annotated Alice: The Definitive Edition,* edited and annotated by Martin Gardner. New York: W.W. Norton and Company.
Chrétien, Jean-Louis. 2004. *The Call and the Response.* Translated by Anne A. Davenport. New York: Fordham University Press.
Eliot, T.S. 1943. *Four Quartets.* San Diego, CA: Harcourt Brace Jovanovich.
Hildegard of Bingen. 1987. *The Book of Divine Works: Ten Visions of God's Deeds in the World and Humanity.* Edited by Matthew Fox. Translated by Robert Cunningham. Santa Fe, NM: Bear and Company: 5-266.
_____. 2008. *Causes and Cures.* Translated by Priscilla Throop. Charlotte, VT: MedievalMS, 2008.
_____. 1987. Letter 41, to the Prelates of Mainz. Translated by Ronald Mille. In *The Book of Divine Works: Ten Visions of God's Deeds in the World and Humanity.* Edited by Matthew Fox. Santa Fe, NM: Bear and Company: 354-59.
_____. 1990. *Scivias.* Translated by Columba Hart and Jane Bishop. Mahwah, NJ: Paulist Press.
_____. 1998. *Symphonia.* Critical edition with introduction, translations, and commentary by Barbara Newman. Ithaca: Cornell University Press.
MacKendrick, Karmen. 2013. *Divine Enticement: Theological Seductions.* New York: Fordham University Press.
_____. "When You Call My Name." *Glossator,* 5, 2011: 57-67.
_____. *Word Made Skin.* 2008. New York: Fordham University Press.
Mackey, Lewis. 1997. *Peregrinations of the Word.* Ann Arbor: University of Michigan Press.
Markson, David. 1988. *Wittgenstein's Mistress.* Elmwood Park, IL: Dalkey Archive Press.
Masciandro, Nicola. 2012. "What is This that Stands before Me?: Metal as Deixis." In *Reflections in the Metal Void.* Edited by Niall Scott. Oxford: Inter-Disciplinary Press: 3-17.
Nancy, Jean-Luc. 2008. *Dis-Enclosure: The Deconstruction of Christianity.* Translated by Bettina Bergo, Gabriel Malenfant, and Michael B. Smith. New York: Fordham University Press.

_____. *Listening*. 2007. Translated by Charlotte Mandell. New York: Fordham University Press.

Online Etymology Dictionary. http://www.etymonline.com/

Pfau, Marianne Richert. 1998. "Music and Text in Hildegard's Antiphons." In Hildegard of Bingen, *Symphonia*. Critical edition with introduction, translations, and commentary by Barbara Newman. Ithaca: Cornell University Press: 74-94.

Rilke, Rainer-Maria. 1990. *New Poems (1907)*. Translated by Edward Snow. New York: North Point Press.

Treitler, Leo. 1984. "Reading and Singing: On the Genesis of Occidental Music-Writing," in *Early Music History* 4: 135-208.

Karmen MacKendrick is a professor of philosophy at Le Moyne College in Syracuse, NY. She works primarily in philosophical theology and on bodies, language, and temporality. Her recent works include *Divine Enticement: Theological Seductions* (Fordham, 2013) and, with Virginia Burrus and Mark Jordan, *Seducing Augustine: Bodies, Desires, Confessions* (Fordham, 2010). She also studies flamenco, and often wishes that she had a decent singing voice.

Glossator publishes original commentaries, editions and translations of commentaries, and essays and articles relating to the theory and history of commentary, glossing, and marginalia. The journal aims to encourage the practice of commentary as a creative form of intellectual work and to provide a forum for dialogue and reflection on the past, present, and future of this ancient genre of writing. By aligning itself, not with any particular discipline, but with a particular mode of production, *Glossator* gives expression to the fact that praxis founds theory.

GLOSSATOR.ORG

Made in the USA
Lexington, KY
29 July 2013